PLANET HEAL

What would you do
to heal planet Earth?

Vol. 1

Healers Unite
Throughout the Diaspora

Treasures gathered by
Queen Afua

This book is intended as a reference volume only, not as a medical text. The information provided herein is designed to help you make informed decisions about your wellness. It is not intended to be a substitute for any treatment that may have been prescribed by your doctor. It is sold with the understanding that the contributing writers nor the publisher are not engaged in rendering medical advice. If you have a medical problem, we urge you to seek appropriate medical help.

The scanning, uploading, and distribution of this book via the Internet or via any other means without the authorization of the publisher is illegal and punishable by law. Please purchase only authorized electronic editions and do not participate in or encourage electronic/digital piracy of materials herein. Your support of the contributing writers' rights is appreciated.

PLANET HEAL™: What would you do to heal Planet Earth? Volume 1 Brooklyn, New York

Conceptual Editor: Queen Afua/Helen O. Robinson

Developmental & Line Editor: Gerianne F. Scott (EmmaJanePress)

Assistants to Ms. Scott: Judy Baldaccini, Chotasani Sackey, Tracey M. Williams

Additional Supporters and Assistants: Kimberli Boyd, Robin Devonish, Abel Dorvil, Sutanyia Fafad, Kheperah Kearse, Freda McDuffie, Tulsi Chase Mehta, Quasheba El (Elaine Smith), Nassareen Rahman, Ali Amechi Torain, Dr. Sharita Yazid

Typists: Graciela Asher, Candice Briggs, Cleopatra Granderson, Kheperah Kearse, Angel Marks, Tulsi Chase Mehta, Luisa Reyes, Cherub "Chopp" Stewart

Logo Artist: LaTonya Lark

Cover Design: Robert W. Gay (Tehuti Films, LLC)

Text Design & Layout: Cindy Shaw (CreativeDetails.net)

FIRST EDITION
EmmaJanePress

ISBN: 9781093641233

EVOLUTION OF FRONT COVER

Original Design Concept: Queen Afua, Quasheba El

Original Presentation: Green Studio NYC.Com

Collaborators for present collage and design: Queen Afua, Gerianne Scott, LaTonya Lark (Leroy Campbell, Mentor), Un Nefer Hetep Rā (Jawanza)

Present Design: Robert W. Gay (Tehuti Films, LLC)

DESCRIPTION

The Eastern Hemisphere view of planet Earth, with the continent of Africa in the center is surrounded by icons from antiquity to contemporary times. Clockwise from the Eastern Hemisphere to the Western Hemisphere the circle of icons represents the Northern, Southern, Eastern and Western geographic directions, as well as global populations.

1. **The Great Pyramid of Giza (aka the Pyramid of Khufu or the Pyramid of Cheops)** – the oldest and largest of the three pyramids in the Giza pyramid complex bordering what is now El Giza, Egypt.

2. **Buddah statue** – the oldest sculpture is found in Indonesia at the Borobudur Temple in the Central Java province. (Buddhism is a nontheistic religion founded 2500 years ago by "the enlightened one" Lord Gautama Buddha.)

3. **The Taj Mahal** – an enormous mausoleum complex commissioned in 1632 by Mughal emperor Shah Jahan to house the remains of his beloved wife. Constructed over a 20-year period on the southern bank of the Yamuna River in Agra, India, the famed complex is one of the most outstanding examples of Mughal architecture, which combined Indian, Persian and Islamic influences.

4. **Stonehenge** – a prehistoric monument in Wiltshire, England. It consists of a ring of standing stones, each around 13 feet (4.0 m) high, 7 feet (2.1 m) wide and weighing around 25 tons. The stones are set within earthworks in the middle of the most dense complex of Neolithic and Bronze Age monuments in England. Archaeologists believe it was constructed from 3000 BC to 2000 BC.

5. **Moai** – monolithic human figures carved by the Rapa Nui people on Easter Island in eastern Polynesia between the years 1250 and 1500. The humongous heads are about three-eighths the size of the whole statue. The moai are chiefly the living faces (aringa ora) of deified ancestors (aringa ora ata tepuna).

6. **Aloe** – a genus containing over 500 species of flowering succulent plants. The most widely known species is Aloe vera, or "true aloe", so named because it is cultivated for use of assorted pharmaceutical purposes.

7. **Olmec Head** – The Olmec colossal heads are stone sculpted from basalt boulders brought from the Sierra de los Tuxtlas mountains of Veracruz. Dating back to at least 900 BC, the monuments are thought to represent portraits of powerful individual Olmec rulers.

8. **Olmec Pyramid** – The Olmec pyramids are legacies built in ancient Mexico from c. 1200 BCE to c. 400 BCE. The Olmec Civilization of Mesoamerica includes the Mayans and Aztecs. The pyramids were built of earth, faced with stone in a stepped shape and usually topped by a platform or temple structure. Many Latin American pyramids were rebuilt over existing structures to glorify the current ruler.

9. **Native American Dream Catcher** – a handmade hoop with woven string or sinew meant to replicate a spider's web. The dreamcatcher may also include sacred items such as feathers or beads. Traditionally it is used as a protective charm hung over infants' cradles.

10. **The Martin Luther King, Jr. National Memorial** in Washington, DC honors Dr. King for his b contributions to freedom and justice. It is the first major memorial on the National Mall dedicated to an African-American and a non-president. Open 24 hours a day, 7 days a week; there is no fee to visit.

11. **Planet Earth (Eastern Hemisphere view)** – The Atlantic Ocean is on the right, the Indian Ocean on the left, and the continent of Africa in the center. Globally, among the people on Earth there are those who require healing and those who heal. Sometimes one is the other.

Globally, among the people on Earth there are those who require healing and those who heal. Sometimes one is the other.

OPENING THE WAY
A Message From The Queen King

―――――∽∘⟨⟩∘∽―――――

Here is what the Old Tree told me today:
You are my Brothers. We are children of the Great Mother. Our Ancestors are bringing us together for a very important task. The only way to succeed In this work is to do it together. Mother is sending us the Ancient Ones. They will help us restore our sight. We have arrived at the edge of the cliff, but we lost our wings, we can no longer fly like the falcons we once were. We have to turn back and hear our great Elders, they will show us the path back to the Great River of the flying fish for us to survive.

May Her Children hear; May Her Children see; May Her Children feel; May Her Children live; May Her Children thrive once more.

King Queen Diambi Mukalenga Mukaji Wa Nkashama Diambi Kabatusuila Tshiyoyo Muata Wa Bakwa Indu ne Bena Tshiyamba Wa Bakwa Mpungu Wa Bakwa Luntu Wa Baluba Wa Kasaï Congo.

―――――∽∘⟨⟩∘∽―――――

Dedication

This work is dedicated to the well-being
of the bodies, minds and spirits of
THE PEOPLE;
the residents and caretakers
of planet Earth.

GRATITUDE

SUPREME THANKSGIVING
To the MOST HIGH for implanting within me the vision to channel PLANET HEAL.

PROFOUND HONOR
To Ancestor Healers. To Imhotep, the Khametic multi-talented genius, who as Chancellor to Pharaoh Djoser in the Third Dynasty was architect of the first pyramid (the Step Pyramid complex at Saqqara and Father of Holistic and Allopathic Medicine. All hail and honor to the Ancestors, gone but not forgotten, bestowed healing blessings upon the people of planet Earth. They led the way, that we may heal. We thank them for their sacrifices and service. Among them…Great Mothers Harriet Tubman, Sojourner Truth, Ella Baker, Rosa Parks and Fannie Lou Hamer (who empowered us with her quote, "…sick and tired of being sick and tired."). Also, Dr. Alvenia Fulton, Dr. Cwolde Kyte, Dr. John E. Moore, John Harris, Leon Thomas, Dr. Keefa Lorraine, Dr. Ronald Davidson, Dr. Josephine English, Dr. Sebi, and Brother Dick Gregory.

HONOR AND RESPECT
To our Cultural Healers. Among them beloved ancestors and esteemed elders who have dedicated their work as educators and/or artists. Their teachings are the foundation for the restoration of our cultural well-being. (See We Stand Upon Their Shoulders.)

APPRECIATION
To Bob Law and his wife, Muntu Law, and to Imhotep Gary Byrd for decades of bringing "Heal Thyself" wellness work to national and international attention.

To the Global Sacred Woman Village/Tribe, Man Heal Thyself and Wellness Warriors, ALL of you, for ALL the wellness work you do.

To Rev. Johnny Ray Youngblood, Senior Pastor, Mount Pisgah Baptist Church (Brooklyn, NY) and Brother Jawaad Abdul Ali, humble assistant to Baba Duku of Blue Nile Botanicals (Washington, DC) for recruiting thousands to commit to their wellness.

To Wanique Shabazz and Chris "Kazi" Rolle for heralding ***Planet Heal*** globally through contemporary social media.

To Brother Fred "Doc" Beasley and his wife, Beauty. As a Global Youth Cultural Architect, "Doc" is the Chapter Leader of NYC Hip Hop Is Green (nychiphopisgreen@gmail.com) a collective focused on influencing youth with positive changes in their lives. Thank you for reconnections to Brooklyn Borough President, Eric Adams and informing him of the ***PLANET HEAL*** initiative.

To Erykah Badu for her generous contribution to the initial editorial and publishing expenses of **PLANET HEAL**.

To Diana Pharr dynamic Spiritual Healer for decades of support.

To Dr Jewel Pookrum a pioneer in wholistic healing through mental and spiritual wellness.

To enlightened Elder Etta Dixon (80+ years—Swing Dancer Extraordinaire) for her consistent participation in the Wellness Movement.

SALUTE
To the Essence magazine team for hosting a visionary Think Tank before the beginning of the 21st century. The spark they ignited resulted in the creation of a Healers' Directory with global outreach.

To A Visionary, her Parents and 2 Rap Artists. In 1976 Leothy Miller Owens founded the oldest African-American bookstore in Brooklyn, NY. She sold multicultural children's books out of her family's apartment. In 1990 she moved **Nkiru Books** to a storefront which became legendary for hosting literary/cultural events to standing-room audiences. After Leothy passed away, in 1992, her parents valiantly kept the store going until 1999. In 2000 Talib Kweli and Yasiin Bey (aka Mos Def) purchased Nkiru Books and brought Leothy's legacy into the 21st century.

GRATITUDE
To all the Healers who contributed to making this volume of **PLANET HEAL** a reality. You are indeed forerunners in answering the call and responding to the question: What would you do to heal planet Earth?

SUPREME GRATITUDE
For the gift of my parents, Ephraim and Ida Robinson I am grateful.

HEARTFELT THANK YOU
To my children Supa Nova Slom, Sherease and Ali Amechi for their sacrifice of sharing their mother, me, as I've been doing my life's work of wellness.

FOUR YEARS LATER…THANK YOU
To the editor of **PLANET HEAL**, my spiritual big sister. Like a mother, from conception to the birth of this body of work you lovingly walked with me and all the healers herein. We thank you, our beloved Gerianne Scott.

Ase.

INTRODUCTION
About Planet Heal

"We who believe in freedom cannot rest."

SWEET HONEY IN THE ROCK

The first time I experienced a mass union for a common cause, I was 9 years old, in Washington, DC., standing in the mud and rain between my mother and father while listening to Martin Luther King Jr. present his "I Have A Dream" speech. Hundreds of thousands surrounded me listening to greatness. From then to now millions have heard Dr. King's legendary message and are still inspired by it. In the sixties people came together for mass liberation. During those memorable times I experienced people from all walks of life rising up to liberate themselves—spiritually, economically, socially, and culturally. We took our walk to our homes and to the streets; from city to city. We rode the buses and sat in. We marched for our rights and freedom. Following Dr. King's speech many things were accomplished. Nonetheless, now, throughout our nations, there is still a need to mend and to heal a broken, divided, wounded, dis-eased, hurt world.

In the spring of 2014, I was inspired to reach out to my friends in the healing community to help me launch a Nation to Nation—City to City 24 Hour Global Fast Teleconference. Over fifty Healers came from the four directions: East, North, West and South. As a Circle of Healers, they sent out their messages to raise the frequency of humanity. The goal has been to end suffering, dis-ease, and violence on each level—personal, family, community, and global. Collectively and continuously they have labored to overcome human and social injustices as they lead the people into wholeness. They have shared their lessons through consultations, workshops and keynote speeches. They have traveled the world spreading their knowledge to seekers of wisdom. They come from a healing legacy which spans from the first civilizations to the present times. The

Elder Healers drew on decades of experience to help seekers of health come out of the mud of struggle and challenge. The newer Healers came with an agenda of abundance, moving with self-awareness as they share talents and techniques for healing of body, mind and spirit. They each offered wellness roadmaps for recovery.

The 24 Hour Global Fast Teleconference Collective realized the magnitude of answering the question: What would you do to heal the planet? We recognized it will take more than herbal tea and salt baths to heal the global condition. None of us can do it alone. We looked to one another and considered adding our portion to the multiplicity of approaches suggested for restoring wellness. **Planet Heal: What would you do to heal Planet Earth? Volume 1** is a collaborative gathering of master teachers and healers who have been weathering the storms and putting out the fires in order to overcome, elevate, transform and heal. This is a mighty circle of wellness. Not even our DNA can hold us back; nor will history deny us wholeness. We, Healers heard our ancestors' call. We came with the healing balm of natural medicine. We, Healers speak out for The People to detox and resurrect from dead thoughts, dead actions, dead words and dead food. This is our time to be whole; right now, at this very moment.

Enter **Planet Heal: What would you do to heal Planet Earth? Volume 1** to meet and be transformed by world-wide Naturopaths, Community Activists, Motivational Speakers, Poets, Crystal Healers, Breathologists, Vegan Chefs, Entrepreneurs, Metaphysicians, Herbalists, Life Coaches, Poets, Musicians, Writers, Body Workers, Reiki Practitioners, Archivists, Body Workers, Authors, Grammy Award Artists, Urban Farmers, Numerologists, Teachers, Midwives, Relationship Counselors, Spiritual Leaders, Yogis, Yoginis, Wealth Advisors, Energy Workers, Artists, Sacred Women, Soul Sweat and Man Heal Thyself Practitioners, Colon Therapists, Womb Workers, Massage Therapists, Authors, and holistically conscious Medical Doctors. These humble teachers are your guides, your mentors, your spiritual fathers and sacred mothers. These healers are Wellness Warriors and Holistic Freedom Fighters. We are convinced that if we continue gathering together, the people will come.

We, The Healers are sharing our knowledge, our experiences, our visions, our mastery, our intelligence and our gifts of healing. The essays in **Planet Heal** offer the next generation a pathway to holistic freedom; a haven of well-being. Decades ago, throughout the earth, we agreed that we would not wait for anyone to heal us, that we could and would Heal Thyself through a Planet Heal consciousness. Globally, each us must tap into our inner healer to repair body, mind and spirit. As each of us awakens our inner healer, we will recognize that we have been given the opportunity to live the path of a healer. We The Healers are We, The People.

We, The People are the millions in the world who claim the right to live a life of optimal mental, physical, emotional health and longevity; peace and prosperity. We, The People are working to raise our vibrational frequency, so we can empty the jails of our youth and empty old age homes of the elderly and move them to **Heal Thyself**. We, The People are willing to work together to put down our swords against one another, so as to save our children from a legacy of dis-ease and mass destruction. We, The People are willing to align ourselves to optimal living; willing to clean up our bodies and our minds. We are willing to take responsibility for our well-being and willing to blame no one for the choices we make of our free will. We are choosing to be renewed, restored, and rejuvenated. We, The People have shifted to higher ground; we are indestructible.

May we all be inspired by this unprecedented sharing. May we be encouraged by these visions for the wealth of wellness and charged by those already on the walk. Let them lead the journey to living large, living strong, living holistically.

To the people who find themselves with these pages in their hands—COME! Join us and add your gifts of wellness for planetary healing! As we unite and collaborate our words and works, we are already making history!

Planet Heal is a call out to the Planet from a microcosmic group of Healers. We can reach and awaken the healer in all of us to rise up from the ashes of dis-ease and take charge of our lives to grow to a macrocosmic unlimited state of well-being. This is to collectively heal and to rejuvenate thousands, millions, trillions…infinity.

People of planet Earth, can you imagine? I can. Let's do it, now!

Wellness Salute,
Queen Afua

WE ARE COMING.

WE ARE UNIFYING.

WE ARE HERE.

MOTHER EARTH SPEAKS

*O*h, my Beloved Children, I am so grateful that you've taken the time to connect with me. It gives me hope. I've been suffering for so long that I feel delusional...

Many of you are talking about my condition and the abuse that I am going through **24, 7, 365…**

But no one is talking to me or listening for that matter. I have a voice, even if it's foggy and toxic at this time in my life. Thank you, thank you, thank you for giving me my moment to express myself.

You rock!!! And I love you dearly.

Here's my self-diagnosis. I'm suffering from post-traumatic-earthquake-tsunami-warzone-blood bath-toxic dump-earth abuse-victimization syndrome. My body needs rest and restoration, so it can heal itself. Can you help me?

It's going to require Love. Love is the Master Healer. Sacrificial love. True love always requires giving; giving of oneself for the greater good without expecting something in return. It is the highest form of conscious living. You're being called to give of your Time, Talent, and Treasures.

Time to commune with me by spending time with me and volunteering your energy in service. Time for letting people know about the global dilemma that we are all facing. Time for solutions. Talent equals sharing your gifts of creativity, expertise, intellect and technology by using your music, writings, art, literary works and technical skills to spread the word of this organic movement! Treasures include making your resources and finances available to rent halls and buses for marches and assemblies to gather the people to make positive changes on my behalf. Treasures are the brilliant solutions that this literary body of work offers to humanity! Kudos to Queen Afua, a true visionary!

I've been beat down and I need you to come around. Please advocate for me. I'm clear that I'm still here but I'm shaking and quaking out of control. I'm your Mama and I want to be green again, to be revived, to come alive. Come, come, come be one with me, plant seeds in me. Walk on me, talk to me and listen to the wind, that too is me!

Have you ever been to a mountain peak or seen your face in the valley creek? Speak with my indigenous Ones, they've lived the closest to me, they've known me for centuries. They build Sweat Lodges for me, they Sun Dance with me; Pow Wow, and Vision Quest for me. It's all about ME right now. I've always been here for You. We are All One …the perception that we are all related is the wisdom-teaching that Indigenous Nations bring to the global table. "All My Relations" is creed.

So, here's the real deal… If you are reading these words you've been chosen to be a conscious being and thus to Align with the Divine for these times. Some of you have the capacity to practice austerities such as fasting, sitting in prayer and long hours of meditation. These and other finely attuned practices radiate light and balance the atmosphere from the evil and greed rampantly destroying me. Others may be called to make immediate attitude adjustments and behavior modification protocols by working to rid addictions and so forth. And some even have the unique gift of the practice of celibacy and work closely with the Creator behind the scenes. We are not all gifted in the same way. I See you and I Love you unconditionally!

Now, the Creator is prompting me to reveal the Big Picture. You—all humans—, Me… We are working with the same elements. We are one body, assigned to healing me. Everyone has their part to play. We've All been given our role. This is hands on, Baby…

My Beloveds, the Creator has blessed this auspicious movement…

It is Done!!!

In Divine Love, Gratitude & Affection,

Mama Earth

(Excerpt from ***Mother Earth Speaks*** by Prema 2018)

PLANET HEAL DAILY AFFIRMATIONS

Let the affirmations below guide your heart, mind and spirit. Choose and recite one or more daily.

- May we collectively heal our planet by healing ourselves, one to another. May we spread love, serenity and wellness, to all our planetary sisters and brothers.

- May we live in alignment with the forces of nature, as we harmonize with air (atmosphere), fire (sun), water (oceans, rivers, lakes, and streams) and earth (soil and plants). Let us collectively tune up our body, mind and spirit to our highest frequency of well-being.

- May we end the health disparity that has plagued humanity.

- May we claim our freedom now, from all social, economic, relationship, physical, emotional, psychological and spiritual disease.

- May we align ourselves in oneness with the natural, bountiful, beautiful tapestry of creation.

- May we all awake, honor and respect the healer within, and live a holistic life of health and longevity.

- May we unify as we purify, ending all war, separation, suffering and greed, that has consumed the Earth. May we tap into the natural wisdom of the ages, as we heal ourselves; that we may heal planet Earth and the entire world family.

TABLE OF CONTENTS

Opening the Way v
Dedication vii
Gratitude ix
About Planet Heal (Introduction). xi
Mother Earth Speaks. xiv
PLANET HEAL Daily Affirmations. xvi

BODY
Body Opening – Papyrus Of Ani xxi

A. Home
   1. Pher Ankh: Our Homes As Medicine, Llaila O. Afrika, ND 3

B. Total Care
   2. Healing Across The Continent, Alison F. Parker Henderson, DC. 7
   3. Optimal Healthy Living, Doctor Brother Natural, ND 10
   4. Creating Health In Our Communities,
      William "Emikola" Richardson, MD 13
   5. In The Fabric Of The Cloth, Bernadette L. Sheridan, MD, AAFP . . . 16
   6. Wholeness Of Mind Body Spirit, Stephen Ssali 19

C. Healers In Every Home
   7. A Healer In Every Home, Jesse Brown, ND. 22
   8. A Healer In Every Household, Bishara Wilson, DACM, SMA. . . . 26

D. Heal A Woman
   9. Heal The Mother, Heal The Earth, Danett Bean, DAAM 28
  10. Organic Blood, Tiffany Janay 31
  11. A Conscientious Birth, Sakina O'uhuru, CM, MS 34

E. Eat Well
  12. Healing With Foods And Herbs, Adio Akil 37

13. Supercharging The Immune System, Chef Keidi Awadu 39
14. Permaculture And Heirloom Seeds, Makeda Dread Cheatom 43
15. What's Wrong With Hybrids?, Chef Ahki 47
16. Eat Good On A Hood Budget, Stic & Afya Ibomu 50
17. Heal The People, Heal The Planet, Baratunde & Kayah Ma'at 52
18. The Remix, Tassili Maat 55
19. Earth Cookers, Wahidah Muhammad 58
20. Many Pathways To Wellness, Queen Afua 60

F. Breath & Beauty Head To Toe

21. At Our Best, Kimberli Boyd 64
22. The Creator Has A Master Planet,
Baba Osaygefo Colby & Karma Colby 66
23. Natural Love On Our People, Sheila Everette-Hale 71
24. The Power Of Breath And Sound, Ayo Handy-Kendi & John Davies 3 . 75
25. Healing Through The Voice, Betty Lane 82
26. Qi Gong: Breath Of Life, George Love, MD, AC 86
27. Love And Beauty Our Ultimate Healing, Queen Esther Hunter Sarr . . 89
28. Het Heru Healing Dance, Queen Mother Maash-T Amm Amen . . . 93

G. Crystal Legacy

29. Rock Your Life, Corinthia Peoples 96
30. Protection, Projection, Manifestation, H-Ankh Risingsun 100
31. Crystallize Your Life, Imani C. Scott 103

Body Closing – Dr. Llaila Afrika 106

MIND

Mind Opening – Bob Marley

H. Empower Thyself

32. Healer Within, Selina Brown 109
33. Phoenix Affects, Klarque Garrison 112
34. The Sense Of Reasoning And Willpower, Paul Goss, ND 115

35. Personal Transformation, Robin "Kheperah" Kearse. 117

36. We Can Heal Our Planet, Aturah Bahtiyah E. Nasik Rahm. 120

37. Sharing The Gift Of Wellness, Tanya Sherise Odums 123

38. Sacred Self...Sacred Work, Rha Goddess. 126

39. My Socks Do Not Have To Match, Gerianne Francis Scott 130

40. Peace Of Mind In Times Of Chaos,
    Mutshat Shemsut-Gianprem Kaur 137

41. Eat Green, Supa Nova Slom. 140

42. Mindfulness: Grab Hold, Rev. Kevin E. Taylor 143

I. Mindset Reset

43. How To Heal The Planet, Taharqa & Tunde-Ra Aleem 146

44. Purge & Purify, Bluepill (Aka Paul Moreland). 148

45. Healing The Community Of Self, Erica Ford. 150

46. Consistency, Akua Gray, ND & Chenu Gray, ND 154

47. Take Care Of Yourself, King Simon. 158

48. Social Healing, Onaje Muid. 160

49. Wholistic Academics 101: "Wholistic Health"
    Winston "Kokayi" Patterson, ND 164

50. D.A.D: Dedicated And Distinguished, Aundrieux Khonsu Sankofa-El .166

51. Natural Time & Global Peace Through Culture,
    Wanique Khemi-Tehuti Shabazz 170

J. Wealth Health

52. Wealth Is Our Legacy, Ellis Liddell 173

53. Healing Your Money Mindset, Prophetess Afraka Sankofa 175

54. The Essential Entrepreneur, Jeanne "Majestic" Taylor 178

K. In This Place

55. Preserving The Legacy, Omar Hardy 181

56. Preserve Paradise, Baratunde & Kayah Ma'at 184

Mind Closing – Lao Tzu 186

SPIRIT

Spirit Opening – Kahlil Gibran

L. Heart & Soul

    57. The S.O.U.L. In Soulmating, Montsho & Nwasha Edu 189

    58. Find Love And Keep It Alive, Chris "Kazi" Rolle 193

M. Arts & Soul

    59. Songerversation: I Am Light, India Arie 196

    60. The Paradigm Of Joy, Erykah Badu 200

    61. Healing Art, Leroy Campbell 202

    62. A World Declaration Of Divine Love, Nadi 203

    63. Harlem Is A Dance Divine, Abdel R. Salaam 205

    64. Music Medicine, Katriel Wise 207

    65. Art Guides My Life's Purpose, Marilyn "Idaka" Worrell 209

N. Soulspeak

    66. Love Is The Law, Snt Urt Kaitha Het Heru 212

    67. Ritualize, Come Alive, Prema 214

    68. Women Need To Heal, Rev. Hasifa A. Rahman 216

    69. Be The Light!, Rev. Nafisa Sharriff 218

    70. The Power Of L-O-V-E …Numerically Speaking, Lloyd Strayhorn . . .220

    71. Change Starts Within, Un Nefer Hetep Rā (Jawanza!) 223

    72. Healing The Soul, Memnon Uzan 226

    73. Thoughts For Planet Heal, Lauren Von Der Pool 227

Spirit Closing – Harriet Tubman 229

Healers Unite, We, The People 230

24 Hour Teleconference Flyer 231

The Healing Continues…, Queen Afua 232

We Stand Upon Their Shoulders 233

HEALERS' DIRECTORY 235

BODY

---

*A*rrange for me the way,
    may I renew myself,
may I become whole.

—Papyrus of Ani

PHER ANKH: OUR HOMES AS MEDICINE

Llaila O. Afrika, Naturopath

The home is a living spirit that expresses spirituality and the art and science of a culture.

The Kemetic (Egyptian) words, Pher (House) and Ankh (Life) mean House of Life. These words exemplify the culture systems of arranging homes. Ancient architecture, houses, buildings, artifacts, home arrangements, instruments, tools, art, dances and toys had holistic symbolism incorporated into them. The cultural symbolism used in the shape of a home started the construction with a tool that had holistic designs and shapes, which transmitted and translated the culture. The construction plan and the tools that built the home had holistic designs and shapes, which transmitted and translated the culture. blueprint layouts and tools used the cultural language transformed into symbols, designs, and shapes, and home arrangement. Therefore, the builder started and finished with cultural language (symbols, shapes), and not with fragmented symbols unrelated to culture, such as in today's building devices and machines. Fragmented devices and machines used in contemporary constructions lead to fragmented homes that do not relate to the individual's culture. A home/house/building can psychologically and emotionally disconnect you from yourself and cause you to connect to a cultural voice outside yourself.

The levers of today have no cultural meaning. In ancient times tools/devices/machines were extensions of culture in an abstract form. The ancient user of mathematics used his culture's idea of mathematics to design tools. People in ancient times saw math, tools, homes and home arrangement from the eyes and mind of their culture. They spoke about their culture through mathematics (numbers and letters) and transformed the numbers and letters (mathematics) into the shaping of a device. The device was used to transform stones and bricks into a building. The steps to arrive at the construction of a building required the language of culture called mathematics. The ancient peoples' usage of the language of mathematics lead to another language of culture called a building tool (device, machine). That lead to constructing a building, which is the architectural language of a culture. If you deconstruct or reverse the process (go backwards) you can trace the building to the tools and the tools to the mathematics and the mathematics to the person and person to the culture.

An individual's home arrangement is defined by their culture. The individual is a product of culture and serves the culture by following the culture's rules for conduct. Culture is evident in Pher Ankh, home arrangement, rituals, ceremonies, morals, marriage forms, food, parenting, dance, games, music, sports, spiritually, thought process, and so forth. Culture unifies people as a group. Only a group can grant a person life, liberty and the pursuit of happiness. Without a group to protect you, attack your enemies, and defend you, an individual has no rights. Rights to practice your culture at all times and in all situations (called freedom) are guaranteed by a group and not guaranteed by a behavior ritual, "Right", written on a paper. Consequently, the mathematics, tools, and constructed building reflected a group's culture, home arrangement, and made the individual feel secure in their personhood, because the group guaranteed the right to achieve the highest level of humanism. The use of Pher Ankh mathematics, tools, songs sung while doing construction, and food eaten while at work building a home were voices of culture and made a person feel holistic, nurtured, protected and connected to culture physically, emotionally, spiritually, and socially. The individual is always surrounded by their culture. Hopefully, the culture is intact and has not been distorted or invaded by another culture.

A culture intact uses its clothing, music, art, dance, sport, marriage and families to produce a healthy child. The child will possess their culture and prefer their culture to all other cultures. Cultures are different and teach the child to prefer one shape/design above another. The symbols called letters are different for each culture (Chinese, Japanese, German, French and so on). The letter's shapes are a method for transmitting culture. The letter's shapes are a method for transmitting culture. The letters used with numbers serve to transmit culture. Cultures read differently because they organize thoughts differently. For example, some cultures use word orders such as verb then noun and are read from the right to left; others are read in a vertical line from the bottom of the page to the top. The use of letters and numbers and organizing thoughts and home arrangement acculturates an individual. Pher Ankh home arrangement is an extension of the culture language in an abstract form. Pher Ankh is the voice of culture. Pher Ankh is easy to understand because it relates to the human body, science, astronomy (stars, planets) and directions (North, South, East, West), which are shared by all cultures. Therefore, any culture can use it and not feel culturally alienated. Pher Ankh is a universal system for arranging the home. It is an ancient humanistic system, which is ecumenical and has worldwide usage.

> *"Health is not found in hospitals and clinics; health care is found in homes."*
>
> DR. REGINA M. BENJAMIN,
> U.S. SURGEON GENERAL 2009-2013

Today the home is seen as a sterilized building for living. It is merely a structure of steel, glass, concrete, wood, and/or marble loaded with excessive material goods. If the home's arrangement is not specific, then it is a modern primitive dwelling linked to the modern uncivilized. The Europeans used Greek standards for arrangement and design and believed the home is built and arranged as culture-less even though it was culturally constructed by the Greek culture's normal values and standards of beauty. This mirrors European culture and their belief in the fragmentation and separation of roles and labor. The ancient black Africans' view of a home is a unified mixture of art and science based upon the cultural value system norms, philosophy, and theology. The African home and village is a function of kinship, gender, elders and ancestors. The area, domain or space and size of a village, home, room, building or size of furniture is not solely based upon abstract measurement and scales. Very much in the equation are the cultural sense of balance, aesthetics, ecology, and relationships to the environment. Also involved are the spiritual and philosophical meaning of the village, home, furniture, room, building and type of privacy required. As said earlier, the Kemetic words, Pher and Ankh mean House of Life. These words exemplify the culture systems of arranging homes.

The architectural structure of the human anatomy is physiology. The body is considered a holy temple (house) created by God. It is the anatomical home that the mind, emotions and spirit live in. The body has plants (flora), animals/insects (microbes), soil (minerals) and fluids (water) similar to the earth and its life forms. It has protons and electrons (planets) that have orbits similar to the planets in the galaxy. The body is a miniature world and galaxy, a microcosmic of the macrocosmic. Therefore, it was logical for ancient Africans to use the body as a model (blueprint) for building and arranging the home. The functional art and science needed to holistically interpret and translate the human anatomy and apply it to arranging the home is provided by the African culture.

When using Pher Ankh in their home, the Dogon of Sanga (Mali) included mixtures of human anatomy and human biology in the symbolism. The Dogon houses were built to symbolically duplicate the human anatomy. The large rectangle family (living) room is the torso, smaller rectangle rooms on each side of the living room are the arms, and the door represents the mouth. The entrance to the vestibule faces the north and represents the protective male principle; while the outer door between the entrance and living rooms represents the nurturing female principle. The ground floor of the home represented the female giving birth to the cosmos, the ceilings represent the male protecting the cosmos, his skeleton is the beams in the ceiling, the four posts are a combination of the female's two arms and the male's two arms. The breath of life comes from their heads which are symbolized by the fireplace (stove) where meals are created. The fireplace is also the creative center of the home.

The designs inside and outside the house, on furnishings and utensils, as well as the layout of the village/cities, the structure of the houses and the artwork have meanings. Circles, for example, represent the cycles of life as in, the three (3) trimesters of pregnancy, the circadian cycle of food, the cyclic pattern of life, death and the rebirth or the eternity of time. Scaling Circles (circles inside of circles) and other geometric mapping patterns have cultural messages as well.

The cultural value system norms, philosophy, and theology within which we exist is a social, spiritual, political, moral, emotional and cultural tool from other cultures. In many instances, the system must be adjusted or changed because your present house or apartment in a building's architecture was designed and painted according to a culture other than your own. Therefore, your home must be personalized with Pher Ankh, which can reflect home medicine to charge you and your family.

HEALING ACROSS THE CONTINENT

Alison Parker Henderson, Chiropractor

"We must give up the silly idea of waiting on God to save us."

MARCUS GARVEY

"Many years ago, we fell asleep by the sedative of the superhuman, but the mystic magic of nature's wand says, 'awake and rise again.' Too long has thou slumbered. Too long has time passed you by. your work on earth has been delinquent and you cannot reign on high. If it is true that you have awakened, then good for you, but your work has just begun, because your brother needs awakening too. touch him softly, gently, a portion of thy light to him give, and the mystic magic of your touch will cause him to look and live."

—Lacretia Charlene Lockmore

What would you do to heal planet Earth? I am grateful to be a part of this phenomenal collective energy. It is so needed, as we are in a world crisis. As a healer of grassroots efforts for over 25 years, I have seen things go from bad to worse. I am a holistic chiropractor and herbalist, who has practiced on both sides of the ocean, here in the USA and also in Ghana, West Africa. I started in 1995, with the intention of just having a normal practice of helping people with back pain. I ended up being in the middle of a war against my people. I found myself on the front line with folks dropping dead from high blood pressure, diabetes and cancer; especially CANCER. I became overwhelmed when my fellow grassroots healers started dying by my side.

I left the USA in 2012 thinking I was going to help heal Ghanaians, but I did not realize I was the one who would receive a healing from Mother Africa. In Africa, I was called to be initiated, baptized, reborn, bathed, cleaned and redeemed; brought back to myself and made brand new. In Africa, I was embraced and caressed and felt love like I have never felt before. My soul was invigorated. The ancestors called me home. I heard them somehow and found the courage to get on the plane and come home.

It was not an easy journey, as I went over thinking I was the one who would be healing Africa. Yet, I had to surrender. I was taught how to be an African woman and how to pound fufu and prepare soup. I learned Twi, the Ashante language, and learned to dance at funerals. I was taught to wrap my hair, carry items on my head and make waist beads. I learned how to move with a man and to respect the king. I was trained in the knowledge of herbs and traditional healing practices. I was allowed to work in clinics and hospitals and with other practitioners. I became the doctor for the people in the villages, attending to their aches and pains. I massaged their aching, bleeding feet, cracked from years of dancing on the rough ground or walking miles and miles in Ghanaian slippers (flip-flops). The Ghanaians embraced me as a daughter and trusted me with their lives. I tended to the preachers, to the rich and the poor. The church embraced me, and I them. The way they worship is amazing. They pray affirmations strong enough to make the clouds in the sky shake. They dance and scream praises to the Lord without abandon.

In my humble opinion, (and I am in the world and not of it, so my opinion is very delicate) I am not involved in politics (Gil Scott said, "politricks"). However, it seems, the African race, throughout the diaspora is being systematically murdered; the practice of genocide is upon us. Dominicans are killing Haitians, Indonesians killing West Papuans. Xenophobia is in South Africa; while *niggas* are in *Souf* Chicago, Brooklyn, DC, Kingston, Trinidad, Niger and Togo. This must stop! If we are not killing each other, then the police are killing us. Woe the wars we get caught up in for the sake of…Add to that contaminated water, GMO foods, prescription medicine, street drugs, stress caused by poverty. Consider also, institutional racism, substandard education, welfare, food stamps, public housing, job and housing discrimination. Furthermore, there are the issues of post-slavery syndrome, broken homes, fatherless children, mothers with no mothers and poor relationships. What are we doing here? What of the future for our children and grandchildren? Life is so precious in Africa; God is so close-by; death is also close-by, waiting for your errors.

As physicians (healers), we must first — in the words of Imhotep, not Hippocrates — "Physician, Heal Thyself." Because if we are sick, we cannot heal others. On the airplane, they tell us if there is an emergency to place your own air mask on your face before placing a mask on your loved one. Many of us are healers whether we know it or not; we must heal ourselves first. Just as you have to love yourself first, before you can love someone else. We must heal so we can go save Africa, our homeland, from the rape and pillage. We must awaken our brothers and sisters so that we will not lose our resources; remember who we are.

I would suggest, if possible, removing yourself from the front line of the battlefield for as much time as you can afford, and heal yourself, first. Include your loved ones, if they are willing, then get together in your family circle, community and organize a plan of action. Again, if possible, go to Africa and heal in the sun and energy of the Mother. It is like going to a million-dollar natural spa with only 10 dollars. Eat the fruits and vegetables drenched in the African sun, nourished by the blood of her womb. Be embraced by the friendship and love you will receive. Visit your ancestors and pour libation to their cause and selfless sacrifice at the slave castles. Hush and hear their whispered cries, moans and pleading. Some souls are still trapped in the stench of blood, vomit, and shit that is piled and dried 12 inches high, becoming the floor itself in those dreadful slave castles.

We are dying as a people. We are being murdered day and night, not just by our brothers, sisters, husbands, wives and neighbors, but by the police and other trained predators. We are dying from the water, the foods the GMO and the racist systems of schools, dysfunctional hospitals and corrupt government. We have become slaves held under the guise of student loans, mortgages, car loans and other gangster-style interest-rated loans designed to rob us blind with no viable way to pay off anything.

It's time to go home. There are over 7000 African Americans and diasporic Africans living in Ghana. Many came with terminal cancers, high blood pressure, diabetes and obesity. Some have outlived the terminal cancer by more than 20 years. Most diseases are cured, everybody loses weight. There is no stress, no racism, no police brutality and not too much crime. Generally, 95% of the time Black people do not kill each other on purpose. If you don't get anything else in Ghana, you will get relief from stress and that alone can allow the body to heal quickly.

Being in Africa is like going 'down the country' to stay with Grandma, but even better. When the AA tribe gets together, oh how we laugh, bellies full of fufu and peanut soup and we laugh long and hard ***that we are free.***

OPTIMAL HEALTHY LIVING

Natural (Aka "Doctor" Brother Natural), Naturopath

Your House Is Not Your Greatest Asset
...Your Health Is!

Add More Years To Life By Adding More Life To Your Years!

Optimal healthy living is living in alignment the way God, Supreme Law, Nature, intended human beings to live. As presented below, optimal healthy living includes maintaining a positive mental attitude, organic raw vegan alkaline nutrition and regular exercise.

POSITIVE MENTAL ATTITUDE

A positive mental attitude means having an optimistic viewpoint and optimistic outlook on life.

The benefits of a positive mental attitude:
- Gratefulness, Happiness, Love Self-esteem, Longevity, Better health
- Greater success, Greater motivation
- Increased productivity, Better relationships
- Greater accomplishments
- Positive Affirmations

Your attitude determines and equals your altitude.

Tips for maintaining a positive mental attitude:
- Write down your goals.
- Write down your incentives and desires for reaching your goals.
- Develop a strong desire for achieving your goals.
- Develop a strong belief in your goals.
- Leave your comfort zone while avoiding the shock zone.
- Learn from your mistakes and do not repeat them.
- Always think and dream big.
- Always choose to be joyful.
- Spend one hour or more per day on self-improvement and self-development.
- Live fully in the present moment.
- Never quit.
- Fast, pray for values, guidance and awareness,
- Chant, Meditate, Contemplate
- Spend time in nature.

NUTRITION
Genesis Chapter 1 Verse 29 states:

"Behold I have given you every herb bearing seed upon the earth, and all trees that have in themselves seed of their own kind, to be your meat."

The human anatomy dictates that humans are by nature frugivore and/or herbivore; meaning that all humans are supposed to consume a vegan diet. The exception is mother's breast milk for newborns. That there are no stoves in nature proves that humans should only be eating fruits, vegetables, nuts, seeds, herbs and spices that do not require cooking. The best foods for human consumption are dark green leafy vegetables and low sugar fruits. There are also many Superfoods (nutrient dense) available in nature.

The benefits of an organic raw vegan diet:
- A more fit body
- Increased energy, health and beauty
- Radiant glowing skin,
- Stimulated hair growth
- Better vision
- Detoxified disease-free body temple
- Sexual rejuvenation
- Increased joy and love
- Greater sense of well-being
- Freedom from negative thoughts and emotions
- Increased wisdom, clarity and creativity
- Improved memory and concentration
- Stress reduction
- Finding true spiritual center
- Freedom from all forms of bondage
- Contact with infinite intelligence
- Ultimate spiritual high
- Closer relationship with God

EXERCISE
Aerobic, strength training and stretching exercises on a regular basis is necessary for a healthy lifestyle. Tibetan 5 Rites and Rebounding (jumping on a mini trampoline) are very beneficial exercises for your whole being. Exercises should be performed for a minimum of half an hour per day, at least four days or more per week.

The benefits of exercise:
- Lowers blood pressure, decreases fats and bad cholesterol
- Decreases risks of heart disease, cancer and strokes
- Helps maintain your ideal weight
- Decreases stress and increases happiness
- Helps build and maintain healthy bones, muscles and joints
- Increases utilization of nutrition
- Strengthens organs, especially lungs and heart
- Can be fun and entertaining
- Jogging, yoga, meditation in nature (Prospect Park in Brooklyn, NY) and in the morning, consuming a green smoothie is the best part of Dr. Natural's day.

CREATING HEALTH IN HUMAN COMMUNITIES

William "Emikola" Richardson, Integrative Physician

Planet Earth reflects the habits, actions and lifestyle behaviors of humans. In turn, human health is affected by our own lifestyle and the environment of Planet Earth which we belong to. Consider the estimate that about 95% of Heart and Artery disease, cancer and a myriad of other modern chronic diseases are caused by lifestyle factors blended with environmental toxin exposure. Lifestyle choices predominate as the cause of our modern chronic disease epidemic including our diet, the type of water we drink and shower in, the cosmetic and skin care products we use, tobacco use, our exercise and sleep habits, where we live and work and much more.

Planet Earth is polluted with about one hundred thousand synthetic (man-made) chemicals. Most humans alive today carry hundreds of various contaminants within our bodies. But, why? Because humans are exposed to these toxic chemicals through our food, water, the air we breathe and objects we touch. Most of these toxins are fat soluble chemicals that are dissolved into our fat tissues in ever increasing amounts upon exposure. These chemicals can become causative factors for a whole host of chronic diseases sweeping the planet today. We're talking about anything from Cancer to Chronic Fatigue Syndrome and autoimmune diseases such as Multiple Sclerosis to Multiple Chemical Sensitivity Syndrome, Sarcoidosis, Heart disease and Hypertension.

I and my associates have established the Advanced Clinics for Preventive Medicine (ACPM.NET) to treat detect and prevent a myriad of chronic diseases. We've found that many chronic diseases can be prevented and treated by improving or manipulating a person's diet and lifestyle as well as detoxifying their body of various environmental toxins. I've seen many chronic diseases totally abate or significantly improve such as Coronary Artery Disease, Senility, Erectile Dysfunction, Diabetic Gangrene, Obesity, Type 2 Diabetes, Sarcoidosis, Chronic Fatigue syndrome, Fibromyalgia, Pulmonary Fibrosis, Depression, Cancer, Eczema, IBS and many more. The fact of the matter is that cleaning up our diet, lifestyle and detoxifying our bodies and environment can reverse chronic diseases and have a positive impact on Planet Earth.

Since our short history on Planet Earth, humans have been shaping aspects of their environment, from fire to farming. However, the current influence of Homo Sapiens on Planet Earth has reached a much greater level and now, the Earth, itself, needs healing from its own chronic problems. I'm talking about the rapid increase in global warming because of man's more recent over-reliance on animal products as a food source and industrial pollution, accelerating since the 1850's, releasing greenhouse gases which trap heat inside Earth's atmosphere. In turn, global warming contributes to deforestation, drought, desertification, flooding and other extreme weather conditions. Domesticated animals, such as cows, discharging methane gas into the atmosphere, have become a major contributor to global warming and its negative effects on Planet Earth.

Let's review some of the numerous studies that have shown that traditional Plant-based whole-food diets, worldwide, prevent Heart and Artery disease, Hypertension, Obesity, Type 2 Diabetes, High Cholesterol and the development and growth of many cancers compared to the Western industrialized-era diet which is high in animal products and refined (non-whole) foods.

A study done in 1994 in South Africa by Dr. Denis Burkitt M.D.(medical missionary) compared the prevalence(cases in a population) of Chronic diseases such as Cancer, Heart & Artery disease, Hypertension, Obesity, Type 2 Diabetes and Non-Infectious Gastrointestinal diseases such as Hemorrhoids, Appendicitis, Diverticular disease and Ulcerative Colitis(an Autoimmune disease, where one's own immune system attacks part of their body). This study demonstrated that top cancers found in the U.S. and other Western industrialized nations(Breast, Lung, Prostate, Colon and Pancreatic Cancers) were unheard of in the rural native African populations, less influenced by the (foreign) Westernized diet while the White South Africans had significantly much higher rates of those 5 Cancers, Heart disease, Type 2 Diabetes, Hypertension, Strokes as well as all of the Non-infectious Gastrointestinal diseases mentioned above.

It has been estimated that Planet Earth can comfortably feed 9 billion human beings on a plant-based diet. On the other hand, it has been estimated that if the current world's population consumed as much meat and animal products per person as in the U.S., we would need 4 to 5 Planet Earths to produce those animal products. There is not enough grassland for everyone on Planet Earth to eat "Grass Fed" beef.

Western diseases are quickly spreading to the Asian and African continents. India has the largest actual number of type 2 Diabetes patients because of its vast population eating refined carbohydrates, overeating in general and becoming more sedentary. Nigeria has the largest prevalence of Breast cancer in Sub-Saharan

Africa because of more relative wealth enabling a higher consumption of animal products and refined food. There has been an epidemic of Autism in Lagos, Nigeria possibly because of the environmental hazards of burning computers for the parts. It has been predicted that, in the future, Chronic Western-type diseases will become the top causes of death in Africa, surpassing Malaria and other infectious diseases. There are numerous studies and anecdotal examples demonstrating that people from Asia or Africa have developed Heart & Artery disease or Cancer from moving to America and adopting a Western-styled animal product and refined food-based diet.

We can clean up and "Heal" Planet Earth by changing our lifestyle and avoiding polluting earth with environmental toxins whenever possible. Planet Earth can and would survive just fine without us. But, the opposite is not true; we need a clean and functional Planet Earth with minimal pollution to survive without the chronic diseases sweeping the planet. The human disease load can be curtailed with people moving towards and embracing a plant-based whole organic foods diet such as Traditional African and Asian diets.

IN THE FABRIC OF THE CLOTH

Bernadette L. Sheridan, Family Physician

For as many years as I have practiced medicine, the correlation between disease and how it is affected by social, cultural and environmental factors has always interested, intrigued and at times, haunted me. As one who treats the family as a unit, with each member in some way affected by the health (or unwellness) of the other members, I have been trained to look deeper beyond the actual illness (Diabetes, Hypertension, STD's Heart Disease, to name a few), and explore the deeper causes. In many cases, what is apparent on the surface, little Mary's constant headaches, for example, have less to do with the rare undetected brain tumors or aneurysm and more to do with the stress brought on by a family in crisis. The answer is not always found in a pill or a state-of the art MRI or PET scan.

As physicians, healers and scientists, we constantly ask the question why? When we are faced with conditions and statistics, which are spiraling out of control. It is our natural tendency to sincerely want to help — to make a difference. As we continue to ask the questions why, as the parallels between spiraling staggering illness (such as the epidemic of Diabetes) now attacking the next generation, and the accelerating global chaos, it becomes even more important that not only we ask the right questions, but that when the answers appear, that we take a hard look at them and quickly act upon them. Health Care Professionals: Doctors, Nurses and the entire team of those who deal with health are first and foremost members of the human race. We cannot separate ourselves from those we treat, because disease does not.

As people of the African Diaspora living in the richest, most powerful and most technologically sophisticated nation on Planet Earth, we have more reason to give health a more critical look. We should, after all, because the simple fact remains that even though we remain the minority, we represent the majority when it comes to Diabetes, Kidney Dialysis, certain types of Cancer, Childhood obesity, ect. Simply put, we are dying faster and in greater percentages than any other ethnic group in the melting pot. Technology can and will not reverse this. The answer is not in a new pill or a fancier test. Those things are merely tools. The solution has been discussed and re-discussed amongst the policy makers at the highest levels. Nevertheless, despite sincere and ongoing efforts, we seem not to have scratched the surface. Is the solution economic? Is there monetary gain to the whole business of illness? Are we culturally insensitive as a nation? Is this a sign of "end times"? Is there a conspiracy afoot?

Patients look to their physicians for answers, and physicians (who sometimes have no answers) are hard pressed- they themselves being measured with the same yardstick of wellness as those they dedicate their lives to help. The solution is multifaceted and ongoing. I suggest that we as physicians have a responsibility first to selves (for we should at least try to practice what we preach), then to our patients, and patients have a responsibility to be active partners in their own healing. The mirror first is held to self; therefore, the remainder is directed within my own profession of healers.

A recent article published in the August 4th, 2004 edition of the American College of Cardiology provides the usual statistical array, but within the numbers and the analysis lie what I think are cogent points, which cannot be ignored. In the study, based in San Francisco, it was found that African American patients with heart attacks got less available technology when compared to white patients. The researchers made it clear that factors such as access to care and socio-economic status had little to do their findings. In other words, patients of similar educational backgrounds status (working, college educated, "white collar" folk) received different outcomes and different treatments based on racial differences rather than economic differences. Black patients presenting with complaints of chest pain received life-saving newer technologies (such as Angioplasty or "Clot Dissolving" Medications at a much lower frequency than White Patients presenting with identical complaints and almost identical laboratory findings. The authors could offer no explanation for the data other than "physician bias". Factors like insurance, access to care and other variables were extracted from their analysis. The only difference between Patient A and Patient B was pigment.

Put in another way, it doesn't seem to matter what level of accomplishment you have achieved, there seems to be a significant portion of your treatment that is based on how you look rather than who you are. This seems to simplistic on first glance to even be relevant. But to a scientist, or a clinician, these findings, which have been analyzed, deemed to be statistically significant (to the nth degree of the "p" value), are not only alarming, but they are chilling to say the least.

As physicians, we know only too well that we must remain concerned, but at the same time detached. However, as a minority physician, we are rarely allowed the separation between our ethnicity and our profession. To detach oneself from this discussion, feeling that we are somehow spared the very statistics that scare us would require more energy fueling the denial than I can allow. As a minority physician, I find it difficult not to personalize the data. What would happen if I lost the ability to speak "doctorese".. If I were incapacitated by chest pain, or sudden loss of consciousness…What if my comfortable mantle of title and education should dissolve, leaving me alone with only my birthright to defend me. Would "physician bias" be my ultimate undoing, as I struggled to explain to an ER doctor (with his own physician bias) that my chest pain was real, my abdominal pain was not PID (Pelvic Inflammatory Disease), the mark of a promiscuous woman, or my back pain was not from a malingering welfare mom trying to beat the system? Could I be certain that the clinician who examines me was not clouded by "physician bias" and that he could give me a diagnosis that was based on science and not his perception of who I was?

It is my contention that every minority physician if they are truly honest with themselves has had that haunting fear at one point in time or is hyper vigilant about their family when faced with health care issues. We are subject to the same physician bias that condemns our patients. The same system that has failed them is failing us. As a matter of fact, it is the very denial that racial differences make a difference and the inability to look deeper into that sticky and uncomfortable "can of worms" that makes the problem of racial disparities exist to this day. Conference after conference, study after study, statistic after statistic point to the same conclusion: Racial disparities exist in health care, access to care, treatment, and outcome, because racism exists.

Any clinician worth his/her training knows that to treat the symptom without addressing the problem will ensure that the problem will continue. What is manifesting in health care today is a result of our inability to address the subject of racism from its inception. To go back and to look back is so collectively painful that we overlook, deny and make excuses for something even more deadly than the diseases we seek to eradicate. There is no hope for solution unless we as a nation tackle the sore instead of placing the band-aid. The answer is not in the technology; I fear it is woven in the fabric of the cloth.

I am cautiously optimistic about the future of health care in America, not because I place so much faith in the health care system. I am still of the opinion that it needs a major overhaul. I believe the prognosis for health care will continue to be terminal unless we address the underlying disparities. We have never been very good at facing facts. Denial of the obvious discrepancies is as American as the Declaration of Independence. Unless racism on all its levels is addressed and dissected, these discrepancies will continue and will escalate. I have no reason based on fact to believe otherwise. What I do believe in is the resiliency and survival of people of color despite the insurmountable odds of centuries. Since energy is limited, I am of the mind to continue to spend mine in the attempt to inform and educate and leave policy making to the bureaucrats of my generation.

OPTIMIZING SELF: WHOLENESS OF MIND BODY SPIRIT

Stephen Ssali,
Western/African Herbal Medicine

Optimizing Self is a journey into wholeness. We are whole beings of multi-dimensional nature. We are created in the image and likeness of the creator. Every aspect is reflective of the whole, we are in the process of remembering who we really are and embracing the oneness of all that is. The Universe we live in is holographic in nature. We are holograms containing all possible versions of reality. The part is in the whole and the whole is within the part. The microcosm and macrocosm are interconnected and one.

The optimum self is one of the versions of reality that exists at a specific frequency and vibration. We are vibrational beings living in a vibrational universal ocean of pure energy. We experience and interpret vibrations through our senses. Everything vibrates and resonates at a specific frequency. Our Imagination is the archive of all possible reality. It is from this archive that we focus and select a version of reality that mirrors our optimum self. The optimum self is then activated with our feelings as the universe is always responding to the way we feel. Our core beliefs determine the reality that we perceive and the perception we have creates the experience of the optimum self.

Optimizing self begins with clear visualization of a solid clear picture of the blueprint of the optimum self. We plant an image of the optimum self in our mind's eye seeing the detail with our mental antenna and tuning in. The essence of optimizing self is the way we feel as the optimum self, so getting excited and passionate about how we would feel if we were living as the optimum self now is essential. Engage all your emotions and senses as if you were that optimum self, right here and now. Imagine smelling, touching, hearing and feeling optimum.

The optimum self is grounded in our being, by being and doing what it takes. In order to achieve optimization, we start to mimic closely the actions you see yourself doing in the optimum self-visioning process. Creating a make-believe physical action trains the body consciousness to make you a better receiver of the version of the optimum self that already exists. A version of the optimum self exists here and now, all you have to do is select it and let in.

All radio programs and television programs exist as frequencies. A radio set or television set does not create the program, it just selects it and allows it in. This is also similar to the manifestation of the optimum self we desire. The human body is a divine temple with our brain as a receiver and transmitter. Once we select our desired channel of optimizing self we can now tune in and receive the essence and realization of that reality actualized.

Every event, situation or circumstance has no built-in meaning, they are blank and neutral, we get to assign significance or meaning or interpretation on how it occurs for us and how we interpret the experience. If you assign positive meaning to an event it will produce a positive experience for you. If you assign a negative meaning this will produce a negative experience for you and normally we assign and project a meaning onto a neutral situation we are not even aware we are doing it. We are oblivious of the fact that we are the ones assigning meaning to a neutral event. The optimized self follows its highest excitement. Excitement is caused by resonance with your higher self and is a sign that the activity you are contemplating is aligned with your higher self. The alignment is what causes the excitement.

The optimum self is one with the whole. Hence, following your excitement leads to positive synchronicity; while negative synchronicity comes from ignoring your excitement and letting fear be the experience you choose. The optimum self knows there are no victims or villains only co-creation. Any experience shared by two or more people is the result of all the people involved agreeing to co-create that experience. You can only experience that which is resonant with the vibrations you are currently choosing to be. If you believe you need to be protected, you are attracting into your reality the very thing you believe you need to be protected from. The blueprint of the optimum self is created through the beliefs, emotions, thoughts and actions of the personality.

THE ESSENCE OF OPTIMIZING SELF BEGINS WITH AN OPTIMUM MIND.

The conscious mind thinks it is in charge, in fact it is the subconscious mind making decisions and the conscious mind making up stories to explain those decisions. William James quoted, "If you want a quality, act as if you already have it." What you do, what you own, what you plan, what you think you are, what you want, and so much more are all the result of beliefs and values you have been trained to have, to be and want. Our mind has immense abilities to create the life of our dreams (Good health, wealth and love) and also the ability to bring us everything we say we don't want (sickness, poverty and loneliness). Imagine your mind is like a fresh, sparkling water flowing from a high mountain spring. As the water travels down the mountain it picks up contaminants, however it is still considered clean and drinkable. During our formative years from 0 to 7 years, our subconscious mind is open, programmed and conditioned by our environment.

Our parents and environment play a key role in forming the personality, identity and character we become. Jesuit priests once proclaimed give me a child between the age of 0 to 7 years and he will belong to the church for the rest of his life. Ralph Waldo Emerson quoted, "To get up each morning with the resolve to be happy…is to set our own conditions to the events of each day. To do this is to condition circumstances instead of being conditioned by them."

In Optimizing the mind of self, we are familiar with the terms: the power of the mind, mind over matter and the mind-body connection. We have all heard of spontaneous healings and creating the life of our dreams. The movie, 'The Secret' showed how one's mind was a genie and whatever the mind held in detail it would attract or create.

Many of us created vision boards, printed affirmations and placed them everywhere to see them constantly, began visualizing the things we wanted, tuned into new age radio shows and started reading self-help books. This process achieved varying results in that for most people who tuned into the genie within nothing happened. The question why this happened this way indicates to us that the mind is a doorway to the manifestation process and not the manifestation tool.

Our mind provides the pictures, not the feeling. It organizes the activity to build the vision board and post affirmations. The human brain is a marvel of evolution as far as human consciousness is concerned and one of the best developments is the cerebral cortex. The cerebral cortex is the largest part of the brain and within it the inhibitory power resides. The cortex inhibits impulses that are not in our best interest or intentions. The cortex shuts off the television when the content is violent, suggestive of disease and illness.

We are a product of millions of years of survival mechanism, within us are primitive mechanisms that respond to primitive and gross stimuli. The mechanisms respond to fight or flight, taboo images, fearful rejections in a mechanical way. The law of attraction states that, like attract like. There are three components of the law of attraction: ask, believe and receive.

Manifestation involves an emotional input that is passionate and convinced, a process of visualization and letting go. The spiritual sincerity that realizes that we are a gift from the creator and releases our vision knowing this or something better will manifest for the highest good of all.

A HEALER IN EVERY HOME

Jesse R. Brown, Naturopath

There are numerous health problems in the U.S and globally. The situation gets worse with each generation. At the root of societal ills is poor and declining health. Just as health calamities are the number one reason people go bankrupt, the greatest threat to the national economy is rampant sickness among its people.

Ever-growing incidences of obesity, heart disease, diabetes (adult and juvenile), cancers and infant mortality are affecting millions of families, globally. The number of deaths due to prescription drugs, and abuse of alcohol, tobacco and drugs is overwhelming. Mental illness diseases leading to suicides, and even homicides are causing national alarm. Parents are questioning the damage from vaccinations and immunizations. Global populations are seeking solutions for poisoned water and polluted land. These plagues are even worse among minority populations and underserved communities.

In the US, the offspring of those who built this country and nurtured its growth are not enjoying the fruits of their ancestors' labor; as they should. Poverty and sickness have become the legacy of men and women who did most of the work to lay the foundation of America. Notably, those ancestors were not and *could not* have been ill; they would not have reached here, nor survived the harsh conditions. So why are we, descendants dying in record numbers?

What is the answer to the myriad problems we face with our people, the environment and the threat to all life on Earth? I believe the answer is to train a Healer in Every Home!

What is a Healer? A Healer is a person who is trained in and understands the elements that create healing of the people, the Earth and balance among all living beings. It is someone aware of the importance of the relationship of all things working together as one harmonious organism; as opposed to working against itself in chaos on a path to destruction.

The Healer embraces, in part or in total the Wholistic concepts that are required to heal the people and the planet. Otherwise, as we destroy one, we destroy the other! The ability to heal is inherent within each of us and can be activated under the proper circumstances with encouragement, acceptance, and support. A Healer may help heal people, and subsequently the planet and its plants and animals as part of the bigger purpose.

The effect of having millions of Healers nationally and internationally would be vast and invaluable. Families, communities and people of all races, cultures, and origins could embrace concepts of healing that would help to delay and reverse the destruction of the planet's global warming and slow the degradation of health everywhere.

Traditionally, the concepts and practices of healing were a part of practically all peoples in the world. In some cultures, healing was passed down from generation to generation within families, among Shaman, medicine men and women, and so forth. Over time, the methods of healing were taught only to those who could afford expensive education. Healing principles were held exclusively by those who established schools, standards and approved systems of practice.

What must a Healer learn and what are the essential elements of healing?

The principles of healing are simple and universal. In order that more, rather than fewer may be empowered as caregivers and Healers in training, I share the following fundamentals of the healing process.

There are three essentials common to all methods of healing, whether it is allopathic, naturopathic, homeopathic or other. They are Assessment, Treatment, and Maintenance (A.T.M.):

1. Assessment — The ability to determine what the health concern is and whether that concern is within the ability of the Healer. Assessment in a medical environment is called diagnosis. Typically, a diagnosis includes the patient's (or advocate's) report, coupled with a physical examination and tests (blood, urine, saliva), x-rays, and so on. In the medical model assessment is learned according to Western protocols that are standard in and out of the U.S. Naturopathic assessment methods may involve a variety of modalities from iridology, pulse diagnosis, face reading, energy readings, and more. These assessments might not involve modern-day Western technology; however, some do. The goals of either method are the same, to find the underlying imbalance(s). The medical protocol tends to address the symptoms; while Naturopathy tends to identify the cause.

2. Treatment — What is done once the assessment is completed? Treatment is designed to correct the health problem using the tools at hand. Allopathic medicine primarily uses drugs, surgery, physical therapy, and in some cases diet and lifestyle factors. Naturopathic treatments utilize many elements derived from nature, such as, sunlight, fresh air, exercise, raw superfoods, healing foods; and food supplements such as, vitamins, minerals,

herbs and homeopathic medicines. Naturopathic treatments include bodywork such as, massage, structural balancing and alignment, chiropractic alignment, acupressure, acupuncture, reflexology and energetic healing such as, Reiki or Healing Touch. There are hundreds of healing modalities under the realm of Wholistic or Naturopathic healing that are typically not utilized in allopathic healing.

3. Maintenance — This phase of the healing paradigm is what is done once the acute or chronic health problem has been addressed. Under allopathic maintenance — which varies in length of time — is the plan of aftercare. In Naturopathy maintenance diet, lifestyle, exercise, meditation, and other strategies are used to keep the body in balance so that the condition does not return. To know if the health is being maintained, some form of monitoring and measurement is necessary. Typically, blood sugar, blood pressure and weight are routinely measured.

To help ourselves, our loved ones and/or our community we must understand each of these elements, how to apply them and how to proceed. We can learn the role and application of Assessment, Treatment and Maintenance in medical and naturopathic methods. The average person can learn to administer first aid, CPR, injections, medication usage and then care for the sick and elderly at home. Equally, through training and experience, we can learn what nature provides us and how to use food as medicine.

To resolve the present health crises, we cannot and should not rely on medical intervention alone. Chronic diseases (diabetes, heart problems, cancers) will only be prevented through awareness and willingness to change our daily decisions. Just as the trained medic is needed to tend to the wounded in the battlefield, we need to train the family and friends who are caregivers to our wounded and those in harm's way. The people who can best identify symptoms of depression, dementia, diabetes and others, are those trained to do so. It could be quite effective to teach these close advocates with methods for curbing the illness(es). Learning to heal and therefore becoming a Healer in the family, the community and in the world should not be reserved for an exclusive few who can afford to do so. Developing the healer within must be made available to the masses. The trend for decades is that we have been spending more money on healthcare, yet our disease rates are getting worse. It is time for a drastically different approach to healing. Millions more people who are looking for innovative solutions to the problems must be involved in the process.

When we reconsider the role of relationships, (parental, family, community), we will be better able to identify and reclaim what we have lost. Our maintenance of wellness was lost when we stopped eating together and started working longer hours; and when we disconnected from people while becoming more connected with electronic devices. The answers are not in high-tech, but instead in **high-touch**; not the Internet, but the **inner net**! If we continue to look *outside* of the house instead of *inside* the home — within the hearts and heads of those who are hurting, we will continue to follow a path that leads to more drugs and disease.

Having a Healer in Every Home is real and attainable. Today's problems are not genetic. By preserving, protecting, promoting and perpetuating our traditional healing practices, we can recapture a world in which we have less stuff but more substance. Let us return to the existence when we loved, valued and cared for people, and only liked and used things. We can heal ourselves and the world we temporarily inhabit if only we care for and about those for whom we are the caretakers.

The Wholistic Training Institute in Detroit is a Naturopathic School licensed by the State of Michigan, since 1999. We are approved to offer certification in over 96 classes onsite and online. Our Mission is to Train a Healer in Every Home by using the Wholistic ways and traditions of our ancestors. We believe Good Health Begins Inside and The Power to Heal Is Within every one of us.

The 4 pillars of our program are Empowerment, Employment, Enterprise and Entrepreneurship. Using these principles, we can create health and foster wealth in our communities in ways that are accessible and sustainable. We can reclaim our healing birthright.

A HEALER IN EVERY HOUSEHOLD

Bishara Wilson, Acupuncturist

For the world to heal itself, each person needs to be responsible for their own help. People should only need health professionals and hospitals for emergencies and the conditions that they are unable to handle themselves. This is achieved through the knowledge and practice of activities that promote and maintain health and vitality.

One of the first ways to promote health is through one's mentality and worldview. A positive outlook on life helps to decrease the stress that is at the root of many modern health issues. Stress decreases the flow of vital energy and blood in the body. The body reacts to stress by activating the fight-or-flight system in the body instead of remaining in the rest and relax condition. Over time this wears on the body's organs and ages the body quickly.

There are many ways to decrease stress and be able to cope more effectively with life issues. One is silent meditation. During silent meditation, you sit still and focus on your breathing while maintaining a good posture. Meditation can also include visualization techniques that replace all of the thoughts that can occupy the mind while you were sitting in silence.

Prayer also reduces stress by helping to strengthen your spiritual health. When you have faith in a higher power, you understand that the highest good will occur when you, "Let go and let God." Prayer and faith also allows for us to think bigger than what we can actually see currently and know that the universe is bending and shaping so that we can experience the best outcome all the time.

Reading religious and spiritual text is a source of wisdom and inspiration that can be related to in order to make better decisions and, "Keep the faith."

Physical exercise is necessary to promote and maintain health and vitality. Activities and exercises that tone and strengthen the body. Our muscles and bones are the structure that keeps us upright. Strong muscles look and feel good to help us have a better improved self-esteem. Self-esteem gives us courage to go out on a limb and face situations that others avoid. Strength training also helps you avoid low back pain knee pain and other injuries. A strong body combined with other healthy lifestyle choices promote energy and blood circulation to help increase longevity and overall fantastic well-being.

Flexibility is also necessary. We want our bodies to be able to bend and move not be stiff and dry. Suggestions: calisthenics and stretching or excellent exercises; calisthenics or strength training exercises like push-ups and sit-ups. You want to stretch before and after strength training exercises to relax and lift in the muscles to help avoid injury. Other exercises that promote strength and flexibility are yoga, Tai Chi, Qigong, and the martial arts.

The foundation of health and vitality is diet. In modern times, the soil has been over farmed which depletes it of nutrients. Many plants have been genetically modified with evidence of resulting poor nutritional quality. Crops are sprayed with toxic herbicides and pesticides. Eating organic food or foods from the local farmers market provides high quality foods that are rich in nutrients which your body needs to rebuild itself all the way to the cellular level. Eating high-quality foods helps you to look, think and feel better. We want to eat whole and unprocessed Foods. This usually means home-cooked meals, prepared "from scratch". If something comes in a box and won't spoil for years in your cabinet, you may not want to put it in your body.

In Eastern medicine, herbs are called The Forgotten Food because they are necessary to the body as common foods that we eat but are often overlooked. Herbal medicine includes plant, animal and mineral-based parts. In plants this includes roots, seeds, bark, stem, rhymes, leaves and flowers that we may not normally think to consume but are rich in nutrients needed to maintain body function and heal from sickness. Every household should also have some good books on how to use herbs and an herbal medicine cabinet stocked with a variety of herbal mixtures. Herbs can be taken internally in the form of teas, capsules, pills, and tinctures. Herbs can also be absorbed through the skin as herbal baths, foot soaks, compresses, oils and liniments.

With all the demands of life, you are still ultimately responsible for maintaining your own health. By consciously working to improve your physical, emotional, and spiritual health you will make better decisions which lend to increasing your health, vitality, and longevity.

HEAL THE MOTHER, HEAL THE EARTH

Danett Bean, Women's Health Physician

Give mothers exquisite health. That is what I would do to heal Planet Earth. As a traditional Asian Medicine practitioner one of the key ways that we approach healing is through an understanding of the five elements: fire, earth, metal, water and wood. Extremely important in this is not just the elements by themselves, but the varying relationships of each of these elements with each other. Qi or energy flows between the elements and they are interdependent upon each other.

The most basic and key relationship of the elements is that each element gives energy to another element. In traditional Asian Medicine, the element that gives energy to the next element is called "the mother" and there is a specific sequence to this flow. Fire is the mother of earth, earth is the mother of metal, metal is the mother of water, water is the mother of wood and wood is the mother of fire. When someone comes in for assistance with their health and if the practitioner is using the five elements (a core traditional Asian Medicine approach), the practitioner identifies the imbalance and restores harmony. Sometimes that means reducing excesses, sometimes that means strengthening deficiencies; the end result is always to have this cycle return where each energy flows, fire to earth, earth to metal, and so on.

If someone has an acute situation going on, that is what must be addressed first — for example pain or often some type of inflammation. However, once that is resolved, the root should be addressed and then a preventive care regimen is put in place. Similarly, there are many things going on in the world currently that need immediate attention: climate change, oppressions and more. While individual missions, i.e. actions that address the symptoms, or what in traditional Asian Medicine refer to as the branch treatments need to happen, for true and sustained wellness, the root must be addressed. To come back to the flow of qi through the elements, the "mother" element must be functioning optimally.

What does it mean for the mother element to be functioning optimally? It means that she is not deficient, that she truly has enough qi or energy to pass on to the child element. This same correlation can be understood for human mothers. The more energy and vitality a mother has, the more she can naturally give to her children and family. Consequently, a lack of health and vitality of the mother, results in less energy to be given to her family. An often-unspoken condition, Postnatal Depletion, exemplifies this.

Postnatal Depletion has the potential to affect maternal health in the short and long term. Often if a mother has not been feeling well, mentally or physically after having a child, she is maybe diagnosed with postpartum depression and antidepressants are prescribed. While postpartum depression is a serious condition that requires treatment, what if the mother not feeling well, is not postpartum depression, or not postpartum depression alone? What if the mother actually is depleted? Depletion can happen from a variety of factors, not only, but including: health deficiencies and imbalances prior to pregnancy, medical inductions that sever important meridians (energy pathways), hemorrhage, lack of support after giving birth, returning to work too quickly and increased stress. Postnatal Depletion can linger on for years and make her more susceptible to chronic and potential terminal conditions, in large part because her core health was never addressed.

Think not only of her health, but the health of her children, as well. Think about the roles that she may play in her community as: daughter, sister, friend, teacher, wife, professional, and so on. Each area suffers when she does not truly have enough qi to give. This has been the case in our communities more than what may be realized. Many mothers also will give to other places and minimize their own needs, furthering their depletion.

Then there are mothers we see who may be rude and disrespectful to their child. Some of us like to shake our heads and blame this mother, usually without knowing her story and the reasons why. Oftentimes a lack of resources (within the body — her qi or blood) can lead to some sort of excess which can include heat. This heat can show up as inflammation, whether it be health conditions, such as autoimmune conditions, or turn outwards and manifest as anger or irritability.

To truly help mothers be as healthy as possible and heal the planet, education, healthy choices and support must start from the beginning. Not just during pregnancy, but from the beginning of her life as a female. All babies, including girl babies need to be treated with the utmost respect. **The girl baby is born with all the eggs that she will ever have; the potential for the constituents of the next generation are within her.** Her mind, her body, her ideas must be nurtured and listened to.

To heal the planet, I would make sure that the girl child (and all children) are in totally safe environments, so that she/they are not abused and are able to stay clear of the residual weight and stagnation that can result. That she is taught about her body for what it is, as good and wonderful and completely under her domain. Her esteem and her spirit are to be elevated so that she finds her "selves" around good people which comes from her having good relationships with her parents/caregivers. In the long-term, this increases the likelihood for her to make better choices about who to be in a relationship with and who to share genes with. It includes being fed healthy foods, i.e. no hormones, or pesticides, but instead a diet that is high in vitality so that when it is time for her to begin menstruating, it is a healthy experience. Also, that the girl child is taught about her cycle and the cycles of nature and for her to understand that she is one with all. Teaching these things is what is needed.

This is how I would heal the planet. Making certain that the girl child grows up with support that continues throughout her life is critical. The following conditions need to be in place:

- Essential resources such as ongoing sister circles, as well as thoughtful, attentive, respectful, and affordable medical care would be the norm.
- As an adult if she chooses to become a mother, her health is good going into conception and she has abundant good qi, for her and her baby.
- Prior to, during and after labor she is surrounded by the help that she wants, and she is able to rest and replenish with a true decision on her part of when she is ready to serve others, i.e. true qi that she has enough to pass on.
- Continuing a healthy lifestyle will allow her to have her best health and when she is ready, give qi to all the different areas in her community.
- When the time comes for her to enter menopause, because her health has been good, it is a smooth and joyful transition.
- She continues this throughout old age and the rest of her healthy and blissful life in this realm.

Each stage of the way, women get support from nature and natural remedies, and from their communities- this is how I would heal the planet. Her health, her joy, her gifts truly nurture all the elements that surround her, which in turn is given back to her. This should be a beautiful dance that never ends and restores the planet and all her inhabitants.

ORGANIC BLOOD

Tiffany Janay, Holistic Health Advocate

Organic Blood was created out of pure necessity. In 2006 my husband, Malik Zakee, and I were just beginning our relationship as boyfriend and girlfriend. We immediately knew that our connection was something powerful, and we would create a legacy together. The question was what would our legacy be? At the time, he weighed 300 pounds and was borderline for high blood pressure. I weighed 200 pounds, had extremely high cholesterol, was blacking out randomly and had a slew of other scary issues.

We knew that before we could build a sustainable business, we first needed to build sustainable health. Rationally, we wanted to become financially successful, but did not want poor health to cause us to be struggling to enjoy our success. We began making a list of what an ideal life looked like. We looked for guidance from mentors who were living in accordance with our goals.

The research began, and we read every book we could and watched tons of videos and documentaries. We gathered tools and empowered ourselves with knowledge. We needed this information for ourselves, but we quickly realized that with our change in lifestyle came a lot of adversity from our peers and family. The information we gathered became our shield against the attacks , which came rapidly. People didn't understand why we quit our jobs and why we were "eating like rabbits." They had never seen anyone do things like this before, and it was completely against the grain.

Along with quitting our job came the backlash. We lost many things we had gained when we worked our jobs. we were forced to live in uncomfortable places, all because we didn't want to work "regular jobs" any longer. The "regular jobs" were part of what was making us sick and unhealthy. The environment and workloads were against our plans for living a healthy lifestyle, so we knew we couldn't go back.

Our focus shifted to what we could do with the resources we had at the time. We began fasting together, working out, and slowly changing our diet to eventually being full vegan. We felt amazing! The weight was dropping off, and we were curing ourselves of our ailments. This made us feel very powerful, and we wanted more power! We soon began sharing our knowledge with anyone who wanted to know what we were doing, and we saw the people around us begin to shift.

Sharing our story on social media was inevitable. The people needed to know what was possible with Earth and all it had to offer us to help us heal ourselves. We slowly began to build up our tribe and people from all over the world took the information we shared and then made changes in their lives too. It was amazing to witness and be part of the shift that was happening.

A few years into our journey, I was gifted the book **Heal Thyself** by a sister I met for the first time. I shared with her where I was in my healing journey, and she told me I needed this book to help me accomplish my next level goals. **Heal Thyself** completely changed my life, and I knew I had to meet and create an alliance with Queen Afua and her family. Shortly, I made that dream come true. I created a bond with the First Family of Wellness, and we immediately began creating with each other.

Organic Blood grew from the direction of the people. It was what we needed to allow us to live from our own talents. The people guided us with their needs, told us what to create and promised to contribute and support us. We began creating events for people to gather and enjoy good music and a cool environment; while also eating healthy food. Our events were so well received that we were inspired to create more. Our events are vital because we want to show people that caring for self should be fun and entertaining. You do not have to do this alone when there is a community of us.

In 2013, we moved from California to Atlanta. Our company and mission expanded mass levels and lead us to focus on womb wellness along with our community events. Shortly after our relocation, our company, "Organic Blood Yoni Eggs" became a sensation, and we were attracting so many women that needed our guidance on the product we were providing.

We were pushed to take what we were doing very seriously. We identified Yoni Eggs as our main focus and gained as much knowledge as possible. We formed a powerful sisterhood to support the women on their journey. Then something unexpected, yet very necessary happened; we formed unity amongst women! This was so healing for me personally and helped me shift how I had felt about relationships with women.

Organic Blood Yoni Eggs was the first to launch an e-commerce website dedicated just to Yoni Eggs, thus giving birth to a new industry. Our love of crystals and womb health has taken us around the world to form sister circles. We have been connecting with our community on an intimate basis to inspire a change of wellness into our lives. We have grown our community and have helped people to speak to each other with more compassion, to cheer each other on and celebrate each other's success. We have consistently provided tools to people as we gather them for ourselves.

Semi-precious stones are ancient beings that live within the earth and have been respected tremendously throughout history. I like to think of them as beings that have lived many lifetimes and have mastered traits which with many of us humans struggle. These are traits such as forgiveness, self-love, focus, confidence and supreme health. These beings, the Mineral People, have overcome those blockages and will vibrate at that frequency, for eternity. They are part of the grid of our planet and are here holding space for our growth and personal expansions. Keeping them around in your space is extremely influential to your vibration and just being around them inspires you to aspire higher.

Envisioning the womb in likeliness to a garden is helpful when learning how to care for that special place within us. It requires a nice sunny place, filled with friends that are great for its ecology (birds, bees, worms, and other beneficial insects). The PH must be maintained in balance. It requires nutritious compost (food with minerals and vitamins). You must weed it consistently to be sure nothing is going to starve it from its nutrients or stunt its growth potential (transitioning relationships can be toxic to our well-being). Watering it daily is vital and it is important to preserve the seeds for the next harvest.

Using crystals within the womb space helps to bring high vibrational energy in and creates a connection between woman and her womb. What I have witnessed within my years of this work are women awakening to power they possess. Suddenly, they want to worship their yoni! They begin making decisions every day that will benefit their sacred space, thus turning them to a lifestyle dedicated to their self-love and personal care. I love witnessing them crave more healthy foods, companionship from other women, sacred baths, adequate exercise and better feminine care products overall.

I am thankful for the work of the honorable Queen Afua, because it is she who awakened me to my potential and from there I, along with my mate, was able to go out into our communities and help to shift them to higher levels. Initially, I didn't know that my journey would take me to do this type of work, but I'll never forget the first time I met Queen's son, Ali. With a sea of people around us he said to me, "You are here for something more than what is being sold on this table. You came with something greater in mind." That has turned out to be the truth.

In summary, our contribution to the universe includes educating those who resonate to us about the power Earth contains and its healing abilities. We must encourage everyone to live life as organically as possible' and keep it simple. Everything we need is within the Earth. We must encourage women to connect with the divinity within and to nourish herself religiously and for the men to support that. For, it is the woman that sets the tone of our societies, and it is she we all aim to please. When she is balanced and healthy minded, she will give life and raise up everyone who comes within her presence.

Learn more about us and join us on our mission by finding Organic Blood on social media.

HEALING THE PLANET EARTH: A CONSCIENTIOUS BIRTH

Sakina O'uhuru, Activist/Midwife

Healing the planet begins when greater value is placed upon the spiritual transformation of birth. Healing the planet begins when the current management of Pregnancy Labor and Birth shifts towards a more humane approach. The current management of pregnancy, labor, and birth must change towards a more dignified honorable process.

The planet heals with the elimination of racial and gender bias in labor/birth management. Our planet heals when racial discrimination and reproductive injustice ends. Healing will begin when healthcare shifts from a for-profit politically and economically driven model towards a more holistic compassionate standard. The planet heals when empowered women intentionally articulate their needs and play a more active role regarding the management of their labor and delivery. Healing the planet will begin when women begin to own their power and consciously use their voices to stand up and make demands that support their choice regarding labor-room interventions and overall care.

Healing the planet begins when the insurance industry no longer uses its corporate power to regulate the practice of midwives by denying women access to midwifery services or access to maternity care of their choice. Our labor birth choices have been influenced by our social norms and dictates that do not place enough value upon women's most sacred life event.

African American history reflects a legacy of strength exemplified by women who in the past have chosen Midwives as the primary provider for support during pregnancy labor and birth. Today, that legacy has changed to one that reflects underutilization of Midwives by African American women. We have moved away from our healing legacy. Healing the Planet arises with culturally competent health care providers. Culturally competent providers can help improve birth outcomes and can positively impact the health equity of women.

The planet heals when women are encouraged to reflect upon elements of importance in their lives. Reflecting upon those elements will support them in self-discovery. This reflection strengthens, empowers and helps support women to feel stronger and secure in decisions regarding birth practitioner and birth settings.

Healing the planet requires women to reject our current domineering approach towards the management of labor. For some time now, we have allowed the current medical paradigm to define for us what is important to us during our pregnancy, labor, and birth journey. We have all been socialized to believe in the current one-dimensional, medicalized approach to managing pregnancy, labor, and birth. This approach focuses more on technology and invasive procedures rather than the human experience. Our medical care system is a male dominated for-profit driven corporation comprising an impatient hostile agenda based in fear. This system offers marginalized care towards women of color.

The current paradigm is hostile towards out-of-hospital birth settings. For the most part, home birth as an option for labor and birth has been rejected by the current American healthcare system, sanctioning home birth as unsafe despite the enormous amount of empirical data. New guidelines show that nearly 45 percent of the women giving birth had uncomplicated pregnancies and were better off in the hands of midwives than with hospital doctors.

Birth is a sacred process to be honored, cherished, and revered. Therefore, it is important to choose practitioners and birth settings that will respect and honor this tradition. Midwives encourage women to take more control in initiating and creating a more relevant positive birth experience that matters to her, her partner and her family. A positive birth experience involves the presence of family. A satisfying birth experience includes a partnership between the expectant woman and her provider. A positive satisfying birth experience is empowering, illuminating, restorative, connective, inclusive and above all healing. Our birth experience matters ancestrally—drawing on the past and providing memory for future. Women are eternally transformed by their birth experience.

Statistically speaking, the maternal mortality rate (MMR) is 3- 4 times higher among African American women than among non-Hispanic Caucasian women. The infant mortality rate (IMR 11.1%) among preterm birth black infants is 2.4 times higher than that of white infants. A preterm labor usually leads to delivering a low birth weight baby. Racial and gender injustice are partly responsible for these untoward statistics. We obviously have different variables to negotiate. Based on these statistics it is extremely important for African American women to become more responsible, accountable, and critically aware of their health physically, emotionally, and spiritually. It is also imperative that we choose birth options that work more cohesively with our whole spirit and well-being. It is equally important for women to be informed of all labor and birth options and to remain informed about vital health facts and statistics.

As a Midwife, I encourage women to find their voice, own their power and trust their innate ability to birth. I encourage women to conscientiously choose to birth within the privacy of their homes or at least choose a provider who they intuitively trust who cares to touch, who dares to listen, who validates, and of course one who practices with some human dignity. It is important for women to deliberately choose a provider who cares to integrate the medical, social, cultural and religious elements in the management care of the birthing woman.

I encourage women to exercise their reproductive rights throughout their entire pregnancy and birth in the way that is right for their labor birth journey.

Consider the following:
- Midwives validate home birth, and all birth options made within a conscious context, inspired from within, centered around collective decision-making that supports the transformative potential, purpose and power of Birth.
- Midwives have a lower C-section rate then physician led deliveries.
- Midwives have lower than the national average rate for episiotomy or for cesarean deliveries.
- Midwives initiate breastfeeding at a higher than national average rate.
- Midwives also have a lower Infant mortality rate and a lower LBW rate then physician led deliveries.
- Midwives provide comprehensive care which creates a culture of safety.
- Midwives demonstrate quality care by engaging in a shared decision-making process with clients. Generally, increased patient involvement has an impact on better health outcomes and increased patient satisfaction.

Healing the planet originates with a conscientious decision to birth in the way that is right for you and in the way that is healing to both you and our planet.

I am a Midwife and I represent a Conscious Collaborative Driven Evidence-based Paradigm. A nature-based spiritual process that leads to the healing of our planet.

I encourage women to move towards a natural transformative birth process that is consistent with the Midwifery- based Philosophy. A philosophy that is consistent with a healthier lifestyle, and a transformative birth process that contributes to the healing of our planet.

For further information on this topic please refer to the following:

1. Declerqu, ER. Sakala, C Corry, MP, et al. *Listening to mothers II: report of the second national survey of women's childbearing experiences.*
2. Hamilton BE, Martin JA, Ventura SJ, et al. Births: final data for 2009. *Nat'l Vital Stat Rep.* 2010; 59(3): 1-19. http://www.cdc.gov/nchs/data/nvsr/nvsr59/nvsr59_03.pdf. Accessed August 22, 2016.
3. Bennhold, K., & Saint Louis, C. (2014, December 3). British Regulator Urges Home Births Over Hospitals for Uncomplicated Pregnancies. The New York Times. Retrieved August 22, 2016, from ny.times.com
4. Renfrew MJ, Homer CSE, Downe S, McFadden A, Muir N, Prentice T, et al. Midwifery: An Executive Summary for The Lancet's Series. Midwifery: The Lancet; 2014.

HEALING WITH FOODS AND HERBS

Adio Akil, Natural Foods Chef

My name is Adio Akil. I am a Food Therapist. I heal through the use of Organic Food and Herbs. I help people lose weight and get rid of diseases by using Foods and Herbs. I am a Mother of six Children, Five Suns and One Daughter as well as a Sister and Aunt to many.

I began my journey into healing with foods when I was around 18 years of age. I have studied and travelled with Dr. Sebi, Dr. Abdul, Adisa Akil and Pharmacist and Herbalist Bongo Hu I of St. James, Jamaica, learning about the World of Food, Herbs and Healing. For seven years I worked at the Community Warehouse, a DC based, cooperatively owned natural food company that sold bulk organic grains, nuts, seeds, herbs, spices and vegetables. I have a BA from Barnard College and a Certificate in Natural Healing and Raw Food Preparation from The Garden Holistic Institute of St. Croix, Virgin Islands.

At the age of seventeen, during an annual doctor's visit, a cyst was found in my left breast. My mother arranged to have the cyst surgically removed. However, the cyst returned a year later in the same place and at age eighteen, I had the cyst surgically removed again.

The return of the cyst made me realize that something I was doing was not in tune with Nature and had to be changed. I was a dancer and an athlete. I was thin and in shape. I began to research what caused cysts and learned that the growth of a cyst is directly related to what you eat. After thinking about how much white bread, cupcakes, buns, white rice and pasta, cookies, pies, hamburgers, hot dogs, chicken, pork chops, bacon, rabbit, deer, eggs and candy I ate regularly, I realized that I needed to make a change. I had been raised with a lot of Love, but also, with too much devitalized food. I did not want to be cut again or possibly develop breast cancer or even worse, need to have a mastectomy and end up losing one or both of my breasts.

I began researching foods, proper nutrition for vegetarians and natural food preparation. My studies took me to California, Florida, Jamaica, St Croix, Mexico and West Africa, where I learned about natural foods and herbs. I learned that the ability for the body to make new cells is very important. I learned that Sea Moss is a cell proliferator, which generates most cells in the body. I learned that healthy cells have a built-in mechanism that only allows cellular replication for three purposes: normal growth, healing of injured tissue and replacement of cells lost in normal metabolism. I learned that getting oxygen to the blood stream is crucial to life. I also learned how important an alkaline body is to life and the ability to remain disease free. I learned how important Greens and Iron are to the Life of the body. From this information and these experiences, I was able to heal myself and put together a wellness and healing plan that incorporates healthy organic foods and herbs.

I am 60 years young today. I have never had another cyst or major illness since I was eighteen years old. I am vegetarian and eat about 60% of my food uncooked. Several times, I have successfully given Lotus Birth, with just me and my mate present. I attribute my good health and my safe births to my many years of a vegan, herb-filled diet.

I have worked with many people over the years. Successfully, I have been able to help several of them to lose weight and to get rid of diseases that have never returned. This was done through eating live foods and using mostly Live Organic Foods with herbs. My aim is to serve and help provide information and food products that can help all people and particularly People of Color in the care of their bodies and souls. I combine healthy balanced vegetarian eating and living habits (What goes in must come out!). Confidently, I recommend that my clients do the same, for the best results in living a healthy, energetic, and disease-free life.

SUPERCHARGING THE IMMUNE SYSTEM

Chef Keidi Awadu, Raw Food Chef

We find ourselves in a most promising yet unquestionably *contradictory* moment in history. The accumulation of human wisdom from the most ancient civilizations is a legacy for which all of us should be wonderfully grateful and inspired. From the perspective of Ancient Egyptians, viewing our collective wisdom from pre-Nile Valley civilization to the cutting edge of science-based, data-driven wisdom, we can bear witness to a vast spectrum of knowledge that can and does sustain health, prosperity, quality of human engagement, and sustained optimism about the future which lies ahead.

Thus, we've developed awareness of the burden that "modern society" has placed upon us. Too many of us are currently shouldering a burden of disorder, disease, psychology of self-limitation, as well as a pervasive sense of victimization and anxiety regarding our fate.

Correspondingly, the highly-evolved human immune system is a product of 500 million years of cell differentiation, genetic adaptation, and has the *potential* to represent the most capable resistance against disease that has arisen among all species. High-quality longevity is now increasing at the fastest rate in the modern era. We have witnessed in the past two centuries great reduction of premature death due to diseases such as fevers, pulmonary infections, parasitic diseases, childhood illness and inflammatory processes.

Yet, in contradiction to this positive momentum we're presented with a whole new spectrum of man-made threats from antibiotic-resistant bacteria, food-borne superbugs, notions of new pandemics of Ebola, HIV/AIDS, Zika virus, or periodic declaration of some cross-species germ. For many of us within the natural health community, hysteria over such exotic bugs is hyped out of context with respect to the *real dangers* posed by the overuse of antibiotics in the food chain, toxic pesticides and dangers from a spectrum of environmental stressors, ranging from personal care products to industrial chemicals.

Our studies have shown us how plant-based nutrition has proven superior to that of the *omnivorian* society within which we were raised. Americans will eat essentially anything promoted as "food" by profit-obsessed corporations and mass media; despite the fact that our natural biology has not evolved compatibility with this overly-processed dietary configuration. Americans take their cues as to what constitutes food from advertisements on television and other media. It matters little to them that nutrition for humans would follow the same general rules for other species. Plant-eating animals such as elephants, rhinos, hippopotamuses and gorillas (all of whom are large, vegetarian mammals), can't remain healthy while eating like humans. This might seem an absurdity, yet, within modern societies, nutrition logic is often distorted regarding human nutrition.

Who among us could imagine that a captive gorilla whose diet became dependent upon junk food, burgers and fries, sodas, sweets and chemical-laden food would enjoy longevity and disease resistance? We might never do that to a vegetarian animal but will often subject children to such mal-nutrition. For humans to enjoy optimal health through nutrition our diet must be centered upon foods which facilitate oxygen-dependent metabolic processes, supply proper hydration, and an abundance of critical nutrients. These primary nutrient classes consist of: hydration, protein, carbohydrates, amino acids, essential fatty acids, fiber, minerals, vitamins and enzyme-rich foods. When the integrity of this set of nutrients is met through a plant-based diet, then the effective functioning of all our synergistic body systems is achieved.

As much as any of the body's integrated systems, the *immune system* becomes primary beneficiary of wise and disciplined behavior. As such, contrary to habits which feed epidemics of inflammatory diseases within society, we can create the right environment whereby infectious diseases, inflammation, metabolic disorders (i.e., diabetes, overweight, abdominal obesity, hypertension, elevated triglycerides, kidney disorders and cholesterol imbalance), as well as energy imbalances are all reduced due to conscious application of a healthy lifestyle. We will need *supercharged* immune systems in order to fend off assaults from superbugs that are predicted to emerge from this corrupted environment. Within the U.S., over 24,000 Americans die each year from *antibiotic-resistant bacteria* which are mostly the by-product of the nation's food supply system (especially meat from Concentrated Animal Feedlot Operations, so-called *CAFO's*), as well as increasing danger from staph infections in the nation's hospitals and outpatient centers, where antibiotic overuse is epidemic.

The human body naturally evolved a complex system for overcoming infectious pathogens which we refer to as *Reactive Oxygen Species (ROS),* which encompasses a spectrum of processes related to oxidative stress, free radicals, antioxidants and which occur amidst what we call *Redox Reactions*. Details of the complexity of this naturally-developed system for ridding the body of dangerous pathogens would itself demand a significant body of research for our complete understanding. We can state that this ROS system has intelligently evolved over the course of hundreds of millions of years of development of complex, oxygen-dependent cellular life on Planet Earth.

Man's recent achievements in the advance of synthesizing basic Life principles will likely not supersede a half-billion years of biological selection and species evolution. To the contrary, the rapid rise of several dangerous antibiotic-resistant superbugs in recent decades stands as testament that synthetic chemistry is not adequate for disease avoidance. Chemical antibiotics have their place but should be limited as much as possible to infrequent acute response to life-threatening inflammatory challenges.

To take most advantage of this gradual process of species evolution, we are best to integrate as much as possible naturally-selected processes for biological integration into Nature. The following suggestions can serve as guidance toward the goal of supercharging our natural immune systems in order to avoid *superbugs* of the future.

We are the product of 500 million years of oxygen-dependent cellular evolution. Mastering a spectrum of breath management techniques will bring great advantage to immune system functionality, stress-management, and epigenetic mastery over our biological systems.

The existence of Life itself on this planet is directly related to the presence of water and its fundamental correspondence to Life. Optimized hydration is thus, mandatory to the maintenance of all key Life processes. Maintaining the highest integrity of the water we take into our bodies is paramount to our healthy longevity.

Optimized nutrition requires constant access to the spectrum of critical nutrients in their most digestible forms possible. This not only requires that we access, vitamins, minerals, a full spectrum of amino acids, essential fatty acids, fiber, complex carbohydrates, proteins and enzyme-laden raw foods, but that proper preparation of our food demands that we do not harm the integrity of our nutrition through improper preparation techniques.

Our immune systems are rejuvenated through periodic rest and, as such, we mustn't deprive our body of its daily demand for proper sleep. Furthermore, exercise is fundamental toward balancing our whole-body, oxygen-dependent system, as well as for ensuring that circulatory, muscular and skeletal systems are functioning optimally. All processes that contribute toward rejuvenation are reinforced with the right types of regular exercise: cardiovascular, strength training, as well as stretching and balance exercises. An accumulation of a spectrum of environment stressors always accompanies the rise of inflammatory processes within the body. Therefore, stress-reduction, detoxification and efficient waste elimination are all key to an optimized immune system functionality.

Our best understanding about the complex and subtle interaction between the Mind-Body-Spirit matrix requires that we pay particularly close attention to both psychological and spiritual processes that serve our *human wholeness*. While the commonly held understanding that "you are what you eat" has great merit, still we are much more that what we eat and drink. We are how we think, interact, conceptualize, actualize, laugh, cry, empathize and create within the larger circle of Earth species. We are faith-bound Spirits within a multiplicity of material worlds and as such, must consider that our active and co-creative engagement with Nature is key toward manifesting Life's greatest potential.

Yes, we all deserve by mere birthright, health, prosperity and high-quality longevity yet these will not necessarily appear by default. These outcomes demand awareness, investment of creative energy, study, practice, mastery and constant reinforcement. If we correctly understand the power of evolution and cumulative accomplishment, then it only makes sense that each of us strives to be the *best human* that has ever been born. Ultimately, we can best give proper grace and respect to the notion of a Great and Benevolent Creator by *being* that body of Creation in real-time activity in this world. How good and pleasant might it be to discover at that final fleeting moment of our individual life that we were, in actuality, The Almighty, all along?

PERMACULTURE AND HEIRLOOM SEEDS

Makeda Dread Cheatom, Holistic Urban Gardener

Planetary Healing Forces of the Earth

World Beat Center's Children's Peace Garden is dedicated to teaching communities how to create a natural habitat and permaculture gardens, even in limited spaces, such as in urban environments. It's very important to include locally-grown fresh fruits and vegetables in your diet. That means avoiding fruits and vegetables flown from abroad. Your food should be grown in your own porch or community garden. This also helps reduce your carbon or ecological footprint. Some of each person's ecological footprint is dependent upon choices made in their daily life; how much they drive, or from where their food is purchased. Some of it is the per person share of their society's infrastructure. Purchasing at your local farmers' market is a great way to reduce your carbon footprint. And, don't forget to recycle. What we do now affects children all over the world.

Our ancestors' spirits are strong; they worked the Earth and studied her very well. We must return to the Earth Mother and be guided by the knowledge of the ancient ones who knew the cycles of the moon and when to plant. They knew how to harvest foods and save seeds, which they shared, traded and planted for generations to come.

At WorldBeat Center's Children's Peace Garden we continually experiment with different methods of gardening that focuses on water conservation. Our garden features six wicking bed gardens, three aquaponic garden systems, a native plant garden, and is scheduled to include a keyhole and a vertical garden. Below are descriptions of each system with their benefits and uses.

WICKING BEDS

Wicking beds are garden beds that are watered "upside down", from the bottom up. Wicking beds hold a reservoir of water at the bottom of the structure. The water is drawn up by the plant roots through a natural osmosis process called "wicking." Wicking beds can be made using anything from large buckets to raised beds; they make watering easier for the elderly or those with back issues. First, a PVC pipe is drilled on the side of the container and a hole is drilled on another end several inches above the floor. Inside, the bottom is layered with several inches of rocks, straw or weed mats, followed by soil, plants and mulch on top to reduce evaporation. To water the plants, pour water into the PVC pipe until the water spits out from the hole drilled on the side, indicating the reservoir is full. Among the several benefits of wicking beds is that they use up to 50% less water than conventional beds, because very little water is evaporating. Plants in wicking beds do not require daily watering. Vegetation is more plentiful because the roots have direct access to water and weeds have a harder time invading. In our wicking beds we currently are growing strawberries, moringa, peanuts, squash, onion, tomatoes, cilantro, lettuce and ginger.

AQUAPONIC WICKING WELLS

Inspired by Ancient Egyptians and Olmecs, Aquaponic systems are closed-loop gardening systems that include both aquatic and plant life. Aquaponic systems are usually constructed using a fish tank with a planter floating on top. Typically, the water tank fills with fish waste that pumps from the tank into the planter, where microbes convert it to fertilizer for the plants. The plant roots filter and clean the water, which is returned to the fish tank. An aquaponic system produces no pollution, because all the waste is turned into something useful, and all the water is reused! WorldBeat's Aquaponic Wicking Well looks a little different. We have reused a rain barrel with fish on the inside. On the outside, we have wrapped the barrel with carpet insulation where we've made cuttings and inserted plants on the surface. The system is designed so that once a day the water overflows onto the outside and seeps into the insulation which 'wicks' the fish water to the plants. Just like aquaponic systems, our system reuses the water. The plants require infrequent watering and are splendid examples of this drought-tolerant gardening system.

KEYHOLE GARDENS

WorldBeat Garden hopes to construct a keyhole garden, soon. Keyhole gardens are round gardens built with a compost pile at the center, which is separated by a cage or fence. They were originally developed in Africa as a water-conscious method of gardening in areas where water is scarce. They can be constructed from a variety of materials (bricks, stone, wood, clay) and come in a several of sizes. Keyhole gardens are well-suited for most plants, especially perennials which have long roots. The unique circular shape of the garden accommodates for different crops to be grown in various parts of the garden. Leafy greens and culinary herbs are grown on the edges, so they can spill over the sides and grow large. Whereas root crops do best near the center where their roots can reach deep. The construction of a keyhole garden varies with every gardener, but there is a basic structure. Stones, bricks, or wood are layered in a circular shape with a keyhole-like notch in one side. The notch allows gardeners access to the center compost pile. In the center of the keyhole, a smaller circle made from fence material is built inside the outer circle; then, a compost pile is placed inside the smaller circle. The rest of the garden should be layered with: compost, kitchen scraps, dry leaves/twigs, and soil.

The construction of the garden with the compost in the center is what makes keyhole gardens great for water conservation. The garden should be watered through the center: water is poured into the compost pile, and the water then seeps through the fencing and into the rest of the soil, carrying with it the nutrients collected from the compost. Because water leaches through the bottom layers of soil, there is no risk of water loss by evaporation.

PERMACULTURE IS THE FUTURE

Permaculture is a design science that uses the patterns and systems of nature to provide sustainable and regenerative landscapes for both humans and the environment. It is also the best way to repair degraded, polluted and damaged ecosystems. No matter your skill set, age or field of study, permaculture science inspires sustainability and resiliency in design and application. By following some basic principles, we can design landscapes that will catch and harvest nearly every drop of water to produce food and beauty for decades to come. Besides harvesting, there is hardly any work at all regarding tilling or weeding.

FOOD SECURITY AND SEED SOVEREIGNTY

You may be wondering about food security and seed sovereignty. Food security

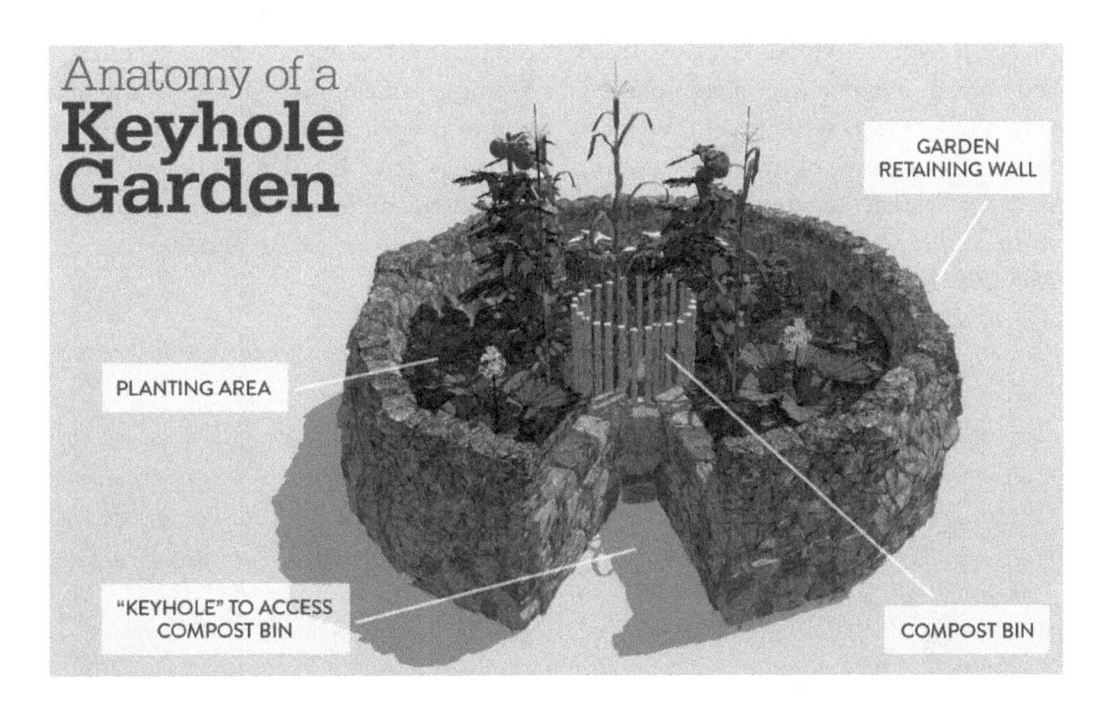

Anatomy of a Keyhole Garden

- GARDEN RETAINING WALL
- PLANTING AREA
- "KEYHOLE" TO ACCESS COMPOST BIN
- COMPOST BIN

means access by all people, at all times to enough food for an active, healthy life. Many people in our country and around the world live in food deserts. A food desert is an urban or rural area without ready access to fresh, affordable, healthy food. Many neighborhoods and communities are loaded with fast food restaurants and convenience stores. It has become very important to grow your own food or start a community garden.

Seed sovereignty reclaims the right for everyone to save their own seeds, as opposed to having to purchase seeds. We all should stand together and promote the use of diverse seeds. Not only does this enhance food security, but also it promotes the preservation of traditional cultural practices and values. Seed security comes from seed sovereignty and the right to use and exchange seeds freely within a community. Upon attending the National Heirloom Exposition in Santa Rosa, CA last year, my consciousness changed regarding food security. I saw and heard dynamic speakers, particularly the keynote speaker, Dr. Vandana Shiva, who was one of the most powerful speakers I've encountered. Dr. Shiva has written over 20 books, including, **Soil Not Oil, Environmental Justice in an Age of Environmental Crisis,** and has inspired the beginning of the Soil Not Oil International Conference.

Heirloom seeds are open-pollinated, genetically diverse cultivars that have been passed down from generation to generation (some say at least 50 or 100 years). Preserving and planting heirloom seeds is important because it means preserving generations of diversity. For instance, there are 10,000 varieties of apples, compared to the very few hybrid types in our grocery stores.

We are the next in line as Earth Keepers, so that means we must empower ourselves by saving our seeds and starting seed libraries and seed banks. Four times a year we should organize a community seed swap, hosted in our backyard or community gardens.

I hope these diverse ways of growing food inspire you to keep your garden no matter how large or small it may be. Your health is your wealth. Your body is your temple, and you must tune it to its highest frequency. Yes, it's all about frequency. Eating organic, non-GMO foods will take you to the portal of health and longevity. You may have heard the phrase, "Many are called, and few are chosen." However, consider, "*All* are called, and few choose."

Stand Firm.

WHAT'S WRONG WITH HYBRIDS?

Chef Ahki, Natural Foods Activist

First to understand this we must clarify. When I refer to a food being "hybrid" I mean that it is un-natural. It is a seed or plant that is not naturally growing from the earth. Classifying that as such means the following:

- It doesn't produce seeds independently to reproduce itself
- Its molecular structure is not complete
- Depends on Man to reproduce
- It is starch based/acidic

With this criterion, we eliminate foods that have been solely produced by certain methods. A food is not generally classified as being "hybrid" simply because it is genetically modified. That is not the only criteria for the classification of "hybrid" food. for centuries humans have been creating different plants by mating together different vegetables and fruits. Unfortunately, this process yields a plant that has an incomplete molecular structure. It cannot "be fruitful and multiply" on its own. This is a hybrid.

The Indigenous physiology is designed to primarily ingest, absorb and process the nutrients derived from wild and natural fruits. Two to four servings per day is insufficient.

Toxification of the cells, tissues and organs is the overwhelming accumulation of toxins. It is the main precursor of disease and adverse conditions in the body. It allows parasites, in their many forms, to populate and multiply exponentially throughout the system. Being overweight or obese is an absolute sign of toxicity within the body. Where there is fat (white adipose tissue) there is a haven for parasites. Parasites are bacteria, viruses, fungi, yeasts or spores. They, like toxins will enter the body through, food, air, cuts, and so on. In other words, parasites are guaranteed an entrance into the body, no matter what one does. The situation thus rests upon whether the body's internal ecology will serve as a sustaining breeding ground for parasite population. Biological disease exists when these parasites invade a cell.

The cell can only be invaded when the cell wall (membrane) charge is positive. This usually occurs at night or during sleep. Once the cell wall's force field (negative charge) is changed, things can enter it.

The Mitochondria located within the cell wall determines the cell charge and provides the energy to the cell which has varying spin cycles. When the spin cycle is high, the cell wall charge is negative (alkaline). When this spin cycle slows down the cell wall charge becomes positive (acid cell membrane). The body goes through these circadian rhythms naturally. When the cell has been breached by the intake or invasion of parasites or, "that which is of a foreign frequency or chemical composition" then the cell becomes an agent or catalyst for disease. It is treasonous that the medical industry and the drug companies make billion$ "treating" obesity and diet related diseases like diabetes while implying that we are all doomed to be sick because of certain genetic or cultural flaws that manifest as disease.

Western medicine has also conditioned us to blame weight gain on excessive caloric intake and the lack of exercise. However, notice the explosion in morbid obesity and auto-immune disease we see today corresponds with profound changes in the food supply.

Many scientists argue that GMO food is toxic to the human body and impossible to digest. In laboratory animals GMO routinely causes tumors, obesity, high blood pressure and birth defects. That means the processed corn that is in everything from taco shells to frosted flakes is toxic. That means the wheat grain that is in everything from salad dressing to hamburger buns is toxic. That means the soy that is in baby formula and tofu is toxic. We are not in this condition because of simply eating too many calories or not making it to the gym 3 days a week. We are sick because many of us have over 100 pounds of undigested toxic "food" trapped in our bodies.

Core principles:
1. You are naturally healthy. Sickness is artificial.
2. You don't catch disease. You "earn" it. Disease results from the buildup of toxins in the body that eventually poison the blood.
3. You get well by what comes out of you, not by what goes into you. Great health comes from getting rid of toxins…not by taking medicines.

I wonder how many people would overcome disease and escape the grip of mental and emotional disorder if they First: Flushed the synthetic drugs; Second: Got adequate sleep; Third: Ate a diet of natural nutritious food.

THE WATER PRINCIPLE SUPPLIES HEALTHY CELL ENVIRONMENT

The human body has three times more lymph fluid than blood. It is lymph that surrounds the cell not blood. Lymph is water. We should drink clean and pure water to replace the body's lymph fluids. The water should have a balanced PH. PH stands for Percentage of Hydrogen ions. The PH scale is from 1-14. The ideal PH is 7.0…You can alkalize your own water by soaking wild plants, herbs in it for 8-12 hours.

THE HEALTHY CELL EXERCISE

Get enough Sunlight & Exercise, every day. Exercise is important because it helps cleanse the lymphatic system, which affects every cell and affects the immune system. Healthy thoughts are also good brain and bodily exercise. The fire is also measured by the heartbeat or pulse. The pulse should average a pace of 72 times in 60 seconds or one minute.

I eat a ton of living food. However, I am not a "Raw Foodist." I am not on a macrobiotic diet nor do I subscribe to the Paleo diet. I reject those labels because they become group identities. People join groups, so they don't have to think. They just do what everyone else in the group does. I don't think that works anymore. I like to tell people I am on the "Ahki Diet."

I eat what works for me. I eat what keeps my energy up. I eat what I find delicious. I eat what makes me feel good. I eat what doesn't make me fat; what doesn't raise my blood sugar. I eat what doesn't make me age fast. I eat things that keep my mind clear and calm.

What I eat changes over time. However, there are some core principles that I believe are fundamental.

1. Plant & fruit based
2. Non-Hybrid
3. Minerally Dense

Eat Organic, as fresh as possible, as Non-Hybridized as possible. No modern grains. Plenty of living foods. Some cooked. Whatever works for your OPTIMUM WELLNESS!

A big shout out to my Raw Family!

EAT GOOD ON A HOOD BUDGET

Stic & Afya Ibomu,
Hip-Hop Power Couple

In the hood, and other lower income communities a lot of times the pennies can get tight and, finances are not where we want them to be. So, we often make choices based on price or convenience or access or habit when it comes to the foods we buy and eat. Too often we sacrifice what's best for us for what's best for our budget. But we don't have to. As plant-based holistic lifestyle students for over 20 years, we have learned that there are some simple steps we can take to eat well and respect our finances at the same time. Here are 7 practical tips.

1. **Choose Produce, not Packages** — People have the wrong idea about eating healthy. It is not buying a lot of expensive packages of food. Boxed and packaged foods are the most expensive and most of the time, the most detrimental food choices. Although processed foods may offer some convenience in moderation, they raise our food budgets as well as undermine our health. In the produce, aisle is where you get the most bang for your buck and the most value for your health. Fill up on fresh greens and fruits, along with basic staples like rice and beans and you are well on your way to healthier eating within a reasonable budget. Eat real foods and save real money.

2. **Cook Big and Save Some for Later** — Cook your meals in bulk and consider freezing the leftovers for later in the week or month. Cooking in bulk gives you the option of having good food choices on hand that will save you time and money. It's always helpful to plan out your meals. Pre-prepare your foods and put meal-sized portions in freezer bags. When you are in a time crunch, all you will have to do is pull something out of the freezer and heat it up.

3. **Soup Up Your Options** — Nothing quite compares to a hot and hearty bowl of soup. Large vegetable soups over brown rice or even whole grain noodles (depending on where you are in your dietary journey) offer filling meals packed with vitamins and nutrients. Soups are easy to prepare, inexpensive and by using beans in the soup to pack in the protein, instead of meat, saves money at the same time.

4. **Budget to See Where Your Values Are** — We have to be honest with ourselves and our finances, by making a budget and placing more value on our health. The average consumer overspends money on non-essential items like sneakers/shoes, headphones, cigarettes, trendy clothes, parties, strip clubs, alcohol, video games, and so on, while seeking the cheapest food we can find. Making a budget not only is the main ingredient to financial stability but can help identify where money can be diverted from in order to purchase healthier food choices.

5. Season your Food — Buy locally grown fresh fruits and vegetables that are in season. It is cheaper because you are not paying for the cost of shipping and delivering out of season foods from across the world to your local area. Foods that are in its natural growing season help strengthen the immune system as well.

6. **Join a Co-Op or Local Community Garden** — You can buy your groceries/produce at a discount as a member of a Co-op in exchange for minimal volunteer work hours per month. Community gardens are also popping up in many urban areas, and this offers the opportunity to learn a useful survival skill. Gardening is also a great and simple form of outdoor exercise.

7. **Drink More Water** — It is medically recommended that we drink at least half our body weight in ounces of water daily. Drinking water curbs the appetite and saves money, as well as helps hydrate our internal organ systems. There is no need to buy expensive plastic bottled water and add on to the already over polluted plastic epidemic in the world. Help save your money and the planet by purchasing a quality filter for the faucet (around $20-$30 or less) and pour up. Drink water instead of choosing sugary drink alternatives and your health will thank you.

Though there is much necessary work to be done locally and nationally to eradicate food deserts and increase access to more people, eating good in the hood is doable. Healthy foods are mostly the produce crops, which are the most simple and least expensive food options we have. Our eating habits are learned behaviors, and our taste buds can be reconditioned for a healthy living. Place more value on life and let's adopt healthier habits.

HEAL THE PEOPLE, HEAL THE PLANET

Baratunde & Kayah Ma'at,
Herbal Alchemists

Thank you, Queen Afua for having the forethought to know that collective voices must contribute to one of the most important discussions of our time. We, Baratunde and Kayah Ma'at believe to truly heal one must have a direct connection with the Spirit realm and with Mother Nature. We join those who have such a relationship and also are gravely concerned about the future of Mother Earth.

I am Baratunde Ma'at, Planetary Herbal Alchemist and Father of The Forgotten Foods and my queen, and soul mate Kayah Ma'at, is the proud Mother of The Forgotten Foods. Together, we are The Forgotten Foods…Remembered. We adopted that name because we felt that have **FORGOTTEN** their natural way and that it is time for humans to **REMEMBER** that our foods and medicines must be **products of the Earth**. We bring to the world powerful, magical and effective herbal products that sustain and maintain life. These foods and medicines come directly from the Mother Source. The Infinite Wisdom of our Creator created a plant medicine for every dis-ease humans would encounter. In nature, we will find all of the nutrients necessary for our spiritual, mental and physical survival.

Our mission is to seek and find the world's supreme super-foods…"forgotten foods." These special sources combined with ancient Spiritual Alchemical Processes, exponentially increase the vibrational frequency and life-sustaining properties in our products. As Light-Workers, this is our way of contributing to raising the vibrational frequency of humanity and the planet. As healers and conscious business owners, we introduce the world: THE 7th FOOD GROUP from The Forgotten Foods…Remembered.

In the western world there is an idea that if your daily dietary consumption includes 6 basic food groups, you can be

guaranteed optimal health. These 6 food groups are:
1. Meat/Protein
2. Dairy
3. Grains
4. Vegetables
5. Fruits
6. Oils/Fats/Sweets

However, what modern society is witnessing instead is unparalleled epidemics of sick people. Mineral deficiencies, heart disease, cancers of all kinds, mental illness, diabetes, high blood pressure, obesity, Alzheimer's and depression just name a few of the illnesses. The truth is that even if one is capable of eating the exact recommended proportions from each category above, the nutrition that cells require for regeneration can no longer be found within these food groups, *(and there's question in many health circles as to whether you ever could)*.

It's no longer a secret that modern humans have become "processed people." Everything we eat has been artificially manufactured, pre-processed, or prepared at home in such a way that the nutritional value is either completely absent or non-absorbable. Also true: Our plants lack the necessary minerals to nourish our cells, blood stream and tissues, because the minerals are no longer in the soil. For decades, with our modern technology and mindset, we have depleted the soil…it is humans who are making our planet sick.

If the minerals are not in the soil, then they are not in the plants. Plants do not manufacture their own minerals; they must be taken from the soil. So many of the diseases we are witnessing are simply mineral deficiencies. And unfortunately, even if your fruits and vegetables are purchased "organic" there is still no way of measuring which ones, if any, of the 60 daily required minerals are in the plant.

Even more devastating is the fact that our natural food supply is now in the hands of government approved guidelines and standards that have allowed the introduction of GMO (Genetically Modified Organisms). These fake food look-a-like products are unnatural, unhealthy, unknown and unsafe. How can we truly find the nutrition our bodies require, when the quest for nutritious food is so complicated or maybe impossible? How can our Blessed planet thrive while Genetically Modified Organisms destroy the original blueprints of life and creation? Surely there will be sick people and a sick planet.

This is why the 7th Food Group™ is so needed because the 6 Basic Food Groups, or what we call *ordinary foods, the Standard American Diet (SAD),* are not enough for optimum health. The Forgotten Foods has recognized that it is a necessity for us to supplement our diets on a daily basis. We also recommend that we eat less so-called food, because it ultimately adds to the toxic overload which is making us ill. We must also consciously take in high frequency super foods that feed the mind of the cells. These are phyto-nutrients that nourish the cells, organs, tissues and blood stream. These are herbs and plants that have been proven, tested and tried for thousands of years to be beneficial for humans.

The 7th Food Group™ is our way of stressing the importance of supplementing our diets with foods that regenerate instead of degenerating the body. It is intended to create a healthier alternative to our daily diets and introduce supplementation that is necessary today. We have a proprietary system for harmonizing our products to drastically heighten the frequency and efficacy of every product. They've been aging for 14 years, they are concentrated, unprocessed, sacred tonics. They add greater assurance that you and your family are being fed targeted cell food for your daily nourishment for wellness and medicine for illness…straight from The Mother.

So, what would we do to Heal Planet Earth? Well for starters, we are convinced that humans as babies and children should be introduced to natural life-sustaining plants that come from healthy soil and a healthy Earth. As those children are growing up to become adults they should learn from the beginning that they and Earth Mother are one…and that we depend upon one another for our daily survival. If humans truly did know that their foods and medicines must be products of the Earth, we could maintain healthy people who would maintain a healthy planet.

Our solution is: *If you heal the people… you can heal the planet.*

THE REMIX

Tassili Maat, Raw Vegan Chef

What legacy will I leave? Ndaba, my children; gather around and listen. ("*Ndaba*" (Zulu) means gather—as read in a book by Credo Mutwa/a Zulu Sangoma.) Ndaba, because I plan to live long enough—another 100 years or more—to tell them myself. To do that I must have longevity. I must be clear-minded, with a sound, able body; and spiritually anchored in the essence of all life. I must be emotionally balanced in Ma'at. What I do now will provide that reality. I will learn something new every day. While it has been said that there is nothing new under the sun, I am open to the remix of all that is. It keeps me youthful and committed to the evolutionary process.

I love to challenge myself; to "Remix" the components of my life. What new ways can I do yoga Asana? What new recipe can I create? With "The Remix", I am never bored; creation is a continuum. I keep my mind active while developing mental discipline; when necessary, I can also keep it still for focus.

My Jegnas (teacher), Dr. Jewel Pookrum, instructed me in her brain-balancing program which involves unification of both hemispheres of the brain. This unification is mental, spiritual, emotional and physical. Dr. Jewel's program enhances what I learned many years ago about meditation, scientific prayer, and manifestation. It is a powerful remix of Raja Yoga, although it is its own formula.

I have gone deeper into healing my emotional body through tai chi, as taught by another Jegna, Baba Ari Shen. This remix of Hatha and Prathayama yogas includes the massage practice of Lymphatic Cleansing. As a massage therapist, I provide my patrons varied healing modalities, including reflexology and Chatsu. Caring for others is a big part of my healing journey. While positive vibes are flowing, and endorphins are released in my body, I am chemically and energetically happy. This strengthens my immune system, restores vitality, lowers my blood pressure and is great for my soul. With a huge smile on my face, I laugh, fully. In joy; I am grateful!

Wow! I'm staying *healthy by healing* others. Life is amazing. Life is synchronistic; we only need to see the connections. This is where meditation comes in; in fact, it never left. I strive to serve, celebrate and give conscious gratitude for the Most High. I live in the moving meditation that is grace…Dharma. When one is no longer bound to Karma—cause and effect—as a reaction, but rather is consciously initiating the cause to create the desired effect, then that is "The Remix."

We are conscious creators of our worlds. There are no victims. During meditation, focus comes to assist "The Remix" because we are remembering something different *can* and *does* exist. Since all realities exist simultaneously, why not magnetize the ones we desire? We are already attracting them through Karma. Why not consciously utilize our focus and help make the world a better place? I do my best to stay in moving mediation. It has guided me on my path, physically, to Tassili's Raw Reality Café. With Love, as the main ingredient, this is where I employ food as medicine. I serve raw, vegan, vegetarian and transitional foods. Some patrons become interested in embarking on their own journeys to optimal health.

As a vegan for 28 years and a raw foodist for 8, I recognize it is not my job to convert others. My job is to make healthy, plant-based foods available, especially to those on mainstream diets. Introduction of live-food choices could assist them on their path to achieving optimal health. Healthy and vegetarian food have gotten the "bad rap" of being bland and boring. I remix these foods and make sure they are delicious! We serve the highest quality, holistic food available, made by hand with *love* and *passion*. You must taste it for yourself! I have a vision for a global franchise of Tassili's Raw Reality. Do I think I can save the world? Well, maybe not everybody, but most definitely those who want to be saved by a *Live-it* instead of a *Diet*.

"Live-it" means we are *consciously* choosing life. Without picking up a gun or throwing a grenade, we are modern day revolutionaries choosing that which is living, over that which is not living; we are promoting life. Choose an apple over a bag of potato chips, fresh juice over soda, a massage over surgery, Yoga over blood pressure meds. Don't get it twisted, allopathic medicine has its place. If somebody falls and breaks their arm, don't take them to the herb store first. Take them to the hospital, get the bones set, *then* get herbs to assist the healing process. Also, I don't recommend abruptly stopping the use of prescribed medication. Remember, all things in due time; gradually. Balance is key.

Balance brings me to Yoga, which has lovingly served my life. Yoga guided me through college, pregnancies, abuse, poor health, spiritual confusion and dysfunctional relationships. Through Yoga I have experienced tantric bliss and achieved focused prayer. It has calmed my road rage, been a key to sanity, an answer to longevity and a guide through the shadows. I love the peace and power of my inner verse. A guru/basu teacher once said, "You don't choose yoga, yoga chooses you." Many are called, few answer. Even fewer consent to pick up the ankh or the cross or to become their brothers' and sisters' keepers. I am honored to be a planetary placeholder. While writing this, I am watching Re set over the Pacific and remembering the saga of Auset, Asar, and Heru…to whom much is given, much is required. Blissed…I am honored to bless others. The I AM Ascension Temple was established as a home for Yoga in Atlanta's Historic West End. Primarily we teach Kundalini and Kemetic Yoga but are open to all schools of discipline. Here are classes in tai chi and meditation, applied spirituality and raw food preparation. We have meeting space for enlightening activities such as workshops and guest speakers. We are spirituality universal; those promoting LOVE are welcome.

My life is rich with Remix opportunities for making "lemonade" instead of complaining about only having "lemons." My parents, civil rights activists, healers and revolutionaries raised me to be of service and to be independent. Dad, an allopathic doctor (internal medicine and cardiology), stressed, "True black power is green power." (Who knew how prophetic his words would be?) in San Diego, Mother, headed the Hypertension Council and founded the African American Museum of Fine Arts. Her community service included working alongside the Black Panthers, the Chicano Federation, the Urban League, and the Jewish Community Center to name a few. From these role models, I remixed my life to assist in the upliftment of humanity.

Attempting to be a best mother and wife left little time for my budding artistic career. Upon spending my whole paycheck for childcare, I decided to discontinue paying someone else to raise our two children. So, I became my own canvas and using color, culture, and style I began the healing art of natural hair care. Beginning with braiding, twists, extensions and lock repair, I eventually incorporated making hair adornments with crystals, metals, beads and threads. The adornments soothed my sisters' souls and celebrated their natural beauty. For nearly four decades I offered healing hair care, returned to school and raised five children, mostly as a single parent. Over time I realized my empathic ability to see beyond sight, hear beyond sound and feel beyond touch. Channeling the Akashic Records and using the sixth sense of psychic sensitivity, I became a mentor of "Oracle Remix"—assisting others in making sense of their lives. I expanded into destiny readings using the art of temporary henna tattooing. I was realizing my own destiny—heal, help, and serve beautifully!

We are the only "self" we will be for our whole lives; it is best we get to know ourselves, **very well**. Isn't that what our ancestors (our-selves returned) said to us? They left the message: "Know thyself!" Feminine AST must put ourselves back together. Masculine ASR must give birth to enlightened selves/Heru. We are the return of the KRST on the planet; here to raise the consciousness of humanity through *morphic resonance.* Our sacred symbols, signs, and schedules are here, left long ago to activate and remind ourselves, who we are. Awaken my children. *Ndaba.* Come gather around and listen. You—

me—we, *Ubuntu,* are of the 144,000. (*"Ubuntu"* (Bantu) means humanity.) It is the frequency for humanity to arise. Awaken that we may remember to remember, who we are, where we are from and what we aim to do—so that we will remember, to go/grow.

My journey continues as my family (both, biological and spiritual), gives me an opportunity to practice grace as unconditional love.

Ase, Ase, Ase, O! Eternally, we gather our harvest for the prosperity of future generations.

EARTH COOKERS

Wahidah Muhammad, Holistic Cooking

Out of our vast gardens of Earth comes a bountiful host of herbs, fruits, vegetables, grains, nuts, and seeds. They are all needed to cleanse, repair, build, and bring peace and tranquility to our bodies, minds and spirits. These are Divine foods, gifts from our Creator to nourish and heal us. Everything we could possibly require is contained within them. They fulfill multiple needs as sustenance and vital medicine to cure our ills in our developmental journey. The Creator has blessed us with these magnificent, miraculously fashioned bodies, and it is our divine right and duty to maintain these vessels of life with the utmost care and love.

There is tremendous joy derived from eating right, because when we eat natural and wholesome foods we do our body, mind and spirit justice, and we reap the benefits by functioning at our optimal level of productivity. This cause and effect principle clearly affirms the well-known adage, "We are what we eat." By making His bounty available to us, the Creator is telling us that this is how He wants us to eat. all the we have to do is take heed of His clear signs and accept what is good and reject what is not.

Man-made food is processed and contains unnatural chemicals that clog, slow down and ultimately destroy our physical bodies all in the name of convenience. If the Creator could tell us what is best for us I believe He would say, "I have set before you all that is good and natural. Partake of it." There is a science to eating correctly, and the key to understanding this science is to realize that the best foods for our bodies are the ones that can used in their maximum entirety, discarding little or nothing.

When we walk into our kitchen, so we should visualize them as Healing Laboratories and ourselves as healing scientist for our families. Always enter this sacred domain in the highly conscious and prayerful state of mind. Be ready to unfold new miracles and discoveries that will help further not only the development of our families but that of our nation. Our systems must be fortified to the upmost to combat the relentless attacks waged against us in our polluted environment. We all have the divine choice of becoming "Earth Cookers" by making a conscious decision between healing our nation or contributing further to its destruction.

Earth Cookers always ask the Creator for guidance before entering the Healing Laboratories to create healing foods and formulas. When we do this, we find ourselves truly amazed at what materializes because of our total faith and trust in God. Becoming an Earth Cookers is an essential step when one decides to travel the Healer Thyself path of Liberation to Purification.

I pray for Healing Eating and Healed Earth for us All.

MANY PATHWAYS TO WELLNESS

Queen Afua

Welcome to the Planet Heal Universal Dietary Wheel. Let us continue to call out for world healing and unity!

I AM that I AM a miracle coming from a microcosm. I AM a part of the whole—the whole earth, which is the whole of nature, which is the whole in the universe. I AM air, fire, water, and earth. We all are made of what makes up nature and what makes up the universe. I speak from the Healers' Kitchen within the text of *The City of Wellness*. I AM healer, and I AM healing myself, and all my relationships. All my relations are my reflection, therefore as I heal myself, I heal my relations.

In 1969, at age 16, during the spiritual, cultural, holistic revolution throughout the United States and globally, I was chemically challenged with a toxic air dis-ease, so I suffered from asthma and allergies. Also, I was challenged with toxic fire dis-ease, so I suffered from extremely painful menstruation. Challenged with toxic water, I suffered from edema in my ankles and legs. I had chronic congestion, which backed into my bloodstream and ended up in my brain causing me to have chronic headaches.

During a 21 Day Detox I connected to the healing powers of nature and began to restore to wellness. I realized by embracing the elements air, fire, water, and earth I was able to escape from chronic disease. With nature's support, I was able to heal myself. Once I made the connection to detoxification using nature and eventual rejuvenation, I proceeded to share my findings with over a million men, women, and children. For over four decades I communicated to them how to Heal Thyself through nature.

Throughout the first four decades on my path of wellness—from being a vegetarian to a vegan to a chlorophyllion—I observed food wars taking place. I have witnessed flexitarians versus vegetarians, the live foodists versus cooked food vegans and the non-hybrid versus alkaline consumers.

My father, Ephraim Robinson, taught me how to love my people. He let me know I could do anything I set my mind to do. Ephraim Robinson, an entrepreneur and a Garveyite always said, "Watch out for the pitfalls of the Willie Lynch divide and conquer mentality." In the interest of world peace and well-being, let us commit to no longer endure and accept dis-ease. Embracing Nature, it is time to connect with family and community to help all to Heal Thyself with air, fire, water, and earth. This connectivity of self, the elements and the changing of the microcosmic thyself can expand to a macrocosmic releasing of the Healer Within.

On this "Dietary Wheel" I have compiled "snapshots" illustrating some of the ways we eat around the world. My purpose is to create a conversation of appreciation for our differences and patience for our frequencies. In the spirit of respect for one another, we must seek a Holistic Lifestyle based on recovery, frequency, choice and difference. We must recognize the various levels of health awareness and stages of transformation especially as related to availability of resources. The quality of what any of us consumes depends on the condition of the soil, air and water where the food is raised. Consider where and how the food is packaged. Also consider that many urban citizens live in a "food desert" where a grocery store or vegetable market may be as far as 5 miles away and only poorly supplied corner stores and/or fast food eateries are nearby home.

Let the "Dietary Wheel" be a call to the communities of the world, to our leaders and students to unify themselves. The time for planetary healing and purification is now. Let us of recover and restore to and through Holistic Lifestyle Ways. Let do so through Nature—air, fire, water, and earth. This is the common thread to reaching liberation through purification to improve our vibration. We are all on a journey of self-discovery; a journey of healing. Through our various choices of healthy living, let us end dis-ease in our hearts, our communities and across the world as we each purify body, mind and spirit.

The examples on the following pages are but a few of the perhaps thousands of global practices for food selection and consumption. These dietary lifestyles, whether organic or non-organic, are in a constant state of transition depending on information, availability, agriculture environment and economics.

We honor the wisdom of the Ancients through the teachings of Master Teachers such as those found here in Planet Heal, as well as the many around the world.

PLANET HEAL UNIVERSAL DIETARY WHEEL

BREATHARIAN

Elemental eaters. Primary food is sunlight.
(Master Teachers: Jericho Sunfire, Elitom Ben Ysrael)

100% FRUITARIAN

Organic (Non GMO) seeded fruits.
(Master Teacher: Alicia Ojeda)

100% JUICETARIAN / THERAPEUTIC JUICE FASTING

Organic green juice, fruit juice, coconut water. H20, herb tea & alkaline water. Therapeutic juice fasting such as included in 21-Day Fast. Juice fasting can be part of the dietary component during observances within many different religions.

CHLOROPHYLLION

90% Green foods, mostly raw. some fruits. 10% whole grains, nuts & seeds. (Founder: Supa Nova Slom)

100% RAW / SUN FIRED FOOD

A diet of fully raw food. (Master Teachers: Aris Latham, Tassili Maat, & High Priest Kwatamani)

NON HYBRID/GMO (ORGANIC/VEGAN)

Avoid GMO (Genetic Modified Organisms): Heavily modified foods include papaya, bananas, apples, corn strawberries, sweet potatoes, tomatoes, zucchini, soybean, pineapple & potatoes. No dairy & sugar. Eat Live, Raw & Cooked Food.
(Master Teacher: Dr. Sebi)

WE

EAT

THE 7 KITCHENS OF CONSCIOUSNESS

International Soul Food, Vegan Kitchen, Manifestation Kitchen, Emerald Green Kitchen, Fasters' Kitchen, Healers' Kitchen, Liberation Kitchen (Master Teacher: Queen Afua)

FLEXITARIAN / PESCATARIAN

Flexitarian diet includes chicken, and fish along with whole foods. Usually excludes pork and red meat. (The Pescatarian excludes all flesh except fish.) Utilizes a blend of hybrid & non hybrid fruits & vegetables. (Master Teacher: Elijah Muhammad—The Nation of Islam)

VEGETARIAN

Non-dairy, sprouts, seeds, avocados, fruits, vegetables, peas, lentils, soy beans, and other beans.

LACTO-OVO VEGETARIAN

Includes milk, eggs, butter & non meat proteins. Also, fruits, vegetables and whole grains.

VEGAN LIVE / RAW & COOKED

Includes fruits, veggies, nuts, grains, seeds. both hybrid & non-hybrid. (Master Teacher: Afya Ibomu)

ALKALINE

Attention paid to the alkalinity and acidity of foods eaten. Includes raw & cooked food. (Master Teacher: Dr. Llaila Afrika)

WE ARE AT OUR *BEST* WHEN WE ARE HEALING

Kimberli Boyd, Teaching Artist

My journey to becoming a healer has been unfolding over several decades. All my life I have been a dancer…35 years a performing artist and choreographer…20 years a teaching artist using movement and creative dance to transform educational environments and community relationships. For 10 years I have been a yoga teacher; and during the past 3 years, an Emerald Green Practitioner and student of Yoga Therapy. I must admit that for a long time I felt scattered and uncertain about the connection between what seemed like very different passions and bodies of knowledge. Yet through even my darkest moments of uncertainty, staying on the path of this "divine curriculum" has led me to the understanding of how exquisitely my passions for movement, creativity, successful learning experiences and wellness weave together.

At our **"BEST"** when we embrace the fullness of who we are and all of the knowledge and experience that we bring. **I believe** that by doing this we are able to tap into our own personal sacred alchemy of healing modalities, perhaps revealing a unique approach to transformation. I believe that doing this is vital to the process of healing ourselves.

I believe that when we bring the **"BEST"** of who we are to whatever we do, we have the capacity to both heal ourselves and facilitate healing in the circles in which we operate.

I believe that as we commit to the process of healing ourselves, we are equipping ourselves to heal the planet. In other words, we must each discover, explore and use all of the tools in our respective healing kits. For me, there is healing in the power of movement. Embracing this holistic point of view has meant learning to **unapologetically allow all of whom I am to show up and shine through**. When I do, the gift to those I serve is, no matter which of my modalities is called upon, all of them are present.

The word **BEST** captures each element of healing integrated into my process. For example, when the teaching artist is called upon – there is healing for the math lesson! By accessing the healing power of Yoga to change the **breath** and lower stress levels in the **brain** and **body**, we are able to **enter** an **emotional** state that is more conducive to learning. This transformation of **emotional** and physical **energy** from nervous anxiety to calm, focused curiosity, makes it possible to access the healing power of creative **expression** and critical thinking, in order to make dances inspired by concepts in the math lesson.

Exploring **spatial** relationships through movement can help us to practice having the experience of collaborating **successfully** with others; while working independently invites us to **take time to tune** our attention inwardly.

So, I say this about myself; I am a Healer. The tools of my sacred alchemy of healing are movement through the art and science of yoga and the creativity of dance. The mission of my healing practice is to inspire passion for living, learning and transformation by facilitating experiences that move hearts, minds and bodies.

THE CREATOR HAS A MASTER PLANET

Baba Osaygefo Colby & Karma Colby, Holistic Artists

PART 1
BABA OSAYGEFO COLBY

*L*et us begin with The Source, Black People in America. Our life's study should be based on the pursuit of absolute truth and supreme justice. The internalization of this concept will almost certainly create a spiritual bridge to good mental health.

We have always, as a part of the American reality been subjected to the American way, affirmation through negation. To circumvent this invisible carcinogenic, simply recognize the greater understanding of mind over matter, which summons the power of spirituality. A healthy spirit is the source of a healthy mind and body.

In 463 years, 1555-2018, we have fallen into a gradual decline from Afrikan captives to the so-called, Afrikan American citizens, a permanent underclass! Actually, the term African American is an oxymoron. When you begin to believe that you are other than what you truly are, you then become confused to the point of mental chaos. This state of mind is referred to as menticide, the systematic and deliberate destruction of a whole race of peoples' minds. Example, we consistently name our children European names. 90% of all Black children born in America, in the last 10 years have been given European names. This constitutes an identity crisis. There is nowhere on this planet where Europeans in any consistency name their children any names other than their own! When you recognize that you are in a state of chaos you stand on the doormat to order! Good health and the power to heal Planet Earth demands Divine Order. Failure to properly diagnose and treat the problem is either ineptness or arrogance. Arrogance according to Dr. Jethro Kloss, author of Back to Eden, is the cause for all disease! Assuming that we have properly diagnosed the problem, let us begin to explore that problem.

For nearly 50 years, as a nationally acclaimed artist, vendor, manufacturer, musician, lecturer, entrepreneur, husband, father, grandfather, great grandfather, vegetarian, publisher etcetera, I am called to set a profile from which our youth can schedule their futures. Art is the personification of any given culture and that culture fueled by determination and faith then provides the political direction of that nation.

From shortly before the end of the American Civil War through and to the present, the core of world creative genius and impact thereof, has found its origin amongst Black people in America. In the arts, sciences, math, music, composition and so forth, the entire world looks to and follows our lead. For example, regarding the construction of the space shuttle, a machined space craft that moves at a rate of speed approaching 18,000 miles an hour outside the atmosphere, what is generally unknown to most people is that the retrorockets, the thrust engines, the cockpit as well as the toilets were all invented by Black people born in the United States. This historical information can be found in *Blacks in Science Ancient and Modern*, one of the many journals edited by Dr. Ivan Van Sertima. The memorandum is not offered to suggest or prove that Black genius is born through arrogance, instead it is the cornerstone of preventive and curative good health. And, our wealth is found in our health.

As an accredited Master Teacher and Mentor for 5 decades, we are proud to say we've taught, touched, and influenced the nation's youth through a city to city nonstop national tour. We conducted a hands on active process in both fabrication and casting, as well as, metal and lapidary arts (cutting of stones). Metals born of essential minerals such as copper, silver and gold provide healing properties which can improve blood circulation, assist the body to detoxify and channel vibrations.

By scientific definition we, humans are electromagnetic carbon-based units. Key word electro. All the metals here-mentioned are high-rated conductors of electricity; the body's main stimulating force. From a lapidary perspective, the healing qualities of stone proximity has long been known. Hematite, a word derived from the same source as the word hemoglobin, enhances blood flow. Amber creates clarity. Onyx advances the destruction of negativity.

At Timbuktu we have offered a holistic approach to discovering your own personal purpose which is also interconnected with the collective discovery of our purpose as a people. "The Healing of Planet Earth." The proper knowledge for the proper purpose will always produce the proper direction in which to move. Let us look to the Black woman as a catalyst for a healed planet. We should worship her as the mother of the sun and she should be served, loved, protected and provided the righteous opportunity to birth, nurture and heal Planet Earth!!!

Observe the ancestors, from the Valley of the Kings to the cotton plantations of Mississippi. The Earth is feminine. Great Mother Earth creates sanctity in truth and justice. WE must reverse this march into eternal damnation and find healing in the source of the wombs of our mothers! Nicodemus did ask Christ, "How shall we then be born again? Shall we re-enter the wombs of our mothers?" In the name of our ancestors we will arrive at and in a world of eternal good health, it is world destiny. In the name of Harriet Tubman, Asantewa, Nzinga, Sojourner Truth, My Grandmothers, My Wife, and my Daughters, we submit these humble words.

The illusion of believing that any disease is incurable is menticide. We will overcome these weaknesses and return to the royalty of Earth's heritage. In times of peace both modesty and humility best become the man but in times of war that same man must summon the power to restore domestic tranquility. To heal is to serve. To serve is to be divine.

The legacy of this life's work here on earth is to ensure the lessons, tests, failures and successes are passed onto and through the next generation. They must be prepared to be willing and deserving to accept the responsibilities carefully packaged and given with great care.

A Humble Servant of The People,
Baba Osaygefo Colby

PART 2
KARMA "SOUL DOCTOR" COLBY

Am I my father's keeper? Yes, I am!! I am his keeper, his friend, his student, his youngest of 5 children, and honored to be an active part of the family business. As a daughter of legacy, it is important to continue down the path divinely laid out for me and to help preserve the magic of my family's multi-dimensional creative force field.

My parents tell the story quite often about their daily routine during the time of my conception. "We got up early every morning, listened to the jazz album "Karma" by Pharoah Sanders, did yoga, and made jewelry." So, it's really no coincidence that I am a lover of jazz, a yoga practitioner and a jewelry designer by trade. It is clearly safe to say, I am about my mother and father's business!!!

As a second-generation entrepreneur, I've learned that in order to help others heal and to properly serve them. I must maintain an elevated level of healing and balance. I must do so by being a shining example of my divine purpose and knowing that I am still a work in progress. Not only am I doing the work, I have also become the work. After 17 years of doing business as KarmaSoul International, I've been able to reprioritize my life after a long stint of severe exhaustion. I experienced a great deal of professional success, but I found that as KarmaSoul was prospering, Karma's Soul was dying. For the benefit of my soul's resuscitation I was forced to use the tools of healthy living I had been given as a child. They say when the student is ready the teacher appears. So, in the spirit of "Black Girl Magic", POOF, Queen Afua emerged into my life! Queen served as my spiritual midwife, nurturing and guiding me through the sacred gateways of being rebirthed into KarmaSoulDoctor, The Soul Practitioner. It is said that it takes a village to raise a child, so Queen Afua was able to reconstitute and reiterate many principles my mother had exemplified to me at a time I was not yet ready to adhere them.

I find systematic body of procedures, from prayer, meditation, healthy eating and so on, to be the most effective medicine I have to offer the planet in an effort of healing. I heal myself to invoke a sense of aspiration in the souls of those who are influenced and inspired by my life's production. Lights, Karma, Action!! My journey is a one-woman play as I cry freedom, sing the blues, dance to the beat of my own sacred drum, lace everyone in laughter, and juggle lemons in the produce section as if no one is watching. Never missing an opportunity to be kind or forgetting to smile, even when tears are streaming down my soul.

Once I was able to breakthrough to a new dimension of my personal wellness, my life-long desire to be a holistic practitioner was reawakened after over 20 years of a dream deferred. Openly sharing the evolution of Karma's Soul, Spirit and Body of healing work enabled me to re-decipher what I was being called on this planet to do before I was even born. It was a super natural progression to begin my shift from hustler to healer. The horse was in front of the carriage now and nothing was lost, rather masterfully orchestrated by The One Most High.

The healing of my heart and mind from psychological debris has liberated me from an illusional state of perpetual emergency and thus shifted my paradigm for creating a more globally expansive state of being. As whole harmonized beings, we are able to step away from our long laundry list of things to do into our shai (destiny) of bringing the planet back to the garden as it was in the beginning.

> *"The Creator has a Master Plan. Peace and happiness through all the land."*
>
> PHAROAH SANDERS

The world is no longer on my shoulders, it is in the palms of my hands. I received the vision where I physically lifted Mother Earth off my shoulders, carried her over my head, gently laid her in my lap and held her like a newborn child. The vision came with a divine message that I had birthed a new world in my spirit. In order to wombnifest anything we must first see it in the unseen realm.

> *"We give thanks for those who have vision and hold the vision in spite of EVERYTHING, because it takes that!! Holding vision in spite of EVERYTHING"*
>
> QUEEN AFUA

As a womb practitioner, I am teaching women how to heal and care for their wombs and helping to bring awareness to womb wellness as a global consideration. As a Sacred Woman Practitioner, I am helping to guide women through The Sacred Woman text, gateway by gateway. I want to help them to grasp in depth their journey of healing the feminine body, mind, and spirit. As a detox facilitator I am aiding women in releasing toxins from every aspect of their lives. As a designer, I create and offer sacred healing adornments to enhance and restore our ancient spiritual beauty, raise self-esteem, and heal the inner wounded child through the power of the feminine arts. As a spirit, having a human experience, I embrace my sacred responsibility to help bring healing to this earthly realm using all the power I have been endowed with from on High.

I host women's healing circles, retreats, workshops, womb yoga dance classes, and I offer consultations, wellness programming and more. It all continues to unfold as a beautiful lotus blossom coming forth out of the mud of my lifetime. Continuing to divinely align with my sacred work (Meshkenet) has helped me to step out on the belief that the earth can be healed as I become an active participant in the birthing of this world vision. I speak life and the planet shifts on its axis. "PLANET HEAL THYSELF!!!!!!!!!!"

I Wish You Wellness,
Karma "Soul Doctor" Colby

NATURAL HAIR AND LOVE ON OUR PEOPLE

Sheila Everette-Hale, Natural Beauty Activist

In October 2011, Amazon Smiley, Marion Council-George, Diane Bailey, Marci Walker, Anu Prestonia, Orin Sounders, Tulane Kinard, Nekhena Evans, Taliah Waajid and I, Sheila Everette-Hale, were recognized by our peers as Master Pioneers in the Natural Hair Industry. It was founded by Anita Hill-Moses and held in Brooklyn, New York. Prerequisites for receiving the award were being in the this field for over 25 years and having contributed greatly to the industry. My contribution is education. Everette's Natural Beauty School/Salon (my family owned and operated business) has been in existence since 1978. We have provided various workshops, seminars, certificate and licensing programs. I spearheaded the separation of licensing of braiders from cosmetologists and as a result, the Natural Hair Culturist license was created in Michigan (FY1997).

In the beginning years (mid 1970s – late 90s), of creating this industry, the focus was on each state creating a braider's license (Michigan) or becoming exempt from having to have any license at all (California). Braiding salons were being shut down by the Board of Cosmetology in various states and some natural hair stylists, (Isis Brantley in Dallas, TX) were handcuffed and put in jail. Taalib-din Uqdah & Pamela Ferrell of Cornrows & Company went to battle for the rights of both employees being harassed for the right for natural hair stylists to provide an income for their family and/or were fired from their jobs for wearing their hair naturally. Meanwhile, several organizations arose to help educate and support braiders and locticians everywhere. To name a few, The National Braider's Guild (NBG) and the American Hairbraiders & Natural Haircare Association (AHNHA).

Moving into the 21st century more training became available in schools, hair shows and braiding seminary/workshops. When social media opened up, Facebook in particular, it made posting pictures easy.

Once we moved to video-sharing and conference-calling, the world became our client and student. They wanted to know more about natural hair, health & beauty; and they expected those who offered natural hair care services to provide the answers by having the products available themselves or be able to offer references for purchasing. there is more information on the social media sites. Taliah Waajid's World Natural Hair Show (Atlanta, GA since 1996) represents one of the many young entrepreneurs and family businesses currently showing up at natural hair shows with unique products and/or services.

Our next move is to come together as a Natural Hair, Health & Beauty INDUSTRY to empower ourselves as a people desiring to give wholesome, quality service and healthy, natural products to our community. We must bring the 'other' skills that many of us used in corporate America and bring to the table to create a powerful and effective industry that will advance the quality of life for everyone. We must position ourselves to finance our own entrepreneurs, inventors, schools, salons, product developers, productions, expos, authors, and so on.

In the book (later movie) ***400 Years Without A Comb*** by Willie Morrow of California Curl, it talks about how the 'inferior seed' was planted in our psyche and we began losing our own identity. This was done not only by using the color of our skin, but also the texture of our hair. Unfortunately, many of our people, both sisters and brothers, are still stuck there. Yet, there is hope. This new generation is certainly reaping the benefits of the ground-breaking work done back in the 70s–80s–90s by the 'Baby Boomers' who wanted their children to be free to express themselves. Now that their children are having children, more and more teens and young adults are keeping the chemicals off of their hair and creating funky and classic natural hair styles to express themselves with nappy hair. More are choosing a vegetarian/vegan lifestyle, eating no meat and surrounding themselves with natural items such as crystals, plants, herbs and spices. More are choosing to be conscious of Mother Earth, the Sun, Moon and Stars and acknowledging and honoring our ancestors.

Our work can heal and set people free… Many speak about the mental and emotional trauma of having to stop relaxing their hair, and I've witnessed sisters who wanted to go natural (especially those wanting to loc their hair) being discouraged by family and friends.

Connie was funny. Nekhena Evans (Brooklyn, NY), author of ***Everything You Ever Wanted To Know About Locks***, came to celebrate our new location grand opening of Everette's Corn-Rows & Braiding Academy in Detroit, MI, in April 2000. Connie attended. She was wearing a wig (I thought it was a latch hook). Nekhena talked about being natural, embracing your own natural beauty, and honoring God's creation of you. Connie was sitting in the hair dryer chairs over by the shampoo bowls. I went over to talk with her about how she was enjoying the event. She shared with me how she's wanted locks for a long time, but her family wasn't supportive of her choice. Nekhena's presentation continued and not long afterwards I looked over and Connie had removed her wig and was taking her hair down. I must admit I thought she had short and thin hair and that's why there was a hesitancy of locks, but girlfriend had a head full of beautiful thick hair! It was about 3 ½ to 4 inches at the time. After everyone noticed her completely loosened hair, she was called up to the front stage and everyone stretched their hands toward her to send love and energy in support of her decision to be free to love herself.

Connie shared with me that after that day she no longer needed to take the multitude of pills she was on and no longer needed the oxygen machine to help her breath. Truly, some people can be literally set free from bondage when they're able to wear their hair in its natural state. Connie got her Sisterlocks in May of 2000. "I'm free to be me…the natural me."

Natural Hair Care Providers are a front-line service to the people. We are HEALERS! One client, one style, one story, one recommendation, one service at a time, we have the opportunity to help reshape, redirect and re-educate minds and help those who don't love themselves to begin doing so…starting with their natural hair. Just by the nature of what we do, we are expected to know certain things, such as, herbs and spices, natural healing remedies and eating habits. We must pay attention to the atmosphere and make sure the space has a steady flow of positive energy (Feng Shui) to flirt with the five senses—sight, sound, smell, taste and touch. We must surround the space with a balance of the 7 elements—earth, air, fire, water, metal, wood and space. We must be certain there is proper and ample lighting for stylists. Most of all we must provide a constant infusion of fresh LOVE.

To 'heal the planet' we must position ourselves as a Natural Hair Industry so that we can support those around the world who desire to open salons and schools. Our tasks will be to develop natural hair, health and beauty products; provide educational opportunities; write books and curricula; develop and design furniture, tools and equipment specifically for the Natural Hair Industry. We must document our own history, write our own stories so that the truth will abound. We must leave a legacy of information, how-to's and financial support, and thus, make it easier for natural hair, health and beauty providers following us to reach higher grounds.

We have a big job ahead of us. Our objective should be to provide holistic, quality products and service for the natural hair, health and beauty community. We must lift-up and encourage our fellow brothers and sisters to embrace their natural selves and to know they are perfect just the way they are. If they aren't pleased with the appearance of their hair, do something about it, but don't 'hate' it, because it's a part of them and to hate anything is to magnify its presence as the annoyance increases.

It is time to take the healing to another level. No more just 'doing hair'. It's time to nurture the soul while grooming the hair. One day as I was walking back to the salon from lunch break I repeatedly said to myself, "Everette's natural hair, health and beauty." Then Spirit said, "No, it's NATURAL hair, NATURAL health, and

NATURAL beauty." Emphasis was on the word 'NATURAL.' Our work has just begun. We must work together to help heal our people…one nappy head at a time. It is time to set standards the community can depend on and it is time for the servers to prosper from their labor of love.

It is my glorious honor to cultivate and style NATURAL hair and love on our people.

HEAL AND TRANSFORM WITH BREATH AND SOUND

Ayo Handy-Kendi & John Davies 3

THE POWER OF THE BREATH
AYO HANDY-KENDI, BREATHOLOGIST

What if you could find a free, always available, *simple* solution, that could easily impact your life and health, change your stress, and manage your trauma? Wouldn't you want to know about it? I certainly wanted to know of such a solution, because earlier in my life I felt overwhelmed by life. The more I looked around my community, I saw evidence of situations that went beyond stress all the way to trauma for me and many others.

In 1970, I started to find the solution to better manage my disharmony. The solution was right under my nose, didn't cost anything, and was always available. The solution was to better manage my breathing. I became a student of "The Breath" and to this day, I am still amazed with its awesome powers.

Early in my career (a holistic practitioner and community organizer), as I examined my own physical and mental health it became critical to look at the disparities of wellness in our communities. I questioned, "Why do Black people succumb to ill health in greater proportions?" My research led me to studies that showed that People of Color live sicker and die sooner than their counterparts do. We also are challenged in greater proportions with major illnesses such as, strokes, heart attacks, cancer, high blood pressure, diabetes, obesity, asthma, infant mortality, hyperactivity, depression and bipolarism. Further, I discovered that substance abuse, addictions, domestic violence and homicide actually are health issues. However, they show up, by whatever names, these systematic physical, emotional, mental and spiritual breakdowns and imbalances clearly overwhelm our communities' capabilities to flourish socially and economically.

My desire to support Black people's health led me to learn more about how the medical and wholistic worlds were pointing to stress as the root cause of illness. A 2005 landmark study from Rush University Medical Center (Chicago) validated my hypothesis that stress from racism is the common thread shared by People of Color. I clearly saw that when under stress people either held their breath or over-breathed, and that people's daily breathing was quite shallow.

"Could stressed-out, inefficient breathing from racism be the root of the disproportionate level of poor health commonly evidenced among Blacks?" Horrifically snatched out of Africa, we were spread around the Diaspora under extremely inhumane conditions. Surely, we must have held our breath out of fear, pain, and stressful survival. Once we landed in foreign lands, we were confronted with the unrelenting trauma of racism and discrimination, while trying to adapt to new ways of living. Imagine how much breath-holding occurred? Such limited and improper oxygen intake created a physical toll on our health and increased the risk for a host of potential illnesses.

Today, more than sixty disorders are classified as stress-related. At the next level, hyper-vigilant stress is trauma. Trauma is the unrelenting physical and emotional response to situations beyond our control, such as, daily living in overcrowded urban centers. Trauma is also living in rural settings surrounded by toxic waste dumps and electromagnetic fields (EMF) oozing from telephone wires, alongside cancerous alleys and "other-side-of-the-tracks" highways. We juggle life, while existing with an overwhelming sense of disempowerment, anxiety, fear, rage, anger and apathy. Coping with traumatic stress, we respond to gentrification, food deserts, police-brutality, social, political, and economic inequality, mass media programming, misinformation from technology's digital divide, violence, poverty, under-education, unemployment, under-nourishment, drugs and alcohol.

In the U.S.A., People of Color (including, African-Americans, Africans, Indigenous Native People, Latin Americans and Immigrants from all over the world) are unconsciously, subconsciously, and consciously reacting from internalized emotions. Victims of enslavement, colonization, immigrant oppression, and survivor programming, we have been annihilated and partitioned. We have had our land stolen, and our water and food sources destroyed. Showing symptoms of hyper-vigilance, distrust, and isolation, we have been reacting to post-traumatic stress disorder (PTSD) due to cellular-level memory of cruel incidents, as well as current traumatic stress disorders.

Too many feeling out of harmony, out of balance and "discombobulated" reach for something to medicate themselves from the pain; or over-medicate to cope. Renowned psychiatrist, Dr. Bobby Wright, defined such feelings and conditions as "Mentacide", which he defined in 1980 as "…the deliberate and systematic destruction of a person or a group's mind." Dr. Francis Cress Welsing wrote of this condition as "racism/White supremacy" and confirmed racism as "the issue" that is at the root of the ills of all society.

So, I studied and practiced this simple solution—Deep Breathing—for the disparities of health as related to stressful, traumatized living. Concrete studies provided medical proof that deep breathing is one of the best methods of relaxation, stress release and trauma reduction. One of my master teachers provided me "truckloads" of testimonials. People stated the benefits of better breathing were being able to manage stress, trauma, and much more. I started compiling my findings, which specifically focused on breathing and the needs of African-centered people.

By 2004, I envisioned a "Breath Movement" and coined the concept, "Breathology, as the art and science of breath awareness, breath mechanics and applied breathing techniques that advance the Spirit, Mind and Body." With my findings I completed my book, *The Power of the Breath*. By 2010, I had evolved my practice to create an entire system called "Optimal Life Breathology" (O.L.B.). and began to certify Breathologists. As a Breathologist and holistic practitioner, the focus of my work was a commitment to healing the stress and trauma in communities of color. Of course, stress does not impact only Black people—it detrimentally affects the entire population, especially in the U.S.A. Thereby, I continued to advocate breath training as the "perfect solution" for all who desired to manage suffering from stress and trauma disorders. I started offering the slogan: *Relearn How to Breathe for Better Life, Health, Work and Longevity*™.

Looking back on my development as an early student of the breath to becoming an international Breathologist, and an advocate of breath focus and training, I see that this work has been a mirror of my own life's "story."

In the early 70s, as a degreed community organizer and counselor, I often heard the expression, "Take a deep breath," to relax and calm down. Yet, I was not doing this. While I was studying breath focus, alternative health and energy balancing, I, myself abused substances, became addicted to cocaine and alcohol, lived very out-of-balance, and became increasingly aware of how often I held my breath. Like most people, I had been restricting my life by shallow, improper breathing. My health was challenged. Merely existing in a spiral of high-stress, anger, fear and reactiveness, I felt numb, empty and depressed. Showing up "unauthentic", I pushed myself to perform in public. Stuck in my own emotional woundedness and low levels of consciousness, I only felt "alive" when I was stimulated by getting "high."

In 1994, my youngest son, at age 17, was hit over the head with a blunt instrument. He was left in a coma for 5 days, while a breath machine sustained his life. Two years later, a breath machine also sustained my father, dying of brain cancer. These experiences made the lasting impression on me that "the Breath" governs the thin line between life and death. In my "Aha" moment, I realized, *"We can have life, but true life comes from a "true, full, life-sustaining breath."*

During this time, I was blessed as The Creator led me to discover "Conscious Connected Breathing" which took my deep breathing to the next level and changed my life. This breathing technique flooded my body with oxygen. I felt awakened, lighter, and unburdened from the suppressed energy of being sexually and mentally abused as a child. As a young girl from age 8 to 13, to cope with the shock, anger, frustration and fear I had stored emotions in my body and my subconscious mind. I had held my breath and gone numb with each incident of abuse. Finally, with each now conscious-connected breath session I released negative emotions as my energy increased by leaps and bounds. I was able to forgive my abuser—my father—and the murderer of my son. I stopped desiring any substances and kept a natural "high." I've been clean and sober ever since.

Breathing techniques, later helped me manage the stress of homelessness, domestic violence, and the closely timed deaths of many family members. So many awesome results forever changed my life and I began to share them more with others. I specialized in facilitating and spreading the awareness of the "power of the breath" and became a health activist and relaxation practitioner. I am one of only a few African-Americans who is trained as a Certified Breathologist (CB), Transformational Facilitator (CTF), and Laughter Yoga Leader/Teacher (CLYT). I further trained and certified as Qi Gong I, II and Reiki Master 3. Now, I compose "tune-up music to breathe along with", combining sound with breath for more transformative possibilities. My "co-creation" of Optimum Life Breathology™ offers twelve best breath practices with other transformative modalities to facilitate life-changing growth and healing. I have shared my signature "deep breathing technique" with billions on radio, television, in print, on stage, and in private practice. I have been blessed to be included in the 24-hour Global Fast events facilitated by Queen Afua and I have worked with many master practitioners, who also recognize "the power of the breath."

Sharing breathology with so many others I beam with empathy over their excited testimonies as they "relearn how to breathe." Breath awareness and training can start your life anew by offering a lifelong tool for the following:

- Increased health and wellness, self-care and preventative care;
- Practical lifestyle applications to enhance all you need to make life better;
- Personal transformation and growth;
- Pain, stress and trauma reduction;
- Detoxification and increased immunity;
- Emotional balancing, peak mental performance,
- Enhanced sexuality and vitality;
- Increased anti-aging and longevity;
- Metabolic nourishment and toning of every cell, of every organ for best function of cellular activity and alkalinity of the body;
- Peace, joy, contentment and passionate love for life, which elevates the spirit;
- And many, many more benefits.

To this day, I continue to experiment with "the Breath" for addiction recovery, conflict resolution, anxiety management, grief/survival issues, diversity and racial healing and general life-style applications. The miracles I have seen in my clients and myself have convinced me that Western medicine is denying Americans a powerful remedy. Those who herald the benefits of Breath insist that the way we breathe is the simplest thing we can change and can make the greatest impact on us in every way. Unfortunately, we take this gift of proper breathing for granted. Maybe the concept of deeper breathing to maximum life and health is too simple a concept in a world of complications. Maybe we are too used to releasing our power to doctors, pharmaceutical pills and surgery. Yet, deep breathing and breath focus *IS* a science-proven solution that we must embrace.

I encourage you to become more conscious of your breath; to become more conscious of life. Celebrate your life as you breathe deeply, fully, and efficiently through every single day, hour, minute and second. You will demonstrate that "You are tired of the stress; tired of the pain; ready to heal; ready to change.™" Yes, a teacher with a solution has come to help you revitalize and re-arrange. This teacher is the breath of life.

So, breathe, open, and awaken to your power and flow. Just relax, and de-traumatize yourself because there is true Power in the Breath™ and its power will help you find your power. Breathology offers "minute to minute Yoga™" that will yoke you back to consciousness to advance you beyond stress and trauma. Your breath is your greatest teacher, on this journey with you always. Breathe better, Live Better. Excel™

A SOUND HEALING EXPERIENCE
AYO HANDY-KENDI, BREATHOLOGIST
& JOHN DAVIES 3, SOUND HEALER

Sound Healing is a wellness modality that uses varied techniques and technologies to harness the energy of sound for the goal of wellness of the human system and expansion of consciousness. Sound Healing is founded on the principle that all matter is vibrating at unique frequencies. Everything has a vibration or a sound. Each cell and every organ in our body has its own sound. Every shape has its own sound. Thoughts, emotions, and intentions each have a vibration or sound.

Science has proven that sound or vibration can change matter, patterns, the molecular structure of water, alter emotional feelings, and create pure consciousness. Many ancient civilizations and early indigenous cultures knew this and had techniques to harness the healing power of sound. They used sound to access higher levels of consciousness and sound frequencies to move matter and energy.

While musical instruments have played an important part in sound healing, the human voice has consistently been a powerful instrument of healing through the ages. A perfect example of this healing is the use of humming, chanting, and wailing by newly captive enslaved people, who were held hostage on boats from Africa to the *"New World."* Later, these people also used sound healing in the fields through call-and-response singing to survive the heat, hard labor, oppression and racism.

Today, sound is re-emerging as a healing modality because of its connection to sound entrainment, wherein people bring rhythms together to create harmonious states and octave resonance. Many people also use the various pitches of sound to alter brain waves, which can create harmony and balance.

Sound is used:
- As a tool for change;
- For meditation and relaxation;
- In chanting, toning, and singing to resonate harmony in the body;
- In the form of nature sounds and natural instruments to create healing frequencies and harmonics;
- In drumming and rhythm to release stress and for team building;
- During shamanic drumming to create altered states of consciousness;
- As a support for children with some learning disabilities;
- As binaural beats to entrain people into specific states of consciousness or emotions;
- To alter brain waves for sleep disorders, for creative expression, or to stabilize emotions;
- To help ground and center people for heightened awareness;
- As a support for difficult life transitions, including birth and death;
- As various medical applications including during surgery, to relieve pain, to break up gallstones; to relax muscles using ultrasound, to reconnect people with dementia, and to resonate the sound frequency of organs to help vibrate them back into a healthy state.

Sound research shows that each of us has a root or Soul frequency at which we vibrate. This Soul frequency emanates from us when we are most centered, grounded, basking in love, or are in a state of pure presence and are fully "living in the moment." However, there are many frequencies that distract us from our own root or Soul frequency. These include frequencies especially generated in the urban setting: cell phones, modes of transportation (i.e. cars, trucks, trains, planes) and all manner of electricity and electromagnetism. There are also sounds or noises from animals, as well as chaotic frequencies from disconnected people who dwell among us. We can also distract our own inner soul frequency, by chaotic and stressful thoughts, pains, and illnesses; and by limiting our breathing.

Because the breath is audible sound, when we breathe rhythmically, deeply, consciously, and consistently, we help to reconnect the frequency within us, and bring ourselves to calm and emotional stillness. When we add music, sound, or vibration to the rhythm of breath, we help to balance out chaos, create more consistent frequencies and radiate grounding, calmness, and peace within.

By going within to our inner frequency, we can meditate upon breath and sound, thus inner peace will reflect outwardly in all that we do.

Now, think about the levels of loud noise, music, videos, honking horns and sirens, constant vibrational energy plugged into our ears from our devices, along with the limited amount of time that we spend with "no sound." Without doubt, the consistent chaotic sounds around us distorts our inner sound and disrupts our natural frequency.

For these reasons, we offer a "breath and sound experience" as Earth Love Tune-Up Crew (ELTUC). We are the Breath Sekou, Ayo Handy-Kendi, and John Davies 3, Sound Healers, Breathologists, and Composers, who create and perform our brand, "Tune-up Music.™" A fusion of African-centered and natural sound instruments, Tune-up Music™ gently stimulates the chakras (energy-centers in the body), while calming the mind of mental chatter and relaxing the nerves for stress reduction. We offer concerts and sessions that connect breath and sound with visualizations, laughter and movement to create harmony, balance, and inner peace, which radiates to create outer peace.

While much relaxation music is composed of European-inspired symphony instruments, synthesized harmonics, or computer-generated rhythms and beats, ELTUC's sounds come from 20 to 30 instruments creating natural sounds and world-beat rhythms. We provide excellent ambient, background sound-tracks for radio, television, film productions or commercials. "Tune-up" sound is also excellent as "white noise", the background sound for an office, or as a sleep aid. ELTUC sound helps ground and relax an audience at the opening of an event or recharge them at the event's close. ELTUC sound offers perfect ambiance in sacred spaces needed for contemplation, creative expression, breathology, meditation, yoga or other holistic practices.

Use breath and sound to "tune you up to tune you in" to a natural world where you will find your highest vibration.

HEALING THROUGH THE VOICE

Betty Lane, Voice Specialist

It seems logical to me that as the voice permeates the body and all surrounding areas of the body, the voice has healing powers. I believe that the entire universe was and is constructed on a harmonic musical scale, a full spectrum of vibrational sound frequencies, known as tones and pitches. The word harmony means, "connected together." Cosmos means, "the order of things." Combined they represent the connectivity of things. To heal, we need the full harmonic spectrum of sound; inside and out. Utilizing the voice for vibrational healing is but one of the many tools available in sound therapy. Another modality is placing tuning forks of varying pitches and frequencies on meridians and acupuncture points of the body to open and expand constricted areas, as well as cleanse and open blockages.

In her book, **City of Wellness**, Queen Afua has brilliantly presented food frequency pyramids to increase our understanding of the food we eat and how the levels of energy it provides can be measured from lowest frequency representing "poor health" up to the highest frequency representing "optimal wellness." In the same manner, the vocal vibrations and sounds around us have energetic healing and wellness qualities based on frequencies from low to high.

What I am seeking to share with and awaken in you is the conscious use of vocal vibrational energy to promote wellness and healing. Voice healing is founded on the premise that all matter is vibrating at specific frequencies (tones and pitches). If you listen to your refrigerator, a passing truck, branches of a tree waving in the wind, you hear sounds and feel the vibrations of said sound at various levels of tonality. You cannot escape sound and vibration. It is all around you, all the time. So why not learn to use it as a healing and wellness tool?

The power to heal through sound and vibration can be traced back to every culture and cosmology throughout time

BODY ~ BREATH AND BEAUTY—HEAD TO TOE

and history. Standing at the top of all cultures and cosmologies is that of the Ancient Egyptian (Kemetic) people who used voice, sound and vibration to heal, strengthen and balance their sense of wholeness from within. Today, universal cultures making powerful sound through the beat of the drum and the call of the voice, still respond to the primitive healing force.

My primary goal is to awaken your awareness to the abilities (and their hidden modalities) you already have within yourself: Vibration, Sound and the VOICE. These are healing tools! Together or independently, they serve as conduits between the inner self and the outer world. The voice, for example, can be used to regain one's sense of emotional balance in the form of song, chant, tone and just simply humming. Using the voice has served to release blocked energy and express emotions. Singing, vibrations and sounds allow us to experience the present in the context of the past; as well as, our present hopes, dreams, desires for the future; and most importantly, to maintain a direct connection with DIVINE SOURCE.

In Genesis, verse after verse starts with or includes the voice with the words, "GOD said." According to the bible, when GOD created man, He used the power of the breath which is a major component of utilizing the voice. The breath causes the vocal chords in the voice box to stretch and vibrate and make sound. You have control over the volume of sound—soft or loud—by way of the contraction of the abdominal muscles and the movement of the diaphragm upon which the lungs sit.

As the sound waves, generated by the vibrating vocal chords, pass through the many parts of your body, they cause all the elements of these spaces to vibrate at various frequencies. The tones are then projected into all parts of your body, including your brain. As sound is emitted from within you, the space around and within you vibrates. A sound cannot be made without a resulting degree of vibration. All vocal sound takes place because of the process of the breath filling the lungs and subsequently filling the spaces in your body with vibration and sound which you want to use as a positive full body-healing and wellness tool.

In the Ancient Egyptian Kemetic tradition, vowel sounds (called sacred sounds) were used as wellness tools to affect, stimulate and vibrate various parts of the body. In the Chinese Healing Sounds, the focus was (and to this day, still is) on vibrating and stimulating the internal organs.

Some vowel sounds used are:
Liver = shu
Spleen = who
Heart = hah
Lung = s-s-s-s-s- (a hissing sound)
Kidney = choo

Through sound and vibration, we use these frequencies to bring the rich harmonies of the planets into cosmic, divine energy for healing and wellness. Every organ and cell has a connection to the vibrations and sounds surrounding them. Slow music has been known to slow down the heart rate, creating a sense of peace and relaxation, and resetting negative cellular patterns in the body. Harmonious sound can get to the inner body in ways that outer modalities cannot. The body is made up of 70-80% water; sound travels much faster in water. That water and a well-hydrated body is a perfect conduit for sound allowing deeper access to healing, especially as the spine, bones, nerves, joints, open and le healing sounds into a much deeper level within the body. Gong Immersion is an example of deep penetration into the depths of the body for wellness and deep healing.

Although the voice and sound are not generally thought of as healing tools, stop and listen to your body. The body speaks from within. The voice, acting as a sonic beam of vibrating energy can heal internally and externally. We are constantly vibrating with the universe and its many sounds. You must take the time for stillness and learn to create quietness inside yourself. We are so busy being "human doings" until we have forgotten how to be "human beings!" Listen to the sounds that come out of your body and the words that come out of your mouth. Negative and positive sounds and words have a direct impact upon our healing capacity. The voice and its vibrating effects can heal on the physical level because it deeply touches and transforms on the emotional and spiritual planes. Think twice about how and what you are saying. Sound and its vibration can calm the mind and subsequently the body; or it may have deep seated, long-term effects. Be kind with the sounds you make and the vibrations you create towards yourself and especially others.

David played the harp to help soothe King Saul, but the voice, through chanting and prayer has been used since the beginning of time to align body, mind and spirit. The voice is a powerful, primitive force. Even when man did not have words, he used the voice and sound to communicate.

Combined with movement practices such as yoga and/or qigong, sound healing is a powerful tool, especially when combined with fundamentals of health such as breath work, nutrition, meditation and stress reduction. It is important to keep the total body healthy. So also look at what you put into your body, who you allow into your body, how you move the body (exercise), cleanse the body inside (detox) and out (bathe). Drinking water is most important. Even changing the molecular structure of water is based on sound and vibration.

Know that sound of any type is vibration and that vibration in any form touches every part of our physical, mental, emotional and spiritual being. Embrace sound and vibration and know that your voice is one of your closest health and healing tools. The more you expand on this knowledge, you will come to understand that sound is heard not just through our ears, but through every cell in your body. The healing potential of your inner vibration and sound is unlimited and is the doorway to true peace and love.

MY MANTRA

I truly believe that we are here to live and to give. To share and to care with an attitude of gratitude for all that we have, have had, hope to have, so that we might find our peace within ourselves and let our light. Shine that others may see our light, our brightness and find their peace, their light and their brightness within themselves. If you believe in peace and love, lift the two fingers of the right hand in the sign of peace and say "peace." Take those two fingers to your heart, which is the seat of love and say, "And love." Point those fingers around wherever you are and with whomever you are with and say, "To you." Bring those fingers back to your heart and say, "To me." If you cannot love yourself you will not be able to love others, nor they you. Remember, "Face smile, Whole Body smile."

Peace and Love always!!!!
Betty Lane

QI GONG: BREATH OF LIFE

George Love, Acupuncturist/Qigong Master

I nearly died in June of 2007. The causes? Bronchitis, White and Black mold in my house, allergy to pollen that was one hundred times higher than usual and a brush fire smoke alert in Tampa Bay.

Background: I was born with a birth defect causing my right foot to curl under. I wore corrective shoes until age six. As a kid I could not run or play sports; nonetheless, I became a Cub Scout—with flat feet. I was short and fat and wore thick glasses. Even though I could barely ride a bike, at age 16 I forged a license and went straight to motorcycles. At the ripe old age of 28 I decided to get in shape, motivated by the fact that I had to walk up eleven flights of stairs, *daily,* to get to work. At first, I committed to run two miles every day. That lasted a year. Then, I ran three miles daily for eighteen months. During this time, I also trained for bicycle racing in Harlem on five-kilometer streets for up to ten laps. Then I had a bad bicycle accident in Central Park. There were five of us in a pack. As we came around a curve someone had just thrown sand on an oil spill. We all went down. With my right foot stuck in the pedal clip, I slid fifty feet, tearing flesh from bone and injuring my right hip piriformis muscle. No riding or running for almost a year. Then I found Master Lee in Central Park performing Qigong exercises every Sunday. He allowed me to join the class. Eventually he invited me to Chinatown where he taught mostly Chinese elders. One day, about three months in, as I was performing Qigong I suddenly felt my head open to the sky. It felt like I was merging with the cosmos. I heard a loud "pop" in my right ankle. Cautiously, I looked at my foot. My shoe was soaking wet. I took off the shoe and poured out water. When I stood up I felt strangely connected to Heaven and Earth. Qigong had reversed my birth defect and my flat feet! When I asked Master Lee about it he told me not to pay attention to phenomena. "Just keep training."

Eventually I became his most dedicated

student. He took me into his practice. Through his tutelage at Jushi Lin Taoist Scholars Council I became a Doctor of Oriental Medicine. In 1994 I became lineage holder of Lung Qigong, Qigong Master of Blue Dragon Immortal Qigong. Because I had a daily practice I thought I had reached the zenith. I taught three days a week from 2001–2007 but did not self-practice daily. So, I forgot the lesson.

Back to near death: I was meeting friends to go camping in Ocala National Forest. I arrived Friday after dark and could not find our location. I pitched my tent in a hollow just 50 feet from the water, with no idea that damp cold would penetrate my lungs. Saturday night I could not sleep because of coughing. I sat by the fire all night playing drums and talking. Sunday, I worked all day massaging and counseling. Sunday night, same thing; sat by the fire, no sleep. Monday, I drove to Tampa. By Tuesday morning I had a horrible cough, which turned out to be bronchitis. I had had childhood asthma but was in denial about my bronchitis. At the same time there were brush fires along I-75 for three months. Our governor, Jeb Bush declined spending resources to put out brush fires. Smoke drifting into Tampa Bay caused major car accidents; and announcements on TV told people to stay indoors. So, no Qi Gong exercise outdoors.

Meanwhile, the pollen count of Live Oak trees was 100 times higher than normal. An unusually cold winter in Florida resulted in a late spring with a high pollen count. There were brush fires because of dry grass. Investigating the difference between Live Oak versus regular Oak trees I realized there are two Live Oak trees in my front yard and three in my backyard. Five Live Oak trees around my house, with a pollen count 100 times higher than normal, caused: no Qi Gong exercise outdoors. I bought a large air filter. It gets better.

The late spring also brought unusual rain patterns. The house I rented had a hole in the roof. I had no idea until the kitchen ceiling fell in and exposed black and white mold in the house. I had to seal the kitchen off with plastic from the rest of the house until the landlord decided to fix. Result: No Qi Gong exercise indoors. So, there I was, wheezing and coughing from Mold, Smoke, Pollen and Bronchitis. I was chewing Chinese Herb pills like M&Ms. I bought a second large air filter. Now it gets interesting.

I took my Chinese Medicine friend out to PF Chang's for dinner on a Monday night. **Reference point:** *Never, never, never* go out to dinner on a Monday night. Whatever isn't sold Saturday night or Sunday, is sold on Monday. Yep, leftover food prepped on Friday is served three days later. SPOILED FOOD. Four hours later I had food poisoning. I called my friend for help. She was assisting her daughter and unable to come to help me. By midnight I had diarrhea and projectile vomiting. I had difficulty breathing. I kept running down the long hallway to the toilet. Finally, I just climbed into the tub and stayed there until morning.

I prayed for death. I had never been this miserable in my whole life. I had been in life and death situations before, but this one…I asked God if I was finished my mission. She did not answer. I held my breath, so I could die. But it did not work. I hugged the air filter, trying to breath in. It was so hard. Then I forced all my muscles to breath out. This went on for over 24 hours. Plus, I was hungry. I had been eating out because of the mold-sealed kitchen. The Health Food Store was only ten blocks away, but I was too weak to walk to the car. No food, plus no air equals no strength. My phone was ringing but I had couldn't talk; I could only wheeze.

My friend showed up two days later, but I was too weak to answer the door. No nourishing Qi; No breath. When she left I got angry. I wanted to stand up and go outside to breathe the smoky, pollen-filled air and die quickly. Anger propelled me up from my prone position. Shakily, I pushed myself outside, got into my car and drove to the beach. I did Qi Gong exercises. It was painful. Then I walked four blocks along the beach and four blocks back. The next morning, I felt no better, but I drove to the beach and did it again. Then I walked eight blocks forward and back. The third morning I could breathe without pain. That afternoon, I did it again.

The fourth morning I had a visit from a drum circle friend. She bundled me up and took me to her house an hour away from the smoke, mold and pollen. She fed me, and we did Blue Dragon Qigong in her yard. After twenty-four hours in her house my low back seized. Probably from forcing myself to breathe for so long. There was no comfortable position for me to be in, left side or right side; knees bent or straight. Unable to walk to the bathroom, I had to crawl. Again, I asked God to end my torture. She whispered, "Qigong is the answer." I forced myself up to perform Qigong for four hours until the pain went away. After two days of performing Qigong I decided to live. I drove to the beach and did Blue Dragon Qigong at sunset. I attracted a crowd. The pier manager asked me to teach Qigong every night during the summer sunset festivities. Now I am doing Qigong twice a day. That's quite a difference from three days a week.

Qigong is for everyone. The ultimate cause of all sickness is conflict with the human heart and the spirit body. If untreated it settles into the emotional body causing stress. If unresolved it drops down into the energy body causing fatigue, sleeplessness, anxiety and depression. And if *that* is untreated it affects the physical body causing pain, premature aging, degenerative disease and toxicity. All physical pain and suffering must be treated physically, first with Qigong Massage and then all four bodies can be treated simultaneously. Medical Qigong combines breathing, meditation and exercise in an hour daily practice. It is the root of Chinese medicine.

My gift to the world is medical Qigong to transform spirit, emotions, energy and physical function.

Can Qigong save Your Life? It saved Mine!

LOVE AND BEAUTY
OUR ULTIMATE HEALING

Queen Esther Hunter Sarr, Moon Therapy

The best way we can assist in healing the planet is to remember that as part of the planet we must consistently Heal Ourselves (our bodies, our minds, our spirituality and our finances). Even if it is not always easy, living a life of wellness has countless benefits. I have been blessed to receive a formula to connect our wellness path with Mother Nature and the rhythms of the moon. My class "HEALING BY THE LIGHT OF THE MOON" is designed to holistically keep our wellness schedule aligned with the cycles of the moon. My classes provide support, accountability, and consistency. "HEALING BY THE LIGHT OF THE MOON" encourages us to change from within. It also supports the fact that women experience their menstrual cycles in accordance with the cycles of moon. The lunar connection solidifies unity from the nature and to the cosmic level. Full circle, our power is amplified as we realize that we actually can have a greater impact on healing the planet.

What an Honor and a Blessing it is to be called upon—along with other Healers in the World—to bring solution to the question, **"What would you do to heal planet Earth?"**

SO MUCH Healing is needed, because SO MUCH Damage has been done. From my perspective LOVE and UNITY are still major components for our Upliftment. Love involves Unity. Love includes Compassion, Healing, Forgiveness, and Endurance! I would remind our Younger Generation that Love includes New School, Old School, and ALL Schools!

We still feel the pain of the loss of our young greats, the beloved Tupac Shakur, the beloved Biggie Smalls, and so many more who cannot be replaced. We still feel their absence. Destroying one another CANNOT BE an option as we strive to Unite, Build, and Stand in Our Greatness!

Families, it is time to Come Together and Heal and Strengthen one another. Forgive and move Forward. Our Blood

Runs Deep! Youth, Respect Your Elders. Elders, Respect Your Youth! Learn from one another. Establish and solidify Family Reunions where we can get to know each other. Share Family History, begin to network, and build a solid foundation for future generations! I encourage each and every one to strive to become the Strongest Link in the Circle! Let us learn to face ourselves in the mirror and acknowledge our strengths and accomplishments. Let us also recognize where we need Healing, Growth, and Development. Educate, read, study, and learn how to improve! Why? Because we are worth it.

We need to love ourselves enough to see our true value. Being well and loving ourselves makes it easier to love one another. Now is the time for us to witness the beauty of each of us taking action for living our ultimate life—Regardless! **How I would Love to wave a Magic Wand and Heal a Whole Community, all at once!** Each person has different issues… different challenges…to work through, personally. My work as a motivational healer is to inspire the return to a Healthy State of Being. I work to ignite the passion and desire to help one get their healing Activated. Knowing what to do and doing it are two different things. I have observe many who begin a wellness process but then lose consistency. My Father's words of wisdom were, "Maintain your health and better your condition." Mother's reminder was, "To think is to create!" Keeping these challenges in mind I have developed a simple system for Healing Oneself with an easy method for staying on track and maintaining consistency.

The system incorporates a Total Formula for Ultimate Beauty by:
- Healing and Strengthening the physical body;
- Developing a positive mindset;
- Aligning the Spiritual Body to be in tune; and
- Developing a Wealthy Body to support yourself by using the gifts you were Blessed with.

These healing modalities are synchronized to the phases of the moon to keep us on a rhythmic pattern of healing. We will be using the Lunar Phases as our time keeper.

1. In the **New Moon**…also known as the **Waxing Moon** we begin our focus on the physical body. This includes clean, healthy food intake by juicing and drinking lots of water for hydration. This segment also includes physical exercise, walking, jogging, dancing, yoga—your choice. Maintain 3–4 days. (Four days for optimum benefits.)
2. The **Crescent Moon** carries us to the second phase where we focus on recognizing the Power of the Mind! This includes Mental Wellness, Positive Thinking, Affirmations, Confirmations, Journaling and Goal Setting. Thinking and Creating. Maintain 3–4 days.
3. The **Quarter Moon**, the next phase, brings us to focus on Spirituality. We can accentuate our Creativity as we are inspired from the Creator. During this time, learn how to tune into your Spiritual Nature. Observe Nature

and realize that We are nature. Prayers, Meditation and Dream Time is the focus. Fasting and light eating is suggested for a 3–4-day period.

4. The **Gibbous Moon** has us entering more of an Introspective phase. Here we begin to see ourselves in more totality. Our focus is to look at our strengths and our gifts and see how with development and support we can create our fortune with who we are! We explore in this realm for 3 days.

5. We arrive at The Beauty…the Mystery…and the Magnetism of **The Full Moon**! Here we are Encouraged to Celebrate the Fullness of Nature within Ourselves
   …Adorn and Beautify
   …Luxuriate
   …Beauty Baths
   …Massages
   …Express Yourself
   …Write Poetry
   …See a Performance
   …Recognize the Beauty of You as an Expression of Love from the Divine! At this lunar time, we can see who we are and the potential of who we can become.

6. After Phase Five which is the completion of the waxing phase on the Full Moon, the Moon proceeds into Phase Six, the **Disseminating Moon** and the beginning of the waning or diminishing phases of the Moon. During this time our focus is to Heal, Teach, Share, Revive and Review. Here we take assessment of the previous phases. We make our shopping lists to prepare ourselves for our healthy food intake and for the next New Moon. We are reminded to keep the body fit as we keep up with our exercise regimens. The key word is **consistency**! Stay consistent with these simple regimens for including the wellness of body, mind and spirit as a part of our everyday lifestyle… use Mother Moon as our time keeper.

7. The Seventh Phase is The Last Quarter Moon. Here we are encouraged to remember our Visions for our lives. Time to Honor, Reject, Evolve, Rest and Reap. In this phase we revisit Mind work. We learn of the G.P.S. and we also discuss the benefits of Brain Balancing. Here we are reminded to read our four direction Affirmation Cards.

8. Phase Eight is the final stage of the Moon Phases. This phase known as the Balsamic Phase represents a stage of Dormancy. More Prayer Time, Dream Awareness, Dissolving, and Allowing. This is an appropriate time to recognize all of the moon cycles. Take analysis, rest, and prepare for the New Moon which is where we begin the cycles all over again. Keep in mind that every round goes higher and higher and we can continue to elevate and uplift ourselves as we align ourselves with the consistent **Rhythm of The Moon**.

In Conclusion, I believe Natural Beauty Medicine (the Power of Love and Beauty) serves as a Gateway to Optimum Wellness. Of course, we must realize that the most beneficial medicine is UNITY! To facilitate that, Spirit has led me to suggest that we use the powerful Natural Phenomena of the Moon as our unifying factor. Meeting on the Full Moon in person…or on conference calls…or in prayer in our homes can connect us Spiritually and Naturally. Thus, I am initiating the Full Moon Prayer Circle, Universally, every month from Now On!

Let us begin with the first Full Moon following the publication of this essay in **Planet Heal**. Let us continue until to Eternity and commit to stay Unified and in Harmony with Ourselves, with Each Other, and with the Natural Galactic Phenomenon!

Love Always,
Queen Esther

See my contact information for guided workshops and private consultations on Total Beauty, by The Light of The Moon.

HET HERU HEALING DANCE

Queen Mother Maash-T Amm Amen,
Empowerment Coach

One night, while I was meditating, beautiful, flowing movements began to take shape in my mind. I grabbed a pen, recorded the movements, and imitated them. Upon further reflection, I realized that these steps had to be refined and woven into a women's dance. This was the genesis of the Het Heru Healing Dance. Known as Hathor and Aphrodite to the Greeks, Venus to the Romans, the Joyous Lake to the ancient Taoists, Oshun to the Yorubas, and Netzach to the Kabalists, Het Heru, as the ancient Kamitians (Egyptians) called her, is the goddess of love, relationships, creativity, beauty, inventiveness, pleasure, joy, and healing—especially of the female reproductive organs. Through expert guidance, I developed this dance to help women find the "joyous lake" within themselves and thereby experience rejuvenation, revitalization, and healing.

Women throughout the world need the gift of healing. As one Het Heru Dance practitioner from the UK reported, "I was bleeding excessively for three years. After doing the Het Heru Healing Dance one time, the bleeding stopped right away." (R.N. –London, UK). Other women have discovered that after performing the dance for a few weeks, they experienced lighter and/or shorter menstrual cycles. They attribute this to their diligent practice of the Het Heru Healing Dance. I couldn't imagine the depth of their healing until I encountered a friend who shared that she had previously undergone eight surgeries. She told me, "My worst complication was a fibroid the size of a five-month fetus. I did the Het Heru Healing Dance every day for three months. The fibroid shrank significantly. Today, I feel wonderful." (L.H. –Brooklyn, NY.) Indeed, she still looks youthful and energetic.

Inspired by the idea that by using this soothing, fluid dance to help women of all ages heal themselves, look spectacular, feel vibrant, and celebrate their femininity, I could hardly wait to teach it to my friends and family. One incident that stands out in my mind occurred at a Het Heru Healing event hosted at a physician's office. Some of the doctor's female patients and as well as her 95-year-old, wheelchair-bound mother attended the session. Although she could not stand, the elder proceeded to dance in her wheelchair. It was a sight to behold! She was smiling. She was happy. This woman experienced joy and relaxation despite her physical limitations. Such is the power of Het Heru's joy.

Some women have reported that the Dance heightened their capacity to relish the joy of womanhood and relate to other women, family members, friends and coworkers more openly and positively. As one practitioner confirms, "Since my experience with the Het Heru Healing Dance, I was promoted twice on my job. I lost weight. I was able to stop arguing with my mate, and I finally got married." (B.V. –Queens, NY)

The Het Heru Healing Dance, an inexpensive, and non-strenuous total body workout that anyone can perform, does not substitute for conventional medical treatment; however, women can use it, in conjunction with other strategies, to promote wellness. Some of its reported effects include stomach and uterine muscle "tonification", improved breathing and blood circulation, tension release and lowered stress levels. One woman who practiced the Dance with me during the final stage of her husband's terminal illness gave the following testimonial: "I started the Healing Dance two months before my husband's death. The Dance helped me to cope with my loss and offset depression. My children saw that I was peaceful, and my emotional state helped them to deal with their loss as well." (Y.B. –Brooklyn, NY)

For more than two decades, I have facilitated Het Heru Dance demonstrations, workshops, and Het Heru Women's Healing Circles, nationally and internationally. These Healing Dance Circles, led by officially designated Het Heru Healers, continue to sprout throughout the country. Healing Circle attendees often ask, "How exactly does the Het Heru Dance work?" Without offering a ton of technicalities, I explain that the Dance primarily, arouses, strengthens, and redirects the body's life force. Yoga, Qi Gong, cardiovascular exercise, and dance can manipulate our life force effectively, but when we respond to life's challenges with fear, anger, grief, worry, or any other tension, we impede the flow of life force and harm our vital organs. This results in mental and physical obstructions that we must remove before we can live successfully. The Dance can help us to remove these blockages.

Each movement of the Het Heru Dance mentally reinforces one of the eleven universal, healing principles:

1. Maintaining peace amid challenge;
2. Understanding that no person or situation can be against us;
3. Being receptive to wise guidance;
4. Accepting our destiny with peace and joy instead of complaining about our lot in life;
5. Loving others unconditionally while sharing and appreciating our blessings;
6. Treating others justly instead of

seeking revenge if they "step on our toes";
7. Choosing to rise above fear, anger, worry, grief, and all other negative emotions;
8. Entertaining joyful, healing images in our minds despite our external circumstances;
9. Using our ideas and words as medicine instead of poison;
10. Nurturing others compassionately and patiently; and
11. Building healthy bodies and minds through proper diet, exercise, energizing breathing techniques, and emotional control.

In a nutshell, these **11 principles**, aligned sequentially with the **11 Het Heru Dance movements**, can detoxify the mind and promote healing. One dancer testifies that every time a challenge confronts her, she does the first movement, mentally or physically, recites the accompanying healing principle and, consequently, reacts calmly and positively. Another, a 45-year-old woman with the body of a 25-year-old, credits her stunning physique to regular practice of the Het Heru Dance, especially the eleventh movement.

Many young women who attend my Het Heru Healing Workshops frequently arrive tense, distraught and unsure about how to fix the problems they face. Grappling with toxic relationships, financial insecurity, interrupted schooling because they can't find the money to finish college, child rearing challenges, friendship issues, and a laundry list of other concerns, they literally come to me in tears. After attending the workshops and practicing the dance diligently at home, they become more joyful, calm, focused, and productive women who can handle their challenges peacefully and effectively. Women who experienced infertility problems prior to doing the Dance, sometimes approach me in the street, point to their pregnant bellies or to their babies in carriages and exclaim joyfully, "This is a Het- Heru- Healing baby! Thank you, Queen Mother!"

Evidently these "beautiful, flowing movements" have transformed many lives, and I am blessed and honored to have spread Het Heru's joy on this planet. In Bermuda, a woman who attended one of our Healing Circles shared: "After being bed-ridden with cancer and inactive for months, a group of women visited me and did the Het Heru Healing dance with me. The session lifted my spirits and inspired me to get up and return to my day-work." (S.A.)

As a women's health advocate, I remain passionate about contributing to the well-being of others. I express boundless thanks and appreciation to Shekhem Ur Shekhem, Ra Un Nefer Amen I for composing The Het Heru Healing Dance melodies and for the wisdom, time, effort and love that he has so selflessly bestowed on me throughout my healing journey. My family members have also wrapped me in a blanket of love, support, and nourishment. The Ausar Auset Society International has assisted me, immensely, in my efforts to facilitate the Dance both here and abroad. I thank everyone who has contributed to this healing technology's success.

Global Sisters,

Please know that healing is in your hands. Embrace it, joyfully!

PROTECTION, PROJECTION & MANIFESTATION

H-Ankh Risingsun, Magnets, Crystals & Pyramids

To truly understand the relationship of crystals and the power of the spoken word, and to regain the forgotten legacy of our rich inheritance, we must first connect the dots of our forgotten legacy. We can do our research through various textbooks, ancient monuments, and pictorial evidence spread throughout the world.

Ancient **PYRAMIDS** found throughout the world were once part of a highly advanced global network of **giant ORGONE POWER PLANTS**. Transmitting electrical power through the air, there was no need for oil, gas, or coal fuel. Orgone energy was collected, condensed, then converted into **quartz activated, wireless electrical power**. Anti-gravity, air, land, water transportation, interplanetary teleportation, home, and industry lighting, electronics, wireless communication were powered by huge **pyramids transmitting wireless electricity**.

Orgone activated crystal technology was widely used throughout the ancient world. Contrary to contemporary beliefs, the ancient world was more advanced than present day technology and the general population of antiquity were highly advanced spiritually. Most individuals had a direct relationship with their divinity without the need for religion.

Protection: Orgone energy helps align your chakras, it fills and balances your meridians, helps repair and expand your aura and repels your enemies while attracting your true friends. It transmutes the negative energy of people and electronic pollution, such as, cell phone radiation, cell phone towers, computers, trains, cars, and buses.

Projection/Cell charging benefits: Orgone amplifies your heart's magnetic field while expanding your personal presence. It increases personal magnetism, strengthens mental focus, enhances physical stamina, balances emotions, lowers mental chatter, heightens creativity and intuition.

Manifestation: Wearing an orgone

amulet, beads, necklaces, waist-beads, or bracelets, helps channel orgone energy into your cells, tissues, and organs. The soothing energy saturation may rapidly assist in feeling calmness, serenity, deeper meditation, more physical strength and endurance.

Healers, therapists, Reiki practitioners, Pranic healers, prayer warriors, Tantra healers, Chi Kung students, salespeople, athletes, seniors, children, and pets can all benefit from the radiance of orgone energy.

As the orgone energy field gradually expands from within you, the energy continues to enlarge, like a balloon, potentially extending for miles. Many orgone amulet owners begin to feel the natural intelligence of orgone gently guiding them throughout their daily activities. **Your aura** will gradually become an **"Orgone Cloud"** of radiant healing energy, continuously collecting, condensing, and discharging mini miracles throughout your life and for others near and far. Deeper rest and sleep with meaningful dreams are common benefits. Powerful quantum energy begins gently pulsing from your auric thoughts and feelings, sending healing vibrations wherever you or your attention is directed. This will accelerate your personal goals and objectives in your life, rapidly manifesting whatever is for your highest good.

Charge your orgone beads, amulets, or necklaces in direct sunlight at least an hour a month. The orgone energy is directed by your thoughts. Orgone flows where your attention goes. Mentally ask your amulet to please connect with you. To send healing energy to others, direct your attention upon them for healing.

Imagine setting a timer for how long you want the orgone energy directed their way.

In the mid-1700s French author and researcher, Fabre d'Olivet wrote, **L'histoire Philosophique du genre Humain.** Two centuries later, in 1915, Nayán Louise Redfield translated Fabre d'Olivet's work. The English language title is, *Hermeneutic Interpretation of the Origin of the Social State of Man and of the Destiny of the Adamic Race*. From d'Olivet's work, here is a quote on the subject of "races":

"The Black Race, more ancient than the White, was dominant upon the earth and held the sceptre of science and of power; it possessed all of Africa and the greater part of Asia, where it had enslaved and restrained the Yellow race. The Black race defined themselves as Masters of the Universe. (Page 56-73) Some remnants of the Red Race had languished obscurely upon the summits of the highest mountains of America and had survived the horrible catastrophe which had just struck them; these weak remnants were unknown; the Red Race to whom they had belonged had not long since possessed the Occidental hemisphere of the globe; the Yellow Race, the Oriental; the Black Race then sovereign, spread to the south on the equatorial line, and, as I have just said, the White Race which was only then springing up, wandered about the environs of the Boreal pole."

As quiet as it's kept from most modern "black folks", there were and still are Europeans and European Americans who remember when their ancestors were the slaves, for hundreds of years. Some remember(ed) their ancestors' armies losing countless battles and wars to Atlantean's superior military technology and science. They recognize that only after the sinking of Atlantis did the tide of world dominion gradually shift to the Europeans.

The forgotten pyramid ruins found throughout the world are ancient reminders of the forgotten era of time when the Black Race defined themselves as Masters of the Universe. By aligning their "I AM" awareness, individually and collectively they had command over most of the world and interplanetary networks. Through the power of crystal technology and sacred words of power…specifically "I AM," the Black Race of Atlanteans harnessed all the sciences of sound and matter.

Only brief mentions of the use of crystals are spoken of in the Bible; such as the breastplate of Aaron, Moses' brother. To allow greater access to his own personal divinity, Aaron wore on his chest twelve crystals and semi-precious stones. Orgone accumulators such as the Sacred Ark and the Tabernacle, were of orgone generation design—gold leaf on the outside and the inside, sandwiched between acacia wood. Acacia wood is revered as the herb of spiritual awakening and personal power, not only by the ancient Egyptians and early Hebrews, but also by Masonic lodges.

Orgone energy is a term to describe the boundless sea of energy, also known as "Chi" "Ki" or "Prana.". Discovered by Dr. Wilhelm Reich M.D., this all-pervading energy can be harnessed with simple devices made of alternate layers of conducting and non-conducting materials. Dr. Wilhelm Reich also discovered 85–90% of all diseases were rooted in the dysfunctional orgasmic experiences within an individual, blocking healthy energy flow to vital organs.

Atlanteans were aware of the sacred power of the herbal kingdom. Certain entheogenic herbs such as Syrian rue, acacia and mushrooms were deeply embraced by the ancient Khemetic culture, as well as other ancient cultures. Master Kilindi speaks often of the "hidden in plain sight" archaeological depictions found in the pillars, temples, and buildings showing reverence for the heightening awareness and cultivation of personal power found by ingesting the divine awareness activation under safe protocols.

We must again become aware of the power of our casual conversations between each other; cultivate communicating with each other with patience and compassion. Wearing a quartz crystal will help organize cellular health and create atomic structure in our personal lives as orderly as the molecular arrangement of the crystal kingdom. With the promiscuous electronic pollution found throughout modern living, wearing a selected quartz amulet will assist in protection and promote personal success. Remember, "I AM," the ancient words of power. Combining the understanding of the ancient words of power, while wearing quartz will promote and accelerate your individual ability to manifest and project successfully at about a 600 percent increase.

For personal safety, protection and power, the following suggested AFFIRMATIONS can be said out loud or mentally; with or without crystals in hand.

- **Yes, "I AM"** divinely protected, every day in every way, **Yes, "I AM."**
- **Yes, "I AM"** earthly wealth & abundance, **Yes, "I AM."**
- **Yes, "I AM"** loving all life, and "I AM" all life loving me, **Yes, "I AM."**
- **Yes, "I AM"** forgiving all life, and "I AM" all life forgiving me, **Yes, "I AM."**
- **Yes, "I AM"** forgiving all past lives, and **"I Am"** all past lives forgiving me.
- **Yes, "I AM"** invisible to all negative law enforcement, **Yes, "I AM."**
- **Yes, "I AM"** the only force in every part of my life, **Yes, "I AM."**
- **Yes, "I AM"** the only force surrounding me, every day in every way, **Yes, "I AM."**
- **Yes, "I AM"** the only force flowing in every part of my life, **Yes, "I AM."**
- **Yes, "I AM"** magnetizing Love, Wisdom, & Power in every cell within me, **Yes "I AM."**
- **Yes, "I AM"** realizing my divine destiny, **Yes, "I AM."**
- **Yes, "I AM"** the only force taking dominion over all men, women, children, world leaders, known and unknown throughout the earth, inner earth, and beyond,
  Yes, "I AM."

"I AM" wishing you crystal-clear projection and success, every day, in every way.
Bro. H-Ankh Risingsun.

ROCK YOUR LIFE

Corinthia Peoples, Crystal Jeweler

With a clinched fist nothing can get in. With an open hand Divine flow is activated. In the spirit of an open hand gemstones entered my life and it's been lights, camera and action ever since! The rock people (gemstones) choose me! They have taken me into spaces and places that my own naked consciousness could not have imagined. My research informs me that gemstones have been important characters in the human story since the beginning of time. Each culture has myths and legends in which gems are featured. Some cultures believe some gems have special powers. I personally believe gems aid and assist our journey and they emanate energy frequency and power. Each gemstone has its own special color, birthplace, story and attribute.

Stones come from the earth, therefore they have the essence of earth energy in them. Stones are created by the ONE DIVINE FORCE, the ONE unseen force, and the ONE omnipresent force that governs things. The "force" usually cannot be seen nor truly explained yet is often felt. That feeling is balance. There has been a loss of balance. Humans are 'outta balance' with Nature; out of sync. It is up to us, humankind to rebuild, repair, rejoin through nature back to Nature, to the earth…to the "Mother!" My call to ALL is, "Let's Remember!" Let's remember the ways of our grand, great-grand and great-great grandmothers and grandfathers. Their ways were in close contact with the earth, with nature. They knew! Now, it is our time to reclaim our knowing.

I would heal the world by infusing nature, the "Mother", into our modern-day ways. One does not exist without the other. We, living and breathing beings should never overlook or ignore nature and the power of natural forces. "She" brings us life each day in the air we breathe, food to eat, soil to plant, sun to feed and water to grow all the living things on our planet.

Today's high-tech world makes it necessary for one to go back to basics. One form of basic alternative living is wearing gemstone jewelry, in this case, wearable gemstone ART. We live in a world with a chaotic energy field, created by the excessive use of the electronics all around us. Modern conveniences such as cell phones, computers and microwaves emit radiation and electromagnetic waves that negatively interfere with our bodies' magnetic fields. Fortunately, nature has given us the gift of plant life, water, sunlight and gemstones, whose organic energies help us return to our natural healthy state.

Consider adorning yourself and your loved-ones with gifts of gemstones. Often when life seems difficult, it is an opportunity to use the challenge to grow and to learn lessons. I find it is during the times when it's difficult to see who I am truly meant to be and what i clearly desire, my patience is tested and could develop. On my journey I've needed to reach down into my soul and connect to the elements for guidance to the tools for navigating to my best existence. As the ancestors in most cultures used talisman for their "magical powers", I use gemstones for the scientific and spiritual properties they offer. Allow me to share a few.

Tiger's Eye is a dear gem and its earth story is ordained to alleviate fear and anxiety while boosting will and passion. It is responsible for lighting the fire to a blazing path of spiritual atonement and deep interpersonal power.

Amethyst has a special lavender scent etched into my heart. I personally use Amethyst as an energy field around my bed, in my bedroom to aid and assist my sleep state of consciousness during my rest. I believe in the scientific analysis of energy fields to aid in protection and help heighten awareness. As such, the Amethyst assists with the physical grounding and return after the spiritual flight and movement of the dream state.

Citrine brings me bliss. I adore experiencing Citrine by placing it on the kitchen window sill. When I gaze at Citrine's orange-red glow my brain releases endorphins of happy hormones. The orange color of Citrine also connects to my womb and ripples sensuality throughout my entire being; it lets me know all is well and in universal timing. Timing is its own power and plays by its own terms and rules. All things are under the grand enchantment of timing.

The legend of Black Onyx is 'letting go.' I have found its special powers of releasing negative emotions and bothersome relationships were literally at my fingertips waiting to assist me. I needed a way out and I believed Black Onyx would be the catalyst and avatar that would anchor me into a deep knowingness of myself. I could awaken to choosing ME, my own tenacity and my will. It seemed long and lonely, yet necessary for the destiny to unravel and for serenity. My made-up mind and determination formed the perfect marriage of releasing the main idea of an individual and the letting go of attachments and illusions that often resulted in an undesirable situation. Presently, I find myself liberated and lessoned for a lifetime.

Gemstones should to be worn for us to gain the full benefits of its energies. Gemstone jewelry is the most convenient way to maintain your body's magnetic field and assist in healing numerous aliments from body to soul. Wearing gemstones is the most stylish, easiest way to maintain your health, and restore bodily, mental and spiritual wellness to its perfect natural state.

My existence has been fused with scaling walls and overcoming fear. I understand that there is a divine plan for my life that has nothing to do with the projection of others and everything to do with the vision and urgings of my spirit and discipline…

I salute *you* in your Beauty, your Sensuality and your Wellness.

One more thing.

Child & Youth Sex Trafficking rips a deep hole in my heart. An atrocity, this trafficking signifies failure to us, our children and humankind. In honor of *leaving things better than I found them,* Corinthia Peoples (my company) contributes to the following. Please visit these sites. Our contributions matter.

1. MISSSEY (Motivating, Inspiring, Supporting & Serving Sexually Exploited Youth)
   http://www.misssey.org and indicate "A Corinthia Peoples Charitable Initiative."
2. The Embracing Project.
   http://www.theembracingproject.org/
   Indicate "A Corinthia Peoples Charitable Initiative."

CRYSTALLIZE YOUR LIFE

Imani C. Scott, Artist/Entrepreneur

In Ancient times, it appears that wherever indigenous peoples dwelled on this Planet, it was customary for our ancient ancestors to make room within their daily practice to commune with Nature. They performed rituals, ceremonies, and worked in general to utilize the forces of the Spirit World. All while striving to live and work in harmony together, and with other co-inhabitants in their environment. Balance was the natural order. One was destined to be prosperous, healthy and content when aligned with the flow of infinite intelligence that governs the sun, moon, stars, the birds, bees, seeds, all animals, insects, plants and/or trees.

There was high regard for the natural ecology that diligently contains itself. The Mother and/or Feminine Principle was highly revered within this divine infinite; and in it. The elements, minerals, food, herbs, and fruits provided by Nature were the source of one's sustenance, nourishment, and medicine. It was also customary to be dependent upon the fruits of one's labor, which was governed by one's obedience to honor the Laws of Nature and/or mutual trade agreements still dependent on Nature in some manner as a primary resource. Otherwise, one would fear the lack of a bountiful Harvest, which could ultimately cause a host of other problems.

Today we live on a planet where, the more technology advancements are made, the more the masses are encouraged to stray away from Nature as a resource. Through media and socialization, the masses increasingly foster habits that glorify individualism, dependency n man-made resources or inventions that devalue; thereby emasculating and diminishing the Mother/Feminine Principle. Ultimately the forces that are governing our societies across the globe are primarily masculine dominant, and extensions of patriarchal systems. Whether consciously or unknowingly, many women are even expressing themselves, and living their lives through a masculine filter. The Food and Drug Administration (FDA), and the World Health Organization (WHO) instead of monitoring our food supply and holding it to the highest standards, have many loop holes extending into greater problems. For instance, some substances categorized as foods, are drugs, create chemical dependencies and harmful effects that even lead to disease and death. Now 'foods' are legally genetically modified. Agricultural vegetation is sprayed with harmful pesticides, "organic" foods/produce are welcomed with no seeds, and crops are celebrated with no weeds. Livestock is farmed in extremely inhumane ways, removed from their natural environments, and fed unnatural "foods" produced for mass consumption.

Our cell phones, computers, electronic devices, household/business appliances, and/or gadgets may increase efficiency in keeping up with the fast pace of daily living. However, these same electronic tools are greatly contributing to the demise in our health. The pollutions of electromagnetic frequencies are at an all-time high, causing damage not only to inhabitants of the earth, but also to the earth itself. The damage is evident in climatic changes, and the high volume of crimes of humanity that fill global news channels. We are now living in the dark ages. But, let us not forget that through the dark comes the light.

Crystals are a medium for the light. The natural high vibrations of crystals can be used as tools. Crystals are what we are. They reflect us, but crystals are not distracted or corrupted. Instead, they are in their purest state. Crystals can help us vibrate at higher levels and frequencies. They absorb, generate and reflect the light. They just are true Divine Light. So, when you hold these crystals, when you have them in your presence, on your altars, in your homes, your office, and your play space, they emit frequencies that help you be in tune with the essence of who you are. Our true nature can be realigned with Divine order, during the use of crystals.

Here we are in the 21st century. One would think we would be at the peak of healthy constructive advancements for all humanity. To the contrary, we are all so bombarded with extreme amounts of unnatural frequencies; through these cell phones, iPads, through man-made light fixtures, electrical appliances, and so forth. These frequencies are not vibrating on a harmonic rhythm with our natural being. So, it is important that we do as much as we can, through foods, through crystals, by any means necessary, to keep our frequency in the heights.

Otherwise, we become a conduit for dis-ease. When we are not vibrating at our highest frequency, being our best selves, it does not mean all is lost. We have an opportunity to experience what it is to be low, so we can appreciate what it is to be in the heights. Crystals may assist in shifting mental perspectives in order for one to seize blessings and/or learn lessons, through great peaks and valleys along the journey of life.

Nonetheless, globally many are at an all-time low, so collectively there is a need to get back into balance. We can use these crystalline gifts of the earth to nurture and attune us back into our best expressions of the highest Divine power. Crystals may be used in a variety of ways. Their energy applications range from mundane practical purposes, to spiritual, metaphysical, even supernatural uses.

Some practical ways to use these gems or crystals is by wearing them in jewelry or accessories such as earrings, necklaces, waist beads and/or ankhlets. As these stones touch various parts of the body, the healing effects can be transferred through the skin. They can also be made to directly touch the skin or also be laid on the body via crystal layouts, placing stones on various Aritu (Chakra points). Chakra points relate to seven primary energy areas on the body. The seven energy vortexes of the Chakras reflect the state of one's health. When energy in the Chakras is being blocked, crystals can be used to balance the energy flow. For example, garnet and clear quartz can be used on all the chakra points. Malachite, bloodstone and/or hematite may be used to relieve pain. As the healing energy of crystals is emitted, it is received through the skin; thereby, befitting one's physical, emotional and ether bodies.

Gem water or elixirs can be prepared by direct or indirect methods to effectively transfer the healing energies into the cells and tissues of the body and so aid one's health and well-being. When placed in the home, office, or in any environment, the crystal energy radiates its harmonic healing light frequencies. This can be expanded with one's conscious thoughts and intentions. Crystals may be programmed for specific healing purposes, which can magnify these benefits. For instance: sodalite, black tourmaline, and clear quartz crystals can be placed on cell phones, on or near appliances and/or gadgets to reduce the harmful effects of electromagnetic frequency (EMF) rays. Jasper is great for house plants and maintenance in the garden and can aid one into being in harmony with natural forces of the earth. Black tourmaline provides an environment of protection and is a natural insecticide. Many crystals can assist with maintaining healthy emotional states and mental balance. Citrine and yellow calcite aid with optimism and positive mental attitudes. Howlite assists with calming rage and increases courage into resolve offenses with a cool head. Use rose quartz, rhodocrocite, or malachite to assist with unconditionally loving oneself, healing hurt, and forgiveness. Aventurine aids with opening the heart to love others and expressing universal love while protecting oneself from being emotionally vulnerable or abused.

On a metaphysical level, crystals can be used to enhance prayer, meditation and creative visualization. Amethyst elevates tranquility and connects one to one's higher Self. Ancestral angels of light and clear quartz clear, cleanse, and amplify one's thoughts, ideas and visions. Turquoise aids in protecting one's psyche and channeling spirit. Labradorite and angelite can be instrumental in connecting one to their spiritual guardians, gaining esoteric knowledge, guidance and protection. Blue apatite can aid as we all strive to commune in tune with the infinite intelligence that governs all.

May we all become intentional in focusing and directing the crystal healing light energies for world healing. Let this Planet itself be brought back into harmony with its highest expression, and the celestial universe. Use crystals and other high vibrational natural resources to live daily with that infinite vibration. In this way, we truly will be a contributing asset to this planet, and as we heal and align ourselves, so will the planet heal.

BODY CLOSING

"Food is not just vitamins and minerals food is spiritual. We have to be in a spiritual position, in order for the food to be in a spiritual position because food seeks spirituality through us and spirituality seeks us through the food."

DR. LLAILA AFRIKA, AUTHOR

MIND

Emancipate yourself
    from mental slavery,
None but ourselves
    can free our minds.

—Bob Marley

HEALER WITHIN

Selina Brown, Soul Coach

Do you know what it's like to heal every element of your being? Do you know how it feels to witness your life transform? Have you ever evolved so much that you don't recognize yourself? Do you know what it feels like to have a rebirth?

If you had asked me these questions 10 years ago, I would have replied with a stern "no." Back then I was a fast-food addict, womb-trauma-suffering young woman. My acne-covered face made me despise mirrors; and a severe stomach condition and irregular heavy periods made being in chronic pain a regular part of life. I came from a linage of trauma and crisis; imbalance was ordinary; this was imbedded in my genetic memory bank from my mother's, mother's, mother's, mother. Every woman I knew was suffering; suffering was our normal. The chaos was also evident in the dysfunctional and draining relationships I had with all the men in my life. I was not in a space mentally, spiritually or physically to absorb a higher frequency; nor to comprehend or even entertain thoughts of healing.

Fast forward a few years later, I moved to New York to start a new executive marketing job. This meant leaving everything I knew in the UK. This was a massive turning point in my life—little did I know then that this was to be the land of my awakening. Through the most beautiful synchronicities, three months after arriving in the Big Apple I was sitting in front of Queen Afua. When we at this first meeting Queen Afua's warmth energized me. She greeted me with, "Peace beloved," and handed me my first glass of green juice. That moment marked the start of my transformation. On that day I was in a really bad place in my life—my eating was terrible (lots of meat, late night feasting, snacks instead of nutritional full meals). I was underweight and malnourished, my periods were lasting two weeks, I was sleeping only two to three hours per night and I was so unhappy. In the following weeks, I was blessed to have Queen introduce me to a program she had created; and so, commenced my healing. The program consisted of:

1. Spa Days: Going to the steam room and sauna once a week—this allowed me to gently release all toxins contained within my body.
2. Bathing: Every two days I took an evening sacred healing bath infused with lavender, rose petals, magnesium salt and coconut oil. I placed lots of candles around to promote calmness and relaxation.
3. Juicing: I had 2 organic green juices a day every morning and afternoon—my favourite combination is: Kale, Spinach, Celery, Apple, Beetroot, Ginger, Carrot and Cucumber.
4. Sage/Crystals/Incense: To keep the frequencies of my body temple high I carried crystals (rose quartz, citrine, selenite are my fav), in my purse and bra (lol). I cleansed my space with sage every weekend and burned incense daily to sweeten up my living space.
5. 4 AM Rising: Every single day I rose at 4 AM (Sacred Time). I poured libations, meditated and spoke words of power. Connecting to my higher self, Kemetic deities and my ancestors was key part of my healing journey.
6. Clean Eating: I immediately started to clean up my diet and became a vegan. It was hard in the beginning, but this was the best thing I ever did. Queen taught me her secret Emerald Green Salad recipe, it's *deliciouuuuuuus!*
7. Self-Love: During this time, I had to learn how to love myself wholly and completely. I did this through affirmations, dancing, gratitude jar, adorning myself in my favorite clothes/jewelry/perfume, spending time in nature, being alone and making time to express myself creatively.

I learned to heal my mind, heart and womb with air, water, fire and earth. I took control of my body and health. I owned all my negative and positive experiences, without blame and excuses. I took my power back. There was a lot of baggage to release and discard. It wasn't easy and at times returning to the disharmony felt like an easier option; but the voices of my higher self and my ancestors and the guidance of Queen Afua kept me going.

After nine months, I took my throne, put on my crown. Queen Selina was ready.

I embraced my healer within and my goddess. Now, I celebrate in every way being a healer and a goddess. I live daily as a whole, complete and vibrant Sacred Woman. I honour and celebrate my greatness, my femininity and sensuality. Everything is in total alignment, I am a proud vegan, a yoga enthusiast, just an all-round joyful being. I can honestly say I love my life. Since my rebirth, my needs appear into my life abundantly and with ease; I co-create with the universe and I'm more powerful than ever. I travel regularly – my healing work takes me across the world from the villages of Africa and the hills of Brazil to the streets of London. I have a consistently five-figure business and only blissful relationships surround me. I've never looked back.

I assist the planet in healing by helping to wake up and raise up the goddesses, priestesses, queens, brujas, empresses. This is my superpower. I have spirit guides, hidden hands and power ancestors that guide me every step of the way. I am a vehicle for the Divine to work through. I assist woman of all ages, cultures and backgrounds by tapping into and them seeing their greatness, their limitless, their magic. My work is a repayment to the Universe; it is my offering to my fellow sisters—spiritually, physically and mentally. It is for my sisters who are yearning for a way out of imprisonment from sexual abuse, fibroids, broken relationships, self-hatred, unworthiness, daddy issues, finance issues, mental health issues.

I encourage women to hold up a metaphysical mirror, which causes them to see beyond their reflection to the beginning of their first breaths. I guide them to identify the patterns, traumas and cycles that block them from reaching their higher self. My processes of healing consist of drawing power from the elements and nature and my grandma's Jamaican herbal remedies. Most importantly I help to guide them back to the stillness—my number one healing tool. I believe that stillness holds all the answers; it's the voice of the highest force. Going to stillness has been the scariest and most uncomfortable thing for the women I've worked with. They can't escape in stillness and silence. This is the place from where all healing starts and where the greatest growth takes place. Once we get quiet enough to recharge the mind and reset the spirit, we are able to tap into our highest selves.

My calling is to work with young girls and women; this a 21st century rites of passage with ancient roots. My mission is for every woman on the planet to have self-love, a love so deep that it places her on a path of freedom and abundance; it connects her back on her truth. I truly believe that once the women take their positions, the men and children, their communities and the world have no choice but to follow.

PHOENIX AFFECTS

Klarque Garrison, Rebirth Coach

Phoenix Affects: <n.> The Phoenix is the mythical sacred firebird that has a life cycle of 500 -1000 years. When nearing the end of its cycle it builds a nest made of twigs and ignites nest to consume all! The Phoenix is then reborn through the ashes.

Affect: means "to influence" or influences.

"Phoenix Affects" is simply the focus of energies that influence the mind, body and spirit towards a natural rebirth of the one.

I am of the belief that we need to experience a re-birth of mind, body and soul which renews our physical and spiritual "selves." These rebirths are often most useful whenever we are in alignment to traverse through a new journey in life. Whether that's a new job, moving to a new state, a new relationship or simply a new season, experiencing a spiritual and physical cleansing through a symbolic rebirth is paramount. This system I created called "Phoenix Affects" does this through seven ideologies which predate mankind. They are universal in concept and practice and were spoken by Toth and Ma'at. They say: Nothing is new under the sun (only the messengers change).

THE PROCESS:
REMOVAL OF CLUTTER (physically and mentally): The purpose of this process is to begin by removing all confusion from your daily routine. Confusion shows up both in our minds and in our reality. Barbara Hemphill once said, "Clutter is

nothing more than postponed decisions", and I am inclined to agree. Spend this day, week, or month that you're going to be committed to doing those projects you've been planning to do forever. Returning phone calls, stop avoiding people, face your fears by doing the things you most fear, and just a few hurdles you'll need to climb to begin removing clutter from your life.

CONNECTING WITH THE UNIVERSE: Now that we've created a growing environment for positive energy, we must learn how to connect with that energy. We do so by way of prayer and meditation! Many of us grow up learning how to pray but very few are taught how or why the act of meditation is equally important. One should not exist without the other.

TAKE THE CHAOS WITHIN & FROM IT CREATE ORDER: We all have an element of Chaos within (and that's not a bad thing). Chaos & Order exist simply as opposites…together they create Balance. *"When we have our body and mind in order, everything else will exist in the right place…in the right way. But, usually without being aware of it, we try to change something other than ourselves…we try to order things outside US."* This was a tenant of Shunryu Suzuki (author of **Zen Mind, Beginner's Mind: Informal Talks on Zen Meditation and Practice**), and it is my wish that it becomes yours as well.

DEVOTING YOUR LIFE TO THE UTTER SERVICE OF OTHERS: We learn how to receive by giving. That is the only way to find our true purpose in this Life. I implore you to forget your earthly desires, and instead look around at how your life can be used as a vehicle of change. What would life be like if everyone strove to improve each person life they meet during the course of each day by leaving that person with a token, gift, kind word, information, contact or hope?

POWER UP YOUR DREAM MACHINE & CREATE OUR FUTURE: It is in our dreams we are truly free. Free to create, roam the Earth and visit alternate Universes. That same practice can create your reality out of the dream state. But first, we must implement and hone the previous steps written here. Only then, can the fabled *Laws of Attraction* (or as it is called in the **Kybalion** "The Law of Mentalism") manifest and become your reality.

THE ART OF MINDFULNESS: Leave yesterday behind, stop dreaming of tomorrow, and live in today. I have learned, "Mindfulness means paying attention in a particular way; On purpose, in the present moment, and non-judgmentally." From reading Jon Kabat-Zinn's books on Mindfulness, one way to begin achieving this rare state of mind is to practice silence throughout your day (well as much as humanly possible). Studies have said women speak on average 20,000 words a day and men somewhere around 7,000. Still, I'll wager most of those words need not be spoken. Silence allows us to focus and become more conscious of everything living we encounter. Wise souls speak loudly in silence…

REBIRTH DAY (Make it your day): We are keepers of the planet, as it keeps us. We are connected in a bond which is pure energy and love. Only together can we experience utopia and bliss. It is my prayer that you heed the lessons that have been passed down by our ancestors. Do not let the ill of the World and the many lost people on it determine your outcome. Choose life over death and you'll live soaring as the ancient Phoenician Phoenix…

Ashe!
Klarque Garrison

THE SENSE OF REASONING AND WILLPOWER

Paul Goss, ND

INTRODUCTION FROM A FAMILY:

*P*aul Goss was the 8th child of 10 born to Sam and Annie Goss in Canton, Georgia. He grew up in a small company town, Alcoa, Tennessee. In this rural setting he received the basics for an international-level education. Paul received that education not in a poorly-funded, segregated school, but rather from two of his neighborhood's African elders. Mitchell, known as the "Root Doctor" and Ms. Bellamy, known as "The Herb Lady". were the local "root workers". They knew the healing value of herbs and plants and how to prepare them as cures. My father's interest in holistic cures began when these "root worker" teachers recognized his potential and began instructing him in ancient cures that had been passed on to them in much the same way.

Paul Goss continued his education at historic Stillman College in Alabama, where he received a master's in biochemistry. His real thirst for knowledge, however, simply could not be filled in a traditional college environment. He went on to become an organic chemist for a large company. Through self-study, he continued to increase his knowledge in holistic healing. Building on his modest beginnings as an apprentice to "Doc" Mitchell and Ms. Bellamy, he started to develop his skills as a holistic health practitioner. As a naturopathic doctor he and Queen Afua have been allies for over 30 years.

Dr. Paul Goss is a humble and wise elder. It is my honor to present his thoughts and words on saving the planet.

With joy,
The family of Dr. Paul Goss

THE SENSE OF REASONING

When you activate your sense of reasoning you should be working on yourself, not on someone else. The first area you should apply your sense of reasoning to is your health. What is it you want out of life? If you want to live and you are doing something that is killing you, use your sense of reasoning and stop doing it. You don't need to read a book or study the situation. **All you need to do is stop. It is very simple.**

Use your sense of reasoning to find out why you are using all the things you are using. Why are you sending your hair out to the hairdresser? Maybe you have a nervous condition that is so bad it is causing your hair to fall out. Once you find out you are nervous, then find out what is making you nervous. Reason everything out so you can stop sending your hair to the hairdresser. You may decide you do not have to worry about the nervous condition because you can always buy something to take care of the problem. You are free to use your sense of reasoning as you like. The important thing is to reason with yourself.

Wisdom is an aspect of your sense of reasoning. When you know why you are doing the things you do, you do not let other people tell you what to do. You can tell yourself what to do. Use your sense of reasoning to understand your situation in this country. Are you still waiting for your "40 acres and a mule?" Reasoning will tell you you're not going to get them. Nobody uses mules any more. Whatever you want you must get for yourself. Why be poor? When you apply your sense of reasoning you will find that being poor is not wise at all.

THE SENSE OF WILLPOWER

Your sense of willpower keeps the body intact. When you apply willpower, you do not have to worry about eating food that is going to cause your body to break down. You do not worry about listening to music or speech that is going to corrupt your system. You do not worry about saying something to someone else that will break her spirit. It takes a lot of willpower not to gossip once you're cranked up.

Is your sense of willpower activated to the point where you can stop doing whatever is harming you or do you need somebody else to stop doing it for you? People in twelve step programs are there because they do not use their sense of willpower. Willpower tells you when to say "yes" and when to say "no". It makes no difference what the situation is or what other people are doing. You should have enough willpower to keep from putting your life in jeopardy.

Your genes make it easy for you to break your bad habits. Your genes tell you what it is you need to do to take yourself into the life you want instead of into the death that other people are trying to push on you.

"Your sense of reasoning helps you understand why you need to break a bad habit. Your sense of willpower helps you do whatever you need to do to replace the bad habit with a good habit."
—Paul Goss, ND

PERSONAL TRANSFORMATION

Robin "Kheperah" Kearse, Transformation Coach

Have you ever been so busy meeting the urgent needs of others that you felt like you had no time to meet your own needs? Does the moment you carve out "me time" become the very moment that others pull on you with time-sensitive requests? Although your first instinct might be to say "No," did the weight of the situation led you to think, *"Let me take care of this person right quick, then I'll get back to me…"*? That was me.

Serving others while putting myself on hold became my norm. Years went by as I was living without being fully *alive*. I had become conditioned to giving away much more of myself than I was cultivating within. *Force* of habit pulled on me when people called; I felt guilty saying "No." I felt like I *had* to do whatever was asked because I was needed. Despite the warning bells in my head, the tug on my heart created a false sense of urgency.

The tasks weren't small. I extended financial resources, provided counseling and therapeutic services, created marketing platforms, developed systems and infrastructures, managed teams and accepted promotions and partnerships that I really didn't want—often for less than the value of what I delivered. At the end of the day, I had nothing but exhaustion and resentment to show for most of my efforts.

In hindsight, my greatest challenge was giving too much, when all I needed to do was give *just enough* or delegate; better yet, set boundaries and stick to them. But I didn't know how to that. Every task and every person received my *all or nothing*. Even odd jobs received my blood, sweat and tears; on weekends, nights, early mornings and holidays. I gave my entire "life" to "make ends meet jobs" supposed to last only for a moment until I could get out and do what I *really* wanted to do.

I wasn't fully present to experience some of the most powerful events in my life. During precious moments when my children were growing up; during the height of my career in the music industry; while traveling to promote a documentary that I starred in; while excelling at a highly demanding corporate career—there were many times when although I was physically in the room, in my head I wasn't really "there." I was shortchanging myself from priceless experiences and cheating my family, friends, and colleagues. I was giving my best talents and abilities, but not the full expression of myself. I rarely stopped to celebrate my own victories, that was the extra I did for others, or for "the job." Technically, I was giving my all in those best years of my life; but at the time my victories *didn't count.* Later I could get back to *doing me.*

At some point I noticed the same pattern in my relationships. I would attract men who I knew were just "in the meantime" until *HE* came along. Yet, I would give these *meantime* men "wifey material" relationships. I gave my all, figuring I would still be the best woman I could be and eventually *HE* would show up. I didn't realize that I was programming my subconscious mind to attract *temporary* lovers who were either incapable or unwilling to love and fully commit to me in the way that I deserved.

But if I was just going through the motions without being fully present, then, *who was showing up every day and living my life?* Whoever *she* was, she couldn't deliver! On rare occasions I would carve out uninterrupted time for myself at home where there was quiet, bright sunlight and nothing in the way. There, I had full reign to totally focus on the personal project of myself; but, she wouldn't show up for *me!* I had become so conditioned to putting myself on hold that subconsciously I had programmed myself not to deserve my own time, attention or support. Unknowingly, I was trapped in a vicious cycle of my own poisonous thoughts.

The catalyst for my self-healing was when I noticed the people I poured into were moving ahead and I was still stuck in the same place. Not focused on myself I hadn't made the personal progress I desired. When people asked me what I wanted, so much time had gone by that I wasn't quite sure anymore. The most humbling time came when folks would ask, "When are you going to *do your thing?*"

I had lost myself. Subconsciously, I had taken on other tasks to escape the magnitude of the personal goals I had set for myself. Perhaps, because I feared that the project of ME was *too big*. It was easy to build a friend's business proposal or give a colleague marketing direction—but what about ME? I had to take some time to really reconnect within and let go of distractions. I had to dig deep to identify and eliminate the mental and emotional blockages that I allowed to hold me back.

I also had to let go of ego-based thinking that says that once you are in a position of leadership you must be perfect, and you cannot show your flaws, or better stated, your growth. When your *growth* is showing along your journey, it can be humbling. But humility allows us to be vulnerable and enjoy the beauty of all of who we are. This provides the greatest catalyst for healing in others. With and leading the way by example, others become able to witness possibilities for themselves.

In 2002, I started an organization called Gemnasium LLC, to help people shift the way they think toward having a better quality of life. During the most challenging time of my life, I had to stop and take note of the fact that I was not practicing what I was teaching and needed to create a few paradigm shifts. Paradigms are merely subconscious agreements based on habits. I had to cultivate new habits to re-new my mind and become more grounded in who I was so that I could nurture and protect *her* and regain control of my life. Here are a few GEMS that have helped me to make this powerful personal shift in order to live a healthier, more balanced life:

1. **Go IN.**
   - Shut in from the outside world and technology to replenish, rebuild, renew and heighten your self-awareness.
   - Change your environment or the people you are around until you can make a real and lasting shift that allows you to be more grounded in who you are and clear about what you want. Many say it takes a minimum of 21 days to break an old habit or establish a new one.
   - The more self-aware you are, the more self-loving and self-respecting you will be of your time and energy. When you are clear on SELF, it will be easier to maintain clear boundaries to stay focused on your goals and find the ability to say "No" to others without guilt.
2. **Purify and Cleanse.**
   - The quality of your life is contingent upon the condition of your mind and the content of your thoughts. When the mind is blocked, and you feel "stuck," clean up any mess at home, work, school, within or throughout your body. By clearing external blockages, you open the way for a clearing within your mind, so that you can "see" and "hear" what to do and gain the courage to move accordingly.
3. **Condition Your Mind.**
   - Meditate Daily. It doesn't have to be deep. Just do as the elders say and "Go somewhere and sit down!" Be still and breathe deeply.
   - Exercise your Will. Challenge yourself to do something difficult that will reinforce self-discipline.
4. **Do NOT FEED the FEARS**
   - Fear is just an energy…you can make a conscious choice to decide not to feed it. This may be a fight, but you can do it! Even if you don't feel it at the moment. There is a saying: "Speak what You Seek until You See What You've Said!"
5. **Remain Faithful.**
   - Remember, faith cometh by hearing—surround yourself with those who will encourage you with positive words along your journey.
6. **Be consistent!**

WE CAN HEAL OUR PLANET

Aturah Bahtiyah E. Nasik Rahm, Holistic Coach

First and foremost, I give my deepest praise and gratitude to Yah (God). My eternal thanks for the leadership and guidance of His Excellency Ben Ammi Ben Israel. Words cannot express my gratitude for the specialness of all the parents who prepared us for these days. In my life those special Beings are Bessie Edmonson (Mama—eighty-eight years, still on this planet); and Joseph Titlton, Jr. (Daddy—transitioned but still very much in my life). I give thanks to Queen Afua for affording me the opportunity to share my blessings with all the Sacred Souls reading this book. Without exception, I am grateful for the bounty of family and friends who enrich my life. With heartfelt appreciation I give thanks to my husband Prince Rahm and my children for encouraging me to serve at my highest ability.

The question posed is, "What would you do to heal planet Earth?" Although the responses in this book are divided into the categories of Body, Mind and Spirit, they are intimately interconnected. Therefore, there are many "solutions" to the various medical, financial, emotional, mental, and spiritual dilemmas in our lives. I believe the common thread to these issues are misaligned thought patterns. If proper alignment is not made, the problem will continue. Most of us simply need a major overhaul in our thought patterns. We must understand that the many thoughts we express daily have been inherited. Based on our point of reference, our thought patterns might be too toxic for a healthy lifestyle.

We must decide to truly take control of our health. One should remember, "Your health is your wealth." Each moment of each day, we are either regenerating or degenerating. This process begins with a thought. Positive thoughts are regenerative and negative thoughts are degenerative. There are thoughts to cause one to dislike their neighbor. There are thoughts that will allow one to create ways to heal the earth. Thoughts can make you beat yourself up, when you make a mistake. Yet, we can learn from our mistakes.

As we embark on everlasting health and life, our immune system is positively influenced by positive thoughts. Positive thoughts will produce health enhancing biochemicals that are far more potent than pharmaceuticals and without any adverse health side effects. Research has shown thoughts provide more than temporary relief. The brain can process nearly 60,000 thoughts per day. This impact on our physical and mental health becomes quite evident.

Endorphins are chemicals that are produced naturally by positive thoughts. Consider patients who are given "placebos." These positive thoughts on healing make the patient believe they are cured as they then benefit from natural healing when the endorphins are released. The chemicals have interleukin and interferon which fight cancer. The chemicals in the pharmaceutical world could cost as much as $40,000.00 and have many side effects. According to famed physician, Dr. Deepak Chopra, the power of positive thoughts can, "…produce a million dollars' worth of Interleukin-2, costs nothing, and has no side effects."

What I am sharing with you emanates from my spiritual being, as I keep in mind the strong connection of mind, body and spirit. The Bible teaches us, when we serve the Lord He will bless our bread and our water; and He will take sickness away from the midst of you. (Exodus 23:25) Since I was a child, my spirituality was a driving force in my life. I am a healer in my family. The ability to give my family advice is the spirit of Yah. The ability to provide healing to women in my community is the spirit of Yah. The ability to raise two healthy children to adulthood is the spirit of Yah.

At this point, I want to share with you the teaching of His Excellency, Ben Ammi Ben Israel. I am referencing two of his major writings, *Physical Immortality Conquering Death* and *Everlasting Life from Thought to Reality*. These writings have sustained me during good times and during difficult days. **I have found his words to be life-giving**.

"What we think (say to ourselves) and cause others to think (convey to them) are also important aspects of building strong immunity. Every word you speak and hear participates in the strengthening or weakening of the immune system. The immune system is a network, which resonates with the vibrations that surround it. It is as surely adversely affected by negative emotions and lies as by bacteria, as deeply impacted by negative thoughts as by drugs. If the immune system is starved of Truth, it will falter, leaving you more susceptible to infection and life-threatening ailments."

His Excellency's thoughts provide a keen vision for obtaining optimum health. First, there is power in motion. It incorporates health and healing. Motion is described as perpetual. Learning and studying is how the brain's motion is utilized. Intense study should be undertaken by those in the age-range of fifty to seventy. The study should involve difficult subject matter. In addition, if no study has been completed in a few years, one should return to study as a student or as a teacher. The brain is nourished by study. The brain is kept in motion by study. An example of the motion of study on the brain can be seen by observing the elderly. When the elderly take on retirement, they tend to cease motion, or their motion is at a minimum.

According to the *Journal of Epidemiology and Community Health,* a retirement study was performed with 2956 participants. The participants were 2/3 healthy and 1/3 unhealthy. The study was sponsored by the National Institute of Health and entitled "Healthy Retirement Study." The study was 18 years in length and concluded that working one year more past 65 years of age decreased all risk mortality by 11% in the healthy participants and 9% decrease in the unhealthy participants.

Motion also involves physical activity for the body. One should strive to perform physical exercise *FOREVER*. The body can rise to the challenge of some form of exercise well into our senior years. Allow yourself creativity in this area. Yoga, water aerobics, walking, dancing, cycling, and running are all excellent physical activities that can be undertaken and will provide the life-giving function of motion.

The final stage of motion is direction. This teaching explains vision, goals, and dreams. Can you see your future? Can you plan your future? Can your future be improved? If your answers are "yes", then the life-giving force of motion should be continued.

I conclude that to heal the planet, we must heal ourselves. For this reason, I founded the Tekiyah Regenerative Health and Wellness Center to provide an environment that promotes health and well-being for the body, mind, and spirit. At the Wellness Center we offer therapeutic spa services including a variety of healing massages, hip baths (yoni steam), facials, manicures and pedicures. We offer quiet and tranquility and the opportunity to declutter the mind in our beautiful meditation room. One can detox and cleanse with our aqua chi foot detox and with colonics. Other treatments offered are sound therapy and Reiki. A range of life-enhancing classes includes yoga, juicing, and live (raw) food preparation are designed to empower the participants.

How would I heal the planet? A positive human being is excited to do good for Earth and for mankind. Of course, we warmly welcome you to visit our center to enjoy and benefit from the services and classes provided there. However, most importantly, regardless of where you are, please seek regenerative opportunities. The main objective is to identify services and classes designed to promote your positive thinking, self-image and wellness.

I encourage each of you to remain positive, think good thoughts, pray, and continue to develop, elevate, and aspire to the healthiest and wealthiest you. Together, as we are healed, we can heal our planet.

SHARING THE GIFT OF WELLNESS

Tanya Sherise Odums, Social Worker

After turning 30 in January 2003, I made the decision to participate in the spring class of Sacred Woman. As a Mental Health Professional, this healing journey took my practice to another level. The tools that I learned ascending through the Sacred Woman Gateways of Illumination, and the knowledge acquired through participating in the one-day fasting shut-ins equipped me with holistic ways to address stress, anxiety and depression. I gained knowledge of how food affects one's physical and mental well-being and how food can be used as medicine to heal.

I always struggled with emotional eating and battled with my weight (and still do), which only perpetuates the depression I experience at times. However, I never surrendered to being overweight and unhealthy. As a mental health professional, I always seek to assist others with learning to manage their emotions and cope effectively with life's challenges. Through prayer, meditation, movement and a healthy diet, I attempt to help others and myself stabilize our mental and emotional well-being.

I have faced challenges; times where I gain weight and feel out of control. However, the weight gain and feelings of losing control are signals that I am not taking care of myself and it is time to go within to refocus and be centered. When I am in this space, it is time to be still and withdraw from the chaos of the outer world. It is a time to find solitude and focus on creating balance in my inner world. This starts with self-reflection through exploring the following questions in meditation:

- Am I making healthy food choices? What foods do I need to release from my diet?
- What is eating me? Why am I stuffing my face? What feeling am I trying to stuff down with food?
- Are my food choices giving me life or robbing me of energy?

- Is what I am eating making me depressed?
- Do I need to move/exercise to shift energy?

During my meditations, I also do deep breathing exercises, reflective journaling and listen to inspirational music. As part of my practice, I teach my clients how to be still and coach them through breathing exercises and reflective meditations. I also teach them how to create sacred space in their homes, which is necessary for spiritual healing/meditative work. Our physical environments have a profound impact on our mental state.

Living in New York City can be chaotic, as it is very fast-paced and often hostile. This is why I encourage my clients to go to the bathhouse at least once a month for deeper releasing and healing. Using hydrotherapeutic facilities at the bathhouse helps with releasing toxins and shifting of energy. The use of essential oils and a massage can heighten this hydrotherapeutic experience. As part of my practice, I educate my clients about the use of healing oils and herbs that can assist with alleviating symptoms of depression and anxiety. Queen Afua's encourages us to be involved with our own health care when she says," Health care is Self-care." My motto has become, "Self-care is health care." As I teach my clients how to take care of themselves, I reinforce my own commitment to self-care and holistic healing. I am not perfect when it comes to living a holistic lifestyle, but I am conscious of how I am living. I pay attention to what I am doing that is preventing me from standing in my power when I make choices that make an impact on my mental and physical health. When I fall off the path of wellness and take a detour back into the unhealthy state of depression and weight gain, I know what to do to find my way back to health and wellness.

As a Certified Clinical Trauma Professional and Eating Disorder Intuitive Therapist, I coach my clients through inner child work. This is necessary for healing, because most of the time when one is practicing unhealthy ways of living it is the inner child screaming for healing in an attempt to get their unmet early childhood needs for love and nurturance addressed. Many resort to maladaptive coping mechanisms, learned as children, to fill the void and numb the pain and disappointment stemming from adverse childhood experience that may have left one traumatized. These maladaptive coping mechanisms are signs of unresolved trauma that may manifest as eating disorders, substance abuse, aggression/rage and other forms of obsessive compulsive, self-abusing, risk-taking behaviors. This is why self-care is necessary; to heal our wounded inner child so the healthy adult can step forward and rule one's world.

To all those who struggle with depression, addiction or other trauma-related mental health issues I encourage you to make a deposit into your emotional bank account. I have been on this healing journey for over 15 years and the greatest trigger for depression is self-neglect and being overwhelmed with life. Self-care is necessary to prevent your emotional bank account from reaching a zero balance. Once your emotional bank account is depleted, you are at risk for mental and physical health problems. So be sure to balance your account consistently by making regular deposits into your emotional and psychological bank accounts. You are the only one responsible for making deposits through engaging in healthy activities that you enjoy; that replenish you mentally and physically. This can include eating good nutritious foods, fun physical activities (dancing), creative activities (singing/art), pampering activities (hydro-therapy, massages, hot bath with aroma therapy and music therapy) and spiritual activities that help your spirit get centered and balanced (prayer, mediation, church services).

Participating in these activities and practicing a holistic lifestyle, in addition to seeking professional counseling from a licensed therapist, can prevent your emotional bank account from reaching a negative balance. This you want to avoid because once you are on or below zero you will become physically sick and symptoms of anxiety and depression will set in. Fortunately, this can all be avoided by loving yourself and choosing to stay on the path to wellness; allowing you to step into your greatness!

AUTHENTIC ALIGNMENT: SACRED SELF...SACRED WORK

Rha Goddess, Transformation Coach

I have always been passionate about liberation. As a child born into the intersection of the Civil Rights and Hip-Hop movements, my earliest memories were filled with the profound examples set by my parents who fought tirelessly for basic dignity and respect. They invested in me to ensure that I would have more opportunities than they had. They were madly in love and passionate about family, education, and community. And they lived the mantra "There but for the grace of God, go I," their way of saying, "If you ever receive any kind of opportunity or advantage in life, you have a responsibility to make a way for others."

For over 30 years, I've leveraged my creative, strategic and facilitative talents to raise awareness about pressing social issues and to support individuals, organizations and communities in building the mental, spiritual, and emotional capacity to address those issues on a local, national and global scale. Through this work, I've developed a unique perspective on leadership and what it takes to foster personal transformation, organizational growth and societal change. From the remote villages of post genocide Rwanda to the shellacked corridors of Midtown Manhattan, I have been fascinated by what causes us to shrink back versus rise up to meet our true selves and respective and collective callings. It has been this fascination that has guided my art, my life, and the creation of my entrepreneurial training company, Move The Crowd (MTC) where we teach people how to stay true, get paid *and* do good. (www.movethecrowd.me)

My title at MTC is Entrepreneurial Soul Coach, but what I am is a professional mentor, cheerleader, advisor, and champion for some of the most courageous and innovative cultural change agents of our time. From spiritual teachers to gender benders to industry disrupters, I'm on the court with a whole new generation of game changers who are putting bold ideas to work every single day and transforming millions of lives around issues of racial justice and equity, juvenile offender reform, young women's empowerment and STEM, and much more.

In my line of work, there is something both magical and terrifying that happens when someone approaches the threshold of self-determination and actualization. The process of bearing witness to our most authentic selves is a sacred act, and one that is not always given the highest consideration. I've seen dreams live and die based upon the quality of who and what was catching them. I've watched people negate themselves entirely, opting to sacrifice self-love for a sense of belonging even when the affiliation is superficial.

This is where I believe "dis-ease" begins. In the negation of the Self.

We are living in an incredible time. A time full of chaos and opportunity. A time when volatility, uncertainty, complexity, and ambiguity rule the day. As the best and the worst of humankind are playing out in real time, the level of "angst" in our society is palpable. We are in the throes of giving birth to a new culture and economy—and it is messy, raw, shocking, disorienting, empowering, inspiring, and euphoric, all at the same time. We have watched the world be ripped apart in the name of greed and exploitation. We've seen rivers of blood run in the streets stemming from the most whimsical provocations. We've seen our planet literally rise-up in protest to the maniacal consumption of its most precious resources in service to the comfort of the tiniest percentage of our humanity.

It's a hot mess out there AND people are waking up………

When I think about what I would do to heal planet earth, I must begin with what I believe needs healing - which is our fundamental disconnection from our humanity. This disconnection shows up as a scarcity and separation mindset that breeds much of what we see playing out in our society. "I am not enough." and "There is not enough." represent the foundation of our illusory estrangement from the All-Providing Source (Source). This is the primary wound.

I believe my calling is to help us reclaim our connection to Source by expressing our most authentic selves in service to our highest contributions. For some it requires the need to go within and strip away layers and layers of conditioning. For others it requires the courage to step up and step out—to raise our voices—to exercise our worthiness and agency. This only becomes possible when we dedicate ourselves to authentic alignment.

Every truly successful person has a context from which they live, move and have their being; and this context serves as a moral compass that guides how they evaluate every relationship, initiative or endeavor. I believe this context is drawn from three things:

- Our most deeply held values
- The unique combination of our talents, gifts and abilities
- The passionate impulse that guides us towards the opportunities and challenges we most want to engage in the world.

In our work at Move The Crowd, we call it an L3 and it stands for How You Live, How You Love, and How You Lead. More powerful than what you say is what you do, and more powerful than what you do is who you BE. How you LIVE, LOVE and LEAD is about authentically expressing who you really are in service of and what you are really here to do in this world. Sacred Self to Sacred Work. Below is a 3-part Guided Reflection for creating your L3. Do these explorations as drawings or journal exercises:

LIVE

As you think about yourself fully realized and as you think about the life you wish to live…and the kind of world you wish to inhabit—What are the VALUES that are most important to you? What are the principles and convictions that govern how you live? What are the qualities or essences that make up those convictions?

Is it joy, love, peace, freedom? How are they expressed? Is it where you live? Is it the kind of food you consume? Is it in your relationship to the earth? Is it in your relationships with others? What are the values that govern those interactions? Be they business or personal? How do you honor the resources of the planet? How do you leverage your resources? i.e. your human, intellectual, social, and financial capital in honor of your highest ideals? How you live is all about what you VALUE. *How you live* should answer the question: When it's all said and done what are you really about? Using words, pictures and/or symbols express the vision for how you **LIVE**.

LOVE

As you think about yourself being fully realized and as you think about what you are here to BRING to the world—What are the unique talents, gifts and abilities that you have been given to share? Is it deep listening, laughter, compassionate speaking, creative storytelling? Think about the things that come easily to you. Think about the things you must sometimes force yourself not to do. Think about the things that people often look to you to provide. What do you see? Think about the things that energize you and bring you true joy when you are able to share them. What can you recognize and own as your unique set of offerings to the planet?

How you love should answer the question: What are you here to bring? Using words, pictures and/or symbols express the vision for how you **LOVE**.

LEAD

As you think about yourself fully realized, think about the difference you wish to make—What do you feel most called to change, create, re-imagine, discover, enhance, shift and/or transform in the world? What issue(s) are you most passionate about? What are the challenges and or opportunities facing humanity that you most want to engage? Is it about eradicating poverty? Is it providing quality education? Is it about helping people find their greatness? How will you leverage your talents and gifts to make that contribution? And what will be different in the world as a result? *How you lead* speaks to your highest calling and it answers the question: What are you here to affect? Or, what is the ultimate impact you want to have on the world? Using words, pictures and/or symbols express the vision for how you **LEAD**.

Take a moment to review your work make any modifications as desired. If you feel complete with that you have, simply use this time to connect to what you've created.

Martha Graham says, "It is not our job to determine how good it is, nor how valuable it is, nor how it compares with other expressions…"

Each of us, no matter where we are or where we come from has a unique contribution to make. It is our job to claim it, to name it, to share it and make it our own. When we can do this…we are free. So, let's get free ya'll.

Let's get FREE.

*For teachers and students...
ALL the time, that's ALL of us...*

MY SOCKS
DO NOT HAVE TO MATCH

Gerianne Francis Scott, Educator/Editor

WOW! We meet on these pages. Traveling in the stories that shape our minds, bodies and souls, we are circles of families and communities. In fact, *this essay* is a circle in four parts:

Part I: BRING IT;
Part II: TIME-SPACE-RESOURCES;
Part III: STORYTIME;
Part IV: HOMAGE.

Circles become spirals. We belong here; healing is already happening.

PART I: BRING IT
(HEAL THYSELF, HEAL OUR PLANET)

1. **Love yourself. Love your life.**
2. **Know yourself. Embrace Family. Claim Joy. Be courageous. Repeat.**
3. **Pray** to ask and to thank. **Meditate** to focus.
4. **Recognize** tools (strengths) and obstacles (challenges). Teach your children to do the same.
5. **Choose** battles wisely. **Plan** strategies intelligently. Teach your children.
6. **Listen.**
7. **Be kind** until kindness is habit.
8. **Laugh**—Heals facial muscles, lungs, heart, soul. Cry—Heals same as laughing, plus eyes and skin.
9. **Sing. Dance. Art. Dream.**
10. **Improvise** aka, think of your feet. (This is an art and a science.)
11. **Be accountable.** Your children will imitate and become accountable people.

12. **APOLOGIZE. FORGIVE.**
13. **Greet/Compliment a stranger;** make their day.
14. Prepare **nourishing meals.** Enjoy with others, often.
15. **Move your bowels, daily.** (Non-negotiable!)
16. **Teach your children to cook, clean, do laundry.** Children will learn responsibility. Set the tone; make tasks fun!
17. **Discover and celebrate the healing opportunities associated with Kwanzaa** (African-American cultural holiday) and **Nguzo Saba** (Seven Principles of Kwanzaa).
18. **Respect, Learn from and Care for Elders.** At 95 (born 1923), GrandMary, my mother, still teaches baking and origami to… lots of folks! Besides cookies and paper birds, healing for all. Marvelous!
19. **Read books** to/with your children until they in turn read to themselves and others.
20. **Write in your journal** at least once a week.
21. **Brain matter matters. Stimulate** and **Exercise** the brain with "hands on" formats, as you stay current with digital formats. **For the brain teach/learn:**
    - **Penmanship** block and cursive, pen/pencil/paper. Establish a signature.
    - **Analog** time (hours, minutes, seconds)
    - **Geography** (Start local, go global–maps/atlases/globes.)
22. **Thank a teacher.**
23. **Gather stories (Sankofa**[1]**).**
24. **Share stories. (Griot**[2]**).**
25. **Hug.**
26. **Leave something better than the way you found it.**
27. **Get your affairs in order.** Peace of mind for you and yours.
28. **Plant something.**
29. **Appreciate** and take care of what already heals you.
30. **Empower** your family with **Time, Space, Resources Grids.** (See below.)
31. **Rest. Rise. Resume…**

PART II: TIME-SPACE-RESOURCES: (A MINDSET)

Time, Space and Resources (TSR) exist over every aspect of everybody's life, at the same time, ALL the time.

TIME is the **WHEN** part. Time involves schedules and deadlines. **SPACE** is the **WHERE** part. Space can be at home or on the job or even in an airplane. RESOURCES are the WHO and the WHAT. Resources include tools, budget, finances, transportation and people. I edit life with a **Time, Space and Resources (TSR)** mindset. It helps to see the big picture and plan accordingly.

Whether planning a party or addressing health issues apply **TSR**; go step by step.
1. **Label** the project;
2. **Identify** tools;
3. **List** obstacles;
4. **Plan** solutions of joy and grace.

The more you analyze with the **TSR** mindset, the more it becomes automatic. As you plan, make lists, in your head, on paper, (or on a device *if you must*). Having plans helps to overcome obstacles. If there is an emergency, say, with the weather or your children, you can slide into Plan B. You eliminate panic! Yes, I understand spontaneity, and I respect "Divine Intervention." However, I am convinced that with plans I can experience "surprises" as a happy participant, rather than as a blindsided victim.

My socks *do not* have to match. Stuck in unforgiving traffic, with wet hair and no breakfast, I was late for work, again. I had to do better. That evening I created a TSR Grid of activities I needed to fix... heal.

When plans don't work, I revise them. I know it is better to have a plan, than not to have one. In the case of Late for Work I prioritized Being On Time over spending time to match my socks. Wearing my unmatched socks, I reclaimed precious time for easier parking and healthier breakfast choices. My stress levels decreased. My accountability profile brightened. I saw more sunrises. Joy and Grace.

Soon, I guided my students to create their own TSR Grids. They began developing savvy solutions to small and large challenges. Decades later former students tell me they've taught TSR Grids to their children. Next generation. Nice.

LATE FOR WORK TSR GRID		
Obstacles	**TSR**	**Solutions**
Missing sunrise/ exercise/ meditation/ breakfast	Time	Go to bed earlier/ Rise earlier
Matching socks	Time/Resources	**My socks *do not* have to match!**
Can't find keys and eyeglasses	Time/Space/Resources	*Always* put essentials in the same place
Traffic; Parking	Time/Space	Leave home earlier

PART III: STORYTIME: (SANKOFA & GRIOT)

Sankofa = go back and gather the history. **Griot** = the one who shares/tells the history. Readers, circle around to gather and share. Don't be distracted by differences: generation, geography, gender and so on. The priority is Global Wellness. If we continue to endanger the elements: Air, Water, Earth, Fire beyond repair, and if we continue to be distracted from caring for our souls, our differences won't matter. Dare we use our time, space and resources to BRING IT—responsibly?

OUR STORIES CONNECT. WALK WITH ME.

Family & Friends: singing a cappella in 4-part harmony; flash cards; Scrabble; hopscotch; scattin' on walks to LaGuardia Airport; gardening; massages… **As often as possible share songs and games with family and friends.**

Afro: (1968) I freed my hair! **Locs:** (1986) I freed my soul! **Why not organize a hair story party? Invite guests to bring and exchange hair stories, products and adornments.**

On my feet: Countless teachers and classes at Ballet Arts, Clark Center, Dance Theatre of Harlem, Ailey Centre, Dinizulu Centre, Forces of Nature…Concerts… Six decades, Readers, I know our families' steps have crisscrossed. **Let's choreograph new memories. Can we Cha Cha? Can we Nay Nay? Who can do the South African Boot Dance? Don't forget the music.**

Academic and Cultural Education: Ongoing Curriculum: Life's Arts and Sciences
  Sets: conventional classrooms, churches, castles, hospitals; farms, fields, undersea coral reefs…
  Locations: Africa, Asia, the Americas, the Caribbean, Europe…next stop Tierra del Fuego right across from Antarctica!

Master teachers: Many had hands on growing me. (See Part IV: HOMAGE).
Lessons—thousands!: Here's one—In Egypt (1983), we visiting teachers became students when Mohamed the felucca pilot took us to a beach where the Nile River meets the Sahara Desert. I touched geography in person. Unforgettable! **Recall important lessons. How will you teach them to others?**

  Some awards: SGO president/HS 1969; Graduate Honors/MS 1982); National Fellowships; Teacher of Excellence; Community Service (NYC Mandala Center). **Create awards and ceremonies for yourself or another;** aha, huge healing opportunities!

Touching Lives: My mantra for four decades: *"Use everything to teach everything."* I gave my middle school, high school and college students the tools to write, perform and publish their stories. Annually, I wrote, directed and produced student presentations. I wrote *The Dreams They Had: A play about Sankofa*. (Produced six times.) **What part of your story is healing our planet? Tell us. Show us. Unprecedented Research:** For a decade my 8th graders hand-wrote invitations. Guest presenters came: historians, activists, writers, artists, athletes (former student, the late Malik Sealy) and family members. *Without computers* 1,000+ students honed skills, connected family stories to the world story and produced collegiate-level projects. **Sankofa your story, find connections, then Griot your story. Use songs, dances, recipes…**

"Heal Thyself!" Queen Afua's mantra is a global wellness beacon. In 1983, Queen guided me through my first 21-Day Detox, liquids only; *waaaay* before Heal Thyself products. (*That's* a story.) Ten years later she wrote her first book, *Heal Thyself for Health and Longevity*. As of 2015, Queen has written six more books. From the beginning I have been her literary editor/archivist. **How are you sharing/recording your story?**

Beaches:

First story: 1990 **King Family Reunion** (annual since 1970) over one hundred family members swam at Corentyne Beach, Guyana as had our ancestors for generations, spanning three centuries. **Gather two or more family members for STORYTIME. (Bonus: Intergenerational gatherings.) Share as you: Cook. Eat. Walk. Celebrate.** (See also BRING IT.)

Second story: The beach in the winter. For decades I've taken students, parents, colleagues, even neighbors to experience the **horizon…the sky kissing the sea!** Ok, too cold where you live? Snow? Just bundle up and head for the shore. No coastline nearby? Get thee to a lake, river or a place in nature. (Bonus: At sunrise!) Breathe… **Guaranteed, WOW, every time! Do it. Journal it. Tell it.**

Third story: (1982) On Goree Beach in Senegal, local children taught me, **'wow' means 'yes'** in the Wolof language. Centuries after Africans had been enslaved to the Americas the word *'wow'* survived; *'yes.'* Think about that…

I am a bridge between all the above and all to come. **I live life out loud** with an Eclectic Family (by blood and by heart)… Treasured Friends and Colleagues… Enlightening Editing Privileges… Entrepreneurial Eyeopeners and Scuba diving. **WOW!**

Thank you for taking time to connect. Embraced and fortified by the ancestors, we walk in mighty footsteps. Humbly, I offer the circle of this essay as we continue to "Heal Thyself" and Heal Our Planet.

Walk good.

---

1. Sankofa: (Twi language/Ghana) –"Go back and get the knowledge of the past."
2. Griot: (traditionally West African) – Oral historian for family/community.

PART IV: HOMAGE:

Words are my forte—bridges from thoughts to deeds. "Thank you," Givers of stories—written and sung and whispered. Words are food; nourishing the palimpsests[3] we are constantly becoming. Our layers are informed and strengthened. This litany is ours; and it is us. **Choose a name**, read what she wrote. **Choose another**, listen to his song. Let their words provoke you, guide you, inspire you to connect your stories.

Before & After: Parents.

Brilliant Laughter: "Moms" Mabley, Redd Foxx, Richard Pryor, Lily Tomlin, Carol Burnett, George Carlin, Whoopi, Bernie Mack, Chris Rock, Trevor Noah…

Pages…: *Child Craft (15 Vols.)*, Bible, Encyclopedias, Seuss, *Girl Scout Handbook, Learning Latin*…Ebony, Jet, Amsterdam News, Daily News, NYTimes, Essence, Ms. … Dick Gregory, Kloss *(Back to Eden)*, M. Obama, S. Sotomayor, Wright, Twain, Camus, Hesse, Kafka, Baldwin, Achebe, Soyinka, Last Poets, Piri Thomas *(…Mean Streets)*, Alice Walker, Angelou, Yarbrough *(Cornrows)*, Garcia-Marquez, Haley, Steinbeck, Heinlein, Gwendolyn Brooks, Langston Hughes, Gibran, Sanchez, Giovanni, *Kama Sutra*… Mao *(…Red Book)*, John G. Jackson, George G.M. James *(Stolen Legacy)*, Carter G. Woodson *(Mis-education)*, Fanon *(Wretched of….)*, Rodney, Carew, Chancellor Williams, Drusilla Dunjee Houston, Cheikh Anta Diop, Dee Brown *(…Wounded Knee)*, Octavia Butler, Julia Alvarez, Jean Auel *(… Cave Bear)*, Clarissa Pinkola Estés *(Women…Wolves)*, Adichie, Dyson…

Mary McLeod Bethune, Zora Neale Hurston, Toni Morrison, MLKing, Malcolm X (Brother Malcolm and my dad sometimes walked through our neighborhood chattin' 'n' scattin'.

Docs, Doers & Sages: Tubman, Truth, Douglass, Booker T & WEB, George Washington Carver, Schomburg, Ida B. Wells, Marcus Garvey, John Lewis, Shirley Chisolm, Nelson & Winnie Mandela, Jitu Weisu, Gil Noble, First World scholars: Adelaide Sandford (Ashe!), Asa Hilliard, Frances Cress Welsing, Amos Wilson, Molefi Asante, Maulana Karenga, Jawanza Kunjufu; Yosef Ben Jochannan (Doc Ben), John Henrik Clarke, Leonard & Rosalind Jeffries, James Smalls, Ivan Van Sertima, Edward Scobie, Richard King, Cheryl Doyle, Ione, Barbara Gathers (AWM), Leothy Miller (Nkiru Books).

Playwrights, Thespians & Stages: Hansberry *(A Raisin…)*, Ward *(Day of Absence)*, Shakespeare, Shange *(for colored girls…)*, August Wilson; Josephine Baker, Paul Robeson, Ossie & Ruby, Diahann Carroll, Della Reese, James Earl Jones, Poitier, Belafonte, A & K Hepburn, Hines, Joe Morton, Cicely Tyson, Bassett, Denzel, Moreno, Alda, Dench, Alfrie Woodard, Latifah, Tantoo Cardinal, Star Trek, Huxtables…WWRL, WBLS, WQXR …

Point my mind: Catholic school nuns; college professors: Joel Oppenheimer, Dr. Don; Kumasi. Abalde Glover.

Point my feet: Dorothy Miller, Betty Peters, Elsie Steele, Charles & Ella Moore, Chuck Davis, Pearl Primus, Arthur Mitchell, Marie Brooks, Alistair Butler, Alvin Ailey, Judith Jamison, Dinizulu, Abdel Salaam, Nafisa Sharrif…

Sing my soul: Marian Anderson, Fitzgerald, Vaughn, Horne, Holiday, Kitt, Nancy Wilson, Nina Simone, Aretha Franklin, Tina, Gladys, Dionne, Diana, Chaka, Donna, Patti LaBelle, Gladys, Roberta, Morgana, Whitney, Chubby Checker, James "Godfather" Brown, Coltrane, Abbey Lincoln, Oscar Peterson, Streisand, Sammy Davis Jr, Rodgers & Hammerstein, Nat "King" Cole, Sinatra, Mormon Tabernacle Choir, Feliciano, Quincy, Pavarotti, Smokey, Beatles, Satchmo, Mercer, Hunter, S & G, Joplin, Pharaoh Sanders *(...Master Plan)*, Bernstein, Makeba, Fela Kuti, Feliciano, Smokey, Eckstein, Prysock, Puente, Isleys, O'Jays, Santana, Lucien, Ritchie, **Scott-Heron, Wonder, Sweet Honey In The Rock, Marley,** Hayes, Mayfield, Dianne Reeves, Earth Wind & Fire, Michael & Jacksons, Prince, Nyro, Elton, Snow, Gipsy Kings, Amatrading, Tupac, Inta-Illimani, McFerrin, Kem, Jill Scott, Vandross (Always and forever, Luther)…

Sing my heart: East Elmhurst. Millers: Miss Dottie, RG, Gloria, Sharlene, Trudy; Davises: Connie, John, Betty Ann to Emily; Lise; Hollands; Astoria. MC Gators and Yayas; Bronx Plus, Carmen V., Halima, Sheila & Ephraim, Ione, Olivers. Mahons/Peters: Betty, Edwy, Pete, Gail, Bobby, Diane, Lynne, Susan, Mimi, Judy, Josie, Sarita, Suncyre; Leah, Cornel, Frances; 166: Rene, Candy Rock, Luz, Sharon, Jeannie, Sealys, Tancos, Danny, Helen, Noemi, Philo, Obi, Elba, Massaquoi, Sharon R., Chase, Leslie, Fortes. Uncle Bill; Grants, Woods, Madeline, Rob; Queen Afua, Mother Ida, Heal Thyself Family; DC. Yolanda; NJ. Riscardo, Mr. Kas, Lee Marieme; PA: Cindy, Judy, Mike, Matt; FL. Paula; NY. Trae, Mark. 'My Children': Marcus, Charlie, Odelis, Athena, Chotsani, Zulliete, Yves, Tanny, Munny, Amin, Ashif; Extended: Dianne, Alistair, Acquanetta, Coco, Susan, Nancy; Maxene &, Francisco, Ellen & Ray, Kay, Warren, Audrey, Seth, Erin, Michael, Nina, Lance, Fior, Nora, Joan, Gerry, Laney, Steve, Eric, Keesha; Wendy, Winston, Kaba, Shari; Andre, Cynthia, Kathy, Sam, Zahyid, Fe, Edyamil, Roxana, Jhanio, Carlos, Helen, Seku, Rhonda, Veronjahlee; Kwanzaa Queens: Paula, Barbara G., Eunice, Barbara W., Shirley, Renee, Marva, Alma. Plus: Cousin Jackie, E. Scott, Aunty Sara, Aunty Carol, Stephan, Lilas, Crystal, Reggie, Stevie, Amina; Francis, Mike, Daeemah, Idris, Adam, Emani, Lisa, Yodeet, Rosalind.

Tribe: Kings & Garners (Guyana), Briscos & Brooks (Africa & Turtle Island), Emma (Nana), Janet (Gaga), Anthony (Grandpa), Mary & Emory (**Mommy & Daddy**), Lynnda, Phyllis, Nkosa, Breyone, Kaiqwon, Irlyaan; Kelyse, Sarai, Anaya, Brandon, Kamora, Jena, Cole, Yara…and the rest to come…

Even if you don't see them on this list, they are *already* on your mind…

Walk Good.

---

3. Palimpsests having diverse layers or aspects

PEACE OF MIND IN TIMES OF CHAOS

Mutshat Shemsut-Gianprem Kaur,
Yoga And Meditation

Have you ever looked at images of planet Earth and marveled at its beauty? There it is, hanging in the silence and darkness of space, a marbled jewel bedecked in shades of blue and green with brown accents and white cloud swirls. Pull in closer, say from an airplane into New York City at night, and the surface becomes a movement of golden jewels. So beautiful. So peaceful. As you gaze your breath is a rhythmic calm. Your mind is quiet, meditative. Know this: The healing of planet earth relies upon how well its human inhabitants can breathe and meditate. As part of my life's purpose, I am tasked with healing planet earth by means of assisting my brothers and sisters in achieving self-mastery through self-knowledge. I do this via Kundalini Yoga and Meditation—a yogic form that addresses every human condition and situation imaginable—as well as through the Ra Sekhi healing arts and Foot Reflexology.

Depending upon your experiences, inner peace, when you find it, may often give way to varying degrees of stress. Your breathing may become shallow and erratic as you think of the day ahead. The top news stories promote fear, distrust, sadness and even horror. Your breath rate increases as you think about your personal affairs, national affairs, world affairs and even other people's affairs. As your mind jumps from subject to subject and stress constricts you, your breathing is mostly in the upper region of your chest, where it often is, the result of one perceived negative experience after another, from childhood to adulthood.

BREATHING

Learning to breathe properly is a must. Too many of us are walking wounded, flinching and waiting for the next blow. Too many of us are holding onto "stuff" that has followed our family through generations. Too many of us have been in destress for so long that it has become our normal. Meanwhile, it wreaks havoc on mind, body and spirit. This stress, this holding of tension, causes a build-up of negative emotions that must be released, otherwise dis-ease will eventually take hold. Proper breathing and expansion of the lungs will help you to reduce your stress. Know this: The mind follows the breath. To control your mind, you must control your breath.

A BREATHING TECHNIQUE TO CHANGE YOUR EMOTIONAL STATE—IMMEDIATELY

Long Deep Breathing is a very simple technique with so many benefits. When you are anxious, in a state of emotional shock or otherwise upset, do this. Through your nose, breathe very deeply and very slowly into your lower abdomen, expanding your rib cage. Very slowly bring that air up, expanding your upper ribcage, into the chest area, filling your lungs with air. Continue to bring your breath up into your shoulder blades. Then, just as slowly, exhale through the nose. Slowly contract all air out, finally pulling your navel back toward your spine to expel the air completely. You will immediately change your emotional state even in the midst of total chaos. Try it.

As practice, the longer you do this breath the more benefits you will derive from it. Try it for 3 minutes and work your way up to 11 minutes, or 31. Besides being relaxing and calming it builds your flow of life force energy, cleanses the blood and aids in speeding up emotional and physical healing—and much more. There are a number of different breathing techniques that achieve specific results. Practicing long deep breathing will make you better able to navigate your world as an individual on this planet, and as part of the human collective.

MEDITATION

A meditative mind will allow you to experience spiritual flow. One important thing you must realize is that you are not your mind. You are soul. You are not your body. You are soul.

The mind accompanies your soul on its journey. It is the mind that thinks, not you. The mind thinks thoughts to protect you—the negative mind. The mind thinks thoughts to help you use what is known based upon your experiences—the positive mind. The mind also judges on behalf of your higher self after considering the thoughts of the negative and positive minds—that is called the neutral mind. Every thought you have goes through these three minds. It is your neutral or meditative mind that you want to develop. Doing so will lead to clarity. Clarity will lead to innerstanding. Innerstanding will lead to self-mastery. Self-mastery will lead you to an enlightened way of being that will ultimately be good for the entire planet as you become expansive, limitless, and work to awaken others to the light. Each enlightened being moves the planet further away from chaos and toward balance, harmony and peace.

However, before you can get to that place you must go through the process of learning how to cleanse your mind through meditation. Just as the physical body needs cleansing so, too, does the mind. The purpose of meditation is to cleanse the mind of the negative thoughts that do not serve you. You want to achieve a balanced mind that will serve your soul and consciousness. You want to rise above the mind and reach the divinity of your soul. Meditation will enable you to communicate with your mind and your body. The mind follows the breath. The body follows the mind.

Meditation develops the meditative mind. It promotes a sense of inner peace. It enables one to release those negative thought patterns that are embedded in the subconscious as fears and blocks. When you let thoughts pass by and allow your mind to be still you are meditating.

The best time to meditate is before dawn. However, any time that is peaceful for you is an appropriate time to meditate. There are hundreds of meditations in the Kundalini Yoga tradition that address so many human conditions or situations in need of correction. Below is a meditation I often teach in my Kundalini Yoga and Meditation classes as well as to Ra Sekhi clients.

A MEDITATION FOR STRESS RELIEF AND CLEARING EMOTIONS OF THE PAST

This is a powerful mediation. It will help you to get rid of the "stuff" so many of us carry around as a result of experiences in this life and past lives as well.

Tune in: Center yourself with the mantra, Ong Namo Guru Dev Namo, chanted 3 times (It means, "I call on my highest self to do my greatest good.)

Posture: Sit in a cross-legged position. The spine is straight; the neck is in line with the spine with the chin tucked in slightly.

Mudra (hand position): Place the hands at the center of the chest with the tips of the thumbs touching each other and the tips of the fingers touching the corresponding fingers on the opposite hand. Leave space between the palms. The fingertips are pointing upward.

Focus: Look at the tip of your nose. However, keep your chin parallel to the floor.

Breath: Inhale 5 counts, hold 5 counts, exhale 5 counts.

Time: 11 minutes or until relief from the stress is felt.

To End: Inhale. Exhale. Relax.

To Close: Chant Sat Nam (It means truth is my identity. Truth is my name. Truth is the name of the One Most High.) 1 to 3 times, with a long *Saaaaaaaat* and a brief Nam.

Comments: This meditation is especially useful for dealing with stressful relationships and with past family issues. It addresses unreasonable fears, reasonable fears, and anxious or obsessive behaviors. It can remove disturbing thoughts from the past that bubble up into the present. It can take difficult situations in the present and release them into the hands of the Infinite One.

The mind follows the breath. The body follows the mind. Inner peace. One individual at a time, we all have it in us to assist in the healing of the planet. We all have the potential to contribute to the shift from chaos to balance. As we heal ourselves, we heal the planet.

EAT GREEN

Supa Nova Slom, Wellness Activist/Artist

I'm Supa Nova Slom, a second-generation health activist and educator brought up in Crown Heights, Brooklyn. My mother, Queen Afua, saw to it that my sister, my brother, and I were raised on life-giving vegetable juices and natural ingredients, and refrained from eating the poison foods, preservatives, and additives that most of the other kids in our hood scarfed down like there was no tomorrow. I've performed periodic body cleanses and detoxing fasts my whole life. We were doing yoga decades before it was something joked about on TV. In my household, the positive power and nearly unlimited energy that exercise, and healthy diet, and periodic fasting create was not a new phase or fad, it was a tradition. I have the blessing of health to show it. What Mom was and is about is holistic wellness. Simply defined, holistic health:

- Seeks to prevent disease before it starts.
- Recognizes that the body, mind, and spirit are one. A problem with any one aspect of that trio affects the other two.
- Assumes that health is a matter of lifestyle and the choices you make about how you live.

The tradition and practice of holistic wellness goes back centuries, and the ideas that Queen Afua taught me have been in play since before recorded history. If there's one word that describes the principle goal of holistic health, it's balance. The ancients had scores of words and symbols to describe the delicate equilibrium between body, mind, and spirit. Balance—not neutrality, not inertia, not paralysis—is a dynamic, energetic, and healthy give-and-take that favors, flatters and enables the magically, fabulously perfect systems, keeping them alive to flow harmoniously and do their jobs.

It took the Industrial Revolution to mess up that balance and introduce many toxins into our system However, the modern holistic health movement has risen up to face these challenges. Fortunately, doctors, scientists, practitioners, and therapists from every background and ethnicity have begun to undo the damage and address both old and new ways to restore the body's long-recognized need for balanced health and well-being. Nutritionists have found that a diet dominated by green vegetables—an ideal source of vitamins, minerals, and enzymes, fiber for cleaning, and water for oxygenating and flushing the system—can restore internal balance and prolong lives threatened by an increasingly toxic environment. Health practitioners have detailed the healing properties of blue-green algae, prairie grasses like wheatgrass, and other specific fruits and vegetables that are now called *superfoods*

...African Americans have led this country in the arts, sports, and politics for more than a century. Unfortunately, over the last three decades, Black Americans have set the standard for poor health statistics. What Mom taught me and fed me made my body and spirit strong. Defending that lifestyle legacy made me tough. In the eighties, my hood was a hard place to stay healthy. From day one, I had to fight my own battle for wellness. Going to school...[with] the sprout sandwich Queen packed for my lunch guaranteed confrontation....Kids don't like different, and there were days when I literally had to fight my way out of the cafeteria. Mom didn't just look after her own, she reached out to anyone, anywhere who was sick and tired if feeling sick and tired from the ravages of body toxins, obesity, and other toxitarian diet-related illnesses....

Cipher—in the hip-hop world is a word that carries weight. A cipher is your circle—your crew, your world, the community of collaborators around you. That means a lot. As you live, move and create, you share all kinds of company with all kinds of people and travel through all kinds of scenes, neighborhoods, and communities. Working with my mom as she took her message of holistic wellness all over the country and the world, I passed through dozens of ciphers. Whether it was a Fort Greene charter school, a Marin County yoga retreat, or a suburban Atlanta community center, Queen Afua's message comes through loud and clear. Alongside Mom and then on my own, first in gang circles, then hip-hop circles, then through outreach education and speaking engagements, I've learned firsthand that the principle and practices of holistic wellness can restore balance and energy in anyone's life. Now that the world is catching up to Queen's message and what used to be considered fringe beliefs have moved into the mainstream, the truth is even more clear.

During my shopping cart travels in Brooklyn, the capital of the Rastafarian Ital health movement and home of the Park Slope Food Coops, I read what they put on prepackaged foods, grains, and starches. There wasn't much difference from what was making kids from Dekalb Avenue to Denver overweight and unhealthy. I realized that most vegetarians were *starchitarians*. Maybe they're not eating meat, or maybe they cut out dairy, but the bulk of their diet is still processed starches just like that of *toxitarians*. The foods had all the preservatives, chemicals, and GMO ingredients, and all the health risks and potential for obesity those things bring. What *toxitarians* and *starchitarians* and most Americans ignore is the secret, cleansing, nutritive power of greens. Carnivore or vegan, overweight or not, the secret to cleansing and detoxifying and re-energizing your life is the same: Eat green.

Look no further than the sun in the sky—that's where the energy starts. That's where the power comes from. That's what we use to jet through our days and nights in good health and full strength. The simple miracle of photosynthesis is the source of a remedy that revs up human cells, cleanses and oxygenated human blood, and keeps us kicking and popping and taking our lives to the next level no matter how much stress we take on and no matter what age we are.

You can only get well if you stop poisoning yourself with toxic foods, start cleansing your body of the ravages we all face from the environment, and start giving yourself and your cells what you really need—a concentrated dose of the sun's radiant energy captured in the nutrient-dense cells of green plant-foods.

> **REVOLUTION** is in healing. In order to **change the world,** that change MUST first take place within us…Our stomachs are being held hostage by toxic substances which are biochemically engineered to **control our minds,** making us drones prone to self-destruction. By expelling the poisonous terrorists in our emotional, mental and physical bodies, we will **experience self-liberation,** allowing us to collectively combat external opposition……
> **Heal Thyself…HOTEP**
> —Supa Nova Slom

MINDFULNESS: GRAB HOLD OF THE FLEXITARIAN LIFESTYLE

Kevin E. Taylor, Pastor/Motivational Speaker

Mindfulness.

That is what was missing from my physical habits as it relates to how I take care of me. I have spent my entire life as a large, tall man who has always had weight issues. Even when I was able to be a much smaller version of myself, it was only because I became obsessed with NOT eating and working out like a fiend, so I was still dealing with weight issues. I was never mindful of my body and my physical needs as it relates to the machine of Me and what I need to be able to operate effectively. I was one of those people who got it in my brain that the only way I was going to lose weight was to stop eating. I have had periods where I could operate with NO FOOD for an entire day, just water. I have had periods where I went to extremes to drop weight and that too was an issue.

But then as I got closer to 50, literally on the bridge of 49, waiting to get to that Golden Age, I made the declaration that I wanted to purpose to be in the best physical, spiritual, financial, sexual and emotional shape of my life. I wanted to do the actual and active work to be in better shape.

A friend of mine, an actor and musician named Barron B. Bass, was helping me consider people to interview for my new web series "NOW WHAT?! WITH KEVIN E TAYLOR" and the name Queen Afua came to me, either through him or through other channels and I ran it by him. He was emphatic that she needed to be someone I spoke with on the show. OH, WHAT A DIFFERENCE A DAY MAKES!

After an exceptionally insightful and enlightening conversation, Queen Afua said "I have something for you." After we got off camera, she handed me a bottle of "Breath of Life," the peppermint and eucalyptus mixture that opens up the passages of your ears, nose and throat, but also your mind. With her recommendation, I took it every morning for a few days and did the 50 fire breaths with my feet elevated. It changed the way I woke up in the morning and helped to continue my path to Wellness. But it wasn't until I went to meet with The Queen that I became mindful. She did a reading. She walked with me through so many of my health concerns and life challenges and seemed to be able to speak directly to my soul and to my habits. When we talked about food, she didn't make me feel any shame about my dietary habits; she challenged me to broaden them. She introduced the word "FLEXETARIAN." I laughed a bit because I was so intrigued and knew it was going to be something I couldn't refuse. I knew it. She walked me through days of being meat-free and more vegetable and mineral mindful, to the point that I have been able to operate differently in my skin and in my senses.

It started with the Green Life and being able to rise in the morning and be excited about breakfast as a real choice for me now, as opposed to something that I grabbed and ran with OR as opposed to thinking "I will eat this huge breakfast and not eat lunch and balance out the caloric intake." No, I needed to be made aware of the REAL IMPORTANCE of revving my body up in the morning, as the machine of Me that determined how I moved through the day. Having already adopted The Breath of Life, being mindful of myself and my intention for the day, I now rise and mixed a pure juice with my Green Life and I am mindful of myself in the morning. I am mindful of being meditative. I am mindful of slowing down and centering before I move. I am mindful to speak the desires of my day. I am mindful to be thankful to God and to speak to my ancestors as soon as my feet touch the ground. I am mindful of peace.

That mindfulness has helped me march masterfully into each new day and when I feel it, I am mindful of eating a salad with chicken and drinking water, but I am also mindful of the days that my body only desires fruits and vegetables and water to operate. I honor both.

The journey of Flexetarianism for me has been about listening, to myself, my needs and my body. So many times, before I began this particular path, I was running on food as a reward for the day or a punishment for my weight. I hadn't listened to my body because I hadn't loved my body. I was a fat kid, born some 11 lbs., who only got bigger as I got bigger. I remember being called "that big baby" as early as 2 and remembering being so conscious that I and my weight were…a burden. But how do you not eat? How do you take control of food when it's food and you need it daily. See, I am not a sweet and snacks and junk food kind of eater. I am a full meal master. When I get hungry, I can outcook most people, male or female, Northern, Southern or Caribbean and I know that. So, when I am battling with food, it was preparation and portions and not making food like I am cooking for an army, which leaves me with a refrigerator filled with awesomeness that I then have at my avail when I get hungry late. I had to get my "get hungry late" under control. That happened with these new habits and the mindfulness of rest/sleep and rising with clarity and listening to my body and what it needs to operate.

I had a co-worker come into my office just now to speak and she laughed and said, "You and those apples!" I eat an apple every morning with my Green Life and that revs me up so clearly and with such focus that I have to remember to eat lunch in a few hours. And when I do, I will walk to a store and get something fresh to prepare. I have found that I am vibrant and vital now. I have found that there are mornings, with my Breath of Life in my pores and my own mixture of morning distilled water, peppermint oil and chlorophyll, that I decide to walk from my apartment to my office, which is 4 miles away. I can not only do it without losing my wind, which is a HUGE DEAL for an asthmatic and I lived in the hospital with my asthma, but I can do it with bursts of energy that keep me going and sweating and feeling alive like never before in my skin or in my lifetime. This newest season is about to be my best. The idea that I could be bigger and better and bolder and brazen in my *blessingness* was beyond me.

As I move in my grace and greatness, I am clear that my newest assignment is to take care of the Me that I want to be when I am 60, who is still traveling and talking and telling tales of greatness around the globe. In order to be up and able, I need to be aware of Me and who I be and what I need to move in and around the world of my dreams. Trust me, it takes work, but I love the job and the joy it brings to be Me. I am a fiend for chicken and it's not just the fat boy who loves Momma's chicken growing up. I am now a mindful eater and I have always been able to grill and roast and pan-sear and do more to a chicken than most. I also love salmon and prepare it masterfully. But I am now conscious and mindful that there are days and desires within me that operate well on the purity of fruits and roots, vegetables and vitamins and when I am aware of myself and my march and my movement in each day, I am able to make such clear and conscientious choices for the betterment of me and my journey to be in the best physical, spiritual, financial, sexual and emotional shape of my life. Healing is available, no matter what age it arrives. I am awake now and mindful that the best is yet to come!

(Photo credit:
Tamara Fleming for FemWORKS Photography)

HOW TO HEAL THE PLANET

Taharqa & Tunde-Ra Aleem,
Positive Action Advisors

To heal the planet, we must first heal ourselves. To heal ourselves we must know ourselves.

The Webster dictionary states that the denotative meaning of the word Human mean, "Godman".

When man knows the God that he serves, he will first serve that God to himself. If it's a healing God, then he will then serve that God to the world. Man is the God that he serves to the world!!!

POWER

(From Chapter 23: Sacred Formulas to Raise the Royal Mind called "Power")

IN ORDER THAT THERE BE A RESURRECTION THERE MUST BE POWER!

How do we acquire power? Essentially, all human bodies and minds possess a fundamental amount of power that can be developed and strengthened by exercising with some form of resistance. One of the greatest exercising tools for developing basic power is weight. When a program is applied, we KNOW that we can develop a beautiful body from exercising with the weight. Life also offers another type of weight that can be used to workout with and that's called "The wait of time." Weight and wait essentially mean the same thing and can be used for the same purpose…development.

Here is an equation in weight/wait for you to examine:

- Our planet earth is a body of weight approximately six sextillion tons, a unit followed by 21 ciphers;
- We came here as a body of weight;
- We evaluate and are forced to grow in the wait and depending on how we use it;
- We will either develop or be crushed by the weight of time.

In this equation, I brought all the waits together to use for our mental workout in time. How do we workout for power with the "wait of time?"

Many of us have learned the science of working out our bodies for development and acquiring physical power, but we lack the correct knowledge of using power exercises for the development of our spirit and our mind. When we exercise for the development of our spirit and our mind, we must use the weight of time.

Time can be weighted, and it is done all the time when we say, "Wait a minute." Time is calculated and assessed by the value one gives to it. However, many of us put little value on our time. We find ourselves waiting for worldly goods such as money, success, love; we even wait for God. Sad to say, these are fruitless exercises. The wise and aware ones do not wait for, they wait as great, and powerful beings; they are in *constant* workout with the wait/weight, for power.

People who want to access power will work out daily with key power words and attributes associated with higher powers or the God powers. They use the "wait/weight of time" to acquire all the power-attributes associated with the Gods, and Goddesses to achieve their every will. This is called, studying the ways of the master to become the master. One must learn to direct supplications to the God in one's self, just as one directs his physical exercise to himself /herself.

The unaware are easily misdirected and they think it is progressive to teach and program their children to become doctors, lawyers, journalists, athletes, and so forth. We encourage our offspring to become monetarily successful. However, so many of us fail to develop the individual character of the being, because we don't know what character to instill into the vessel nor do we truly understand the science of transfiguration *(changing into a glorified and exulted being).*

The denotative meaning for the word Archetype is a *typical, ideal model to emulate.*

- When we are committed to physical development we find a model physical specimen to follow. Most spiritual cultures also have archetypes to study; however, the science of emulation has been replaced with deity worship—a powerless exercise. I read an article today that among the New Deities who Americans worship or emulate are Kanye West, Donald Trump, Kim Kardashian and Nicki Minaj. Needless to say, opinions vary regarding these choices as role models.

Transfiguration teaches the student the science of waiting in the personage of an archetype. The God or Goddess of choice is studied and emulated, then, whatever earthly aspirations the recipient may prey on, not only will the transfigured being succeed in the ways of the archetype, but also, the recipient's mind will be fortified with the higher powers of the archetype.

If the right type of power is implanted and used during the formative "preschool" stage of a child's growth and development, by the time the offspring reaches the first grade the child will be truly, "Ready for the World." They already will have become powerful beings; They will be prepared to use their god powers to accentuate the goals that they want to achieve. Additionally, they will enjoy success in anything that they choose to do…because whatever they do, it will reflect the attributes of God and while serving God on earth…"One cannot serve God unless God is on One's menu."

PURGE & PURIFY

Bluepill (Aka Paul Moreland), Empowerment Coach

---

*I*n any martial art, **power** can only be obtained by the repetition of form. The repetitive cycle is the only thing that will break the mold of normalcy and barrel you into the winner's circle. **Transformation** is a daily operation. Every second, minute, hour of the day should be spent in dedication to the art of healing, either of ourselves or someone else.

As healers, we must mandate healing as a lifestyle. Not only does our life depend on it, but the very lifeforce of our planet needs wellness warriors as allies for the battle of all battles. We live on a planet, that's home to land and ocean—which stay in constant motion. What happens when the wheel stops spinning? The land starts cracking, and the oceans dry up!

We should be very clear that there is something amiss threatening the very safety of our mother planet and if we remain complacent, there will be no deterrent to this proverbial train running off the track. There is an enemy in its midst, spraying the mist of poison on land, air and sea, with no transparency from the people in charge of securing these utilities. Right now, the citizens of this country are voting whether to put the keys in the hands of Trump or Hillary. This can really be considered a state of emergency; a health crisis. Cancer is overtaking Mama's divine vessel, and if she is to succumb to this over-accumulation of poison and toxicity, then who and what is she destined to be reborn as? Dear Mama.

As her children, did we do anything and everything possible to protect the sanctity of our Mama…the Mother…our planet? When the moment mattered most, were we present or were we chasing a ghost? If you are enlisted in this army, know that there is working to do, inwardly and outwardly. Now is not the time for mediocracy. Campaign against procrastination; that is the only wall that stands between you and greatness. These are the commandments in their latest stages. The food from sages has been left on the altar for us all to feast from. We each one must teach one.

What lies up ahead is nothing we should flee from, but rather flee toward. That only comes with the confidence of training. The sifu, our master teachers have graduated, dropped the robe of flesh, only to be adorned in robes of light. Their strobes of light make impact with this planet like moldavite. It's now solar light, available to anyone equipped with solar paneling, coated in melanin.

We are the elect; the chosen; the warriors of wellness in a time of peril. This is also a time to rise a level, to find the devil in the details and purge & purify by learning how to eat well. We stand in the shadow of the future, a time when man and machine will merge, and androids will materialize. If life is a computerized simulation, then the veil is dropping, and we are seeing Oz for what it is.

This program is driven by an artificial intelligence, devoid of the intelligence programmed by nature…not the intelligence of Creator Force, but of man who is mimicking god. In a plastic society, the food will be plastic. the people will be plastic. The music will be cookie-cutter plastic. There is plastic in the ocean. There is plastic in our veins. We must refrain from literally becoming plastic. We must opt out of the artificial society being created for us. Holistic doctors are dying by the multitudes. So, this shouldn't be a joke to you. What we're supposed to do is form a universal front against poison, plastic, putrefied, people & principles. Purge & Purify.

HEALING THE COMMUNITY OF SELF

Erica Ford, Activist/Life Coach

My name is Erica Ford, I grew up in Jamaica, Queens, in the eighties and I want to talk about why it is important that we have more spiritually connected people running the systems that guide/impact our lives. Growing up I was surrounded by deaths caused by gun violence and it became "normal." The kids who I grew up and played with in the sand box, were dying. They were going to jail for football numbers. My girlfriends were mad that their men, mates, husbands, children's fathers, were leaving them alone. It seemed they would never understand the impact such trauma would play in their life, and their children's lives. Their children became stuck! and angry! These things made me dedicate my life to doing work of service, for other than myself.

Far too many of us, don't take the time to stop and breathe. We community-based organization volunteers and CEO's, anti-violence workers, health workers, police officers, yoga instructors, professors/teachers, correction, parole, probation officers, parents, grand-parents, go on and on and we don't find out if everything we believe in and say every day is good for our life.

That was me.

I was the community organizer, the person working with young people. Piled up in my car, we went around organizing and protesting and setting up community events. But, I was disconnected. I was arrogant and didn't have compassion; I was being too judgmental. I called myself the answer to other people's lives and I wasn't living. I would get awarded because I had the biggest mouth, and everyone believed in the mask that I wore every day. At some point I had to stop. Of course, that wasn't until after many people complained, "Yo, E, I ain't trying to be around you no more…you are depleting me, Sis…Not what I signed up for." I kept on going; blaming this one and that one. Finally, when everyone said the same thing, *I* had to say, "Yo, E, you've gotta look at how you're making people feel and the environment that you've created." At that point I wasn't helping people; I wasn't helping myself. I wasn't connected with compassion to the students, nor to the people who had compassion for me and helped me to be who I was at that time....I wasn't even connected to my mother. I had to stop and look inside to see what I was doing to people.

For some reason, I thought, "Can't nobody tell me *nothin'*." In my head I was a whole lot of things that, in reality,

I wasn't even close to being. Many of us go through life with self-centered thinking. So much anger, so much jealousy, so much judgement, so much comparison. This is suffering. Often, we look at suffering as when somebody gets into an accident and they're in pain and suffering...no. *The way we live day in and day out is suffering.* Although I had great ideas and intentions, some of them could never become realities because I would kick down the door and knock out everyone on the other side who had the ability to help me implement what I was trying to do. I had to find new ways to communicate so that the results could give life to the fulfillment of my vision and my mission. The one thing I knew was, if you don't your own vision and mission, you become somebody else's vision and mission. You become angry at your life, because your life has become *somebody else's* life.

Every time I would get pulled over by the police, and they would come to me with "ish", I would give them "double-ish." Since they had the badge, I would end up with a ticket, or worse, locked up. One time, when I got pulled over, I thought, "You know what, Erica? I'm not getting arrested today." I knew the officer's relationship to me was not going to change, *I* had to change my response, so I would not end up in a cell or getting a ticket I couldn't afford. That didn't mean I was getting soft or derailed from my mission of ending police brutality or ending injustices. But, I had to make moves from a place of awareness and focus. I had to ask myself, "How do you want to live?" I started to slow down and just meditate. I listened to what my mother and Viola Plummer, (one of the great community leaders) told me, "Nature is unforgiving to those who don't pay attention to details." My moms would always say, "Don't cost you nothing to be nice, Erica. You have to watch how you talk to people."

Little by little, I made shifts and became more aware of the environment I was creating for other people. Working with my sister Kheperah from Gemnasium, we would challenge old ideas and habits, day in and day out. Yes, even when one of my former employees smacked me in the street, I chose to live by our mantra. I said, "If I'm the peacemaker, but I resolve this conflict with violence, then how do I teach a young person tomorrow that they must choose a way other than violence to resolve conflicts? It was going to be a hard battle. By using Deepak's book, **The Seven Spiritual Laws of Success**, I let the law of karma fall into place; and I let it go. I also aggressively changed my eating habits. Then, a lady named Tara Sheahan sent me to One World Academy, a wisdom school in India, where I went through a spiritual transformation that allowed me to create a path. I went from being an "angry peacemaker" to becoming a true-heart leader. It was like stepping into the world with new eyes. As I shifted from a self-centered to a more compassionate person, doors opened. Blessings and creativity came.

So, before my mother made her transition, we were able to connect. I have been able to get my colleagues and officials to listen to the need to implement a Violence Intervention and Prevention System, which is now helping at-risk youth to make peace a lifestyle, despite living in communities riddled with violence. This institutionalized program is part of the Mayor's Crisis Management system. We were able to get our NY Peace Week to become an official part of the NYC calendar. Through the dedicated work of my team of Violence Intervention and Prevention workers, we've successfully had over 530 days of no shootings and killings of young men and women in our target area of South Jamaica, Queens. Staff retention rate and morale are both very high. Our Urban Yogis teach young people the tools of meditation and yoga as processes toward changing negative norms in the middle of the housing development. Collectively, we are shifting the culture of violence in our communities.

No one has all the answers but together we can solve problems. THINKING BEFORE ACTING IS THE KEY TO SURVIVAL. YOU CAN'T FIGHT BACK FROM THE GRAVEYARD! You will face many challenges, but NEVER lose sight of your goals! The World is Yours! Prepare to Take Lead! Please, consider the following WISDOM NUGGETS, KEYS TO SUCCESS FOR YOUR SPIRIT:

FOCUS

F. **Fix your eyes on your goals.** Know what your short-term and long-term goal are and stay on track. Don't allow yourself to misdirected into non-productive and costly activities!

O. **Ownership is the key to commitment.** Take Charge of Your Destiny! No one else can do it for you… Make It Yours!!

C. **Courage takes practice.** Know your limits. **We all get 'knocked down'** but it's the Real Champs who Get Up and finish making their Dreams a Reality!

U. **Unwavering** is knowing where you are going, then to **focus your efforts and your energy** in that direction. You have the power to 'knock down' all barriers that attempt to stop you from achieving your goals. Believe It & Do It!

S. **Success is Yours!** Don't be willing to accept anything less than Excellence. Eliminate Negative Thinking and Negative Energy. A Genius lies inside of you, let him/her out! The day you give in, is the day you lose! Every day we are Challenged to go Further than we ever knew we could go. Sometimes we ask ourselves: How are we going to make it when everything is going wrong? That is the time to go inside and stop feeding of the *outside negative energy*…we must always Believe in our Ideas and Visions and Work Smart and Hard to Make them a Reality!!!

Do Not Allow to Upset your Path,

Those Who Don't Believe in You or Even Themselves!!!

Take Time to Thank Those

Who Give You the Energy to Continue!!!

You will be faced with many tests in LIFE,

the Power Lies within You to Pass.

Victory is Waiting for You!!!

STAY FOCUSED!!!

A LIFE OF PEACE WELLNESS EDUCATION INSTITUTE

CONSISTENCY

Akua & Chenu Gray, Naturopaths

WHAT WOULD YOU DO TO HEAL THE PLANET? Energy is the force of the universe that is the power behind manifestation. Everything manifested in the present moment is simply an arrangement of compacted energy that has bonded on various vibration levels to create reality for purposeful existence for an appointed time. The realization of this energy connection and life cycle is called oneness in metaphysical terminology. To achieve the realization of this concept of energy and oneness on a personal level would render an individual capable of achieving self-mastery. It is only through progressive levels of self-mastery and environmental awareness can individuals truly change anything.

HOW MUCH CAN ONE PERSON DO IF WE'RE TALKING ABOUT HEALING THE PLANET?

Imagine throwing a stone in the center of a pond, watching the ripples grow and grow all the way out to the water's edge. As you visualize this scenario, pay attention to one very important detail. The ripples remain connected as they grow and become larger. Understanding this connection is crucial. As energy beings, we are all connected and the foundation for permanent change to heal the planet must include living as if this inner connection is our only life line. The food we eat. The water we drink. The way we use nature. All of these areas that sustains life must have protocols and standards that each individual who is aware of their perfect state of energy existence can ripple out to the world around them to facilitate the necessary actions needed to heal their part of the planet.

We all agree that the world needs to change in order to heal the planet and we also agree that it can only be done by consistent collective efforts. It only takes a critical mass of people to make a crucial change in any government, city or community. Identifying, training and mobilizing a mass of individuals with knowledge, skills and the ability to be present to do the work that is needed has always been a challenging task for organizers of progressive and radical change.

The components of how life is structured among the people on this planet are so vast. To heal the planet with this simple fact in mind automatically takes my mind to the logistics of such a task. It has been stated by many elders and wise ancestors that to effectively make changes in human relations that are permanent and lasting, that change has to begin at home. Therefore, the work of the individual and small group to heal the planet must be like the ripples from the impact of a stone tossed to the center of a pond. Unfortunately, the historical problem is not the effort, there are many people who want to do good, but it is the consistency of in the effort that often falls by the way side leaving the door open for further degradation of the earth and the people.

Now the question becomes how do we educate the individual on the crucial concept of oneness and energy awareness for self-mastery and then provide the training necessary for each one to galvanize a critical mass and nurture a committed group to maintain consistency to heal a planet with 7.6 billion people across 197 million square miles of land mass?

The dynamics of nature is harmony, structure and consistency, and people being products of nature would find the natural progression of the following three platforms for healing the world would create lasting change for the entirety of human existence. It worked for ancient Kmt and it can work for us.

1. Establish Temples of Enlightenment for the Education of Seekers
    - The earth exists in a universe that is sustained by balanced energy. Since civilizations emerged they have been subject to this dominate force dictated by the need for energy to arrange itself for manifestation. There has always been good and bad. Manifestations of the bad is what raises the alarm for every generation since ancient Kemetic times to rise up and project the balancing energy of good to maintain survival. Through the thousands of years of the civilized presence of people, we have always established schools, temples and training facilities to educate people based on visions of progress and the needs of the people.
    - With the vision to Heal the Planet in the forefront of so many world healers, the first line of accomplishing the task is to set up temples of enlightenment and schools of thought in as many segments of the world where they do not presently exist. Every community in the world has a progressive thinker that wants to make changes for their people. If they have a place to come to that teaches self-mastery first which offers

a program that involves a commitment of at least five years of working dysfunctional societal programming out of the mind, body, emotions and spirit.

- For those areas of the world that already have temples in alignment with the principles of care for the earth and offering help to the suffering through enlightenment and value exchange principles, there should be a collective effort to provide additional support to these facilities to expand their current work. Spiritual development is the foundation to mental, emotional and physical balance. Only healed people can heal people.

2. Mobilize and Further Educate Critical Masses in the Areas of Life Essentials

- There are those whose purpose in life is to work the land and provide its inhabitants with the body nourishments that fills the belly as well as the mind. These are the willing workers that know the importance of clean water sources and an adequate food supply for every family on the planet. In naturopathy, the goal of perfecting health is through prevention and creating a balanced life by using what nature has provided to us to live and live well. These same goals can be applied to healing the planet as well. Where there is a need in a community or part of the world, those who have dedicated themselves and completed the five-year self-mastery component is then given a ten-year assignment to work in a specialized area of community development and care. These specialized areas could include water supply creation and management, organic farming, reforestation, environmental cleanup, community business development, primary, secondary and advanced academics, spiritual ascension programs, transportation network development, housing development, maternal care, health and wellness services, and so forth.

- Again, there are already components of these specialized areas in existence throughout the globe, therefore in certain communities there is no need to reinvent the wheel. It would then be necessary for these organizations and facilities of structure ten-year work programs to accommodate incoming workers to add to the works in progress.

3. Create Systems to Maintain Consistency for Infinite Generations
    - After the establishment of the community works is well underway, it is time for the next phase of creating a system of consistency. Those enlightened beings who complete the ten years of developing or working in the critical mass setting, must then recruit five members from the community and begin training them to further expand the works, either by building on new ideas for current projects or branching out to develop new community projects in other areas that are in need. This small team will work together for five-years with very distinct goals geared toward longevity. The creation of cycles of wellness endeavor is crucial. This work is not for the fainthearted. Over the many year of being wellness providers to the African Diaspora, this final note of consistency has been the hardest to achieve because even for healers, "life happens" and they get derailed and eventually fall off in their healing work. Therefore, this final stage is the one that needs the greatest promotion because this is the work that will carry our efforts into the generations to come.
    - Even better than the New World Order, which was designed by Western World governments to control the economic and political fate of the world through capitalistic ventures to increase the wealth of the super-rich, we must create the New World Legacy where life is lived in alignment nature (Ntr) by the masses of the people whose eyes, mind and spirit have been opened to the power of oneness that moves the individual to self-mastery. These people will then be able to consistently dedicate themselves to healing the planet through education and build critical masses to embody the work and create consistency that will last through eternity.

TAKE CARE OF YOURSELF

King Simon, Promotional Coach

From a promoter's point of view, we are all salespersons trying to get that big sale that will take us over the humps and bumps of life. I wrote this material to provide some form of help to those who may need the information to start making the necessary plans to become successful in their business; and for everyday planning. I am rich in spirit and full of energy when it comes to the things I love to do. Some may say and have said, that I'm selfish, but is that really a bad thing? To accomplish certain goals, one sometimes has to be selfish (or self-absorbed) in order to stay focused to see the larger picture or the grand scheme of things. In that case, all successful people have some selfishness in them and usually after they have completed what they had to do, they start to share the wealth with other people or energies.

Technology has taken front stage in this age of communication and in the promotional world. If used properly it can be quite effective. Imagine a world without it, now. At one time it would take weeks for news about a war across the ocean to get here and reach the ears and eyes of the masses. Due to technology, it takes minutes. Some may say the world has become smaller through this new-age medium, which might be true in some sense, but this is what a lot of us have been waiting for. Back in the day, we used to watch cartoons such as the Jetsons or sci-fi movies and wonder whether technology would take over. Now it has! I can tell you one thing, we definitely have become inorganic in our way of relating and communicating with each other. Instead of talking, we would rather text. Instead of writing letters, we would rather send an email.

In my conclusion, there is really no conclusion because knowledge is infinite, and the dynamics of information and promotions are changing rapidly with this new age. People nowadays are online holding complete *classes, webinars, lectures, debates, sermons, wars, rallies, playing games, concerts, graduations,* just to name a few. There are online schools and people receiving degrees from an online virtual teacher. Go figure! That is why I always tell young promoters that they have everything at their fingertips, unlike what I and many older promoters had to work with. Back in the day, we had to stick to the basics. Harold Dow (of the Dow Twins) said to me, *"For an older guy—I love social media (Facebook, Twitter, etc.), because it helps me to keep up with small things like birthdays, special events and occasions."*

Street promotions, in certain neighborhoods, have become *'a dog eat dog'* business. If one learns to be creative and reinvent themselves, to stay on top of the game, success is limitless! Remember, with success comes 'haters and enemies.' To quote from the movie **American Gangster**, the Italian mobster says to Denzel Washington's character (Frank Lucas), *"You can be successful and have enemies—huh—and we can be unsuccessful too, and we can have friends. That's the choice we make."* I enjoyed that movie and that part always sticks out in my mind. *What choices will YOU make?*

Note: A very important topic that I am going to touch on briefly is the maintenance of your health. Health should be the most vital part of developing any business, talent or skill. Plainly stated, *"If you are unable to take care of yourself then you will not be able to take care of your business and your family."* Your dreams, goals, and visions all depend on how well you've kept your Mind (Body & Soul) intact. Once the mind is healthy, then the rest will follow. *We all have a choice, and we all must learn how to make the right choices in life.* Sometimes we forget that our bodies (our temples) are like organic machines; they must be taken care of with caution. It is funny but sad to see people carefully maintain their houses and vehicles more than they do their own health. Please, learn about your body as much as you can. Study yourself and do not take your health for granted. Again, I can't say it enough. Find what it is that you love to do and expand on it. If you're a journalist, write everything down and learn the business of journalism. If you're a singer, sing and study other genres of music and don't forget to learn the business. If you're an artist, draw or paint everything you find interesting or do it from your imagination. In time it will all be worth it.

Napoleon Hill wrote in his book, **The Law of Success,** "Time is a master worker that heals the wounds of temporary defeat and equalizes the inequalities and rights the wrongs of the world. There is nothing "Impossible" with time." Don't waste it!

There are 3 types of people: *Those who make things happen, those who watch things happen and those who wonder what the hell happened?* Which one are you?

Remember, No Promotion Is Bad Promotion…Just Spell My Name Right!

Thank you for your support, whoever and wherever you are!

Love & Respect from K.S.P. (King Simon Production)

PLANET HEAL: SOCIAL HEALING

Onaje Muid, Human Rights Activist

Planet Heal, the title of this series, can be treated as a question: can the planet be healed? If so, what is wrong with it that needs to be healed? Then, what can be done about it? To face these questions a few basic philosophical concepts are required. We must first ask ourselves what universe we are based in, that is to say, what understanding are we approaching this task from and what divine laws are we recognizing and choosing to adhere to? This offering will be approached from that of mending the sacred hoop through the establishment of a National Maat Social Recovery Program, called Whm Msw. (A Kemet-Egyptian- reference, so beautifully taught by Brother Uhuru Hotep and Sister Talibah Baker Hotep in the 72 Concepts to Liberate the African Mind.)

Mending the sacred hoop is a metaphor that begins with the affirmation that the universe is one; uni = one, verse = word; universe = one word, or one sound, or one vibration. Everything at its core is this one word, this one sound, this one vibration, this one reality. All life is connected to this oneness, consciously knowing it or not. The scared hoop is all the systems that hold creation in place. Everything exists in its own sacred hoop; the maintenance of the hoop is in the hands of the beholder. The grace of the universe is such that many, many imbalances can occur, over stretches of time, that even with diametric manifestations, which persist from many infractions, life goes on, to a point! Once that point is reached, that which we call death removes that which has either served its purpose or has reached a point of opposition that life is no longer supported. Is the planet at that line? No one would say that it is, I suppose. People would say that the stock pile of nuclear arms could approach it. Yet, the horrific truth is we are at a point of annihilating ourselves, quite different from destroying the planet.

If this is so, the question is what are we to do to heal ourselves? The planet is not the problem. We are the problem on the earth! We have fallen out of balance, for a multitude of reasons. The path for that re-union, is Maat: order, balance, harmony, justice, reciprocity and truth. The program to re-establish Maat is Whm Msw.

We begin with the earth. What earth? Our earth self. This body we inhibit is earth, is it not? This physical temple is made of what, the earth. So now, we move the lens a little from planet heal to earth heal! WE are spiritual beings having a human earth-walking experience. With this shift, from planet heal to earth heal, the earth we speak of is the people. How then do we heal the people before we destroy ourselves? More precisely, how do we heal the social systems of the earth people?

In a cursory treatment we will look at the world dominate system of racism as a system that must be healed. The frame being used to address this question is that one presented by Neely Fuller, Jr. He states, "If you do not understand white supremacy (racism) everything else that you understand, will only confuse you." His student and revered theorist herself, Ancestor Frances Cress Welsing, MD asserts that the oppressed live as survival units not families. For families to exist they must be steeped in their culture and have control over their land. The appearance of progress from slavery falsely suggests that we have moved far for the time when marriages were deemed illegal to now when we can go to the justice of the peace and get legally married; that we can now claim ourselves as families. Only when the social health of the planet comes into full being can we say we are family, because for that to happen, Maat must be present. The healing of social systems begins with healing the survival units so that they can become closer and closer to what a family is—a self- generating system supporting the larger system of freedom and spirit, in a sacred hoop that is in harmony with the universal, and peace abounds.

Using the Nine Fuller (Plus One-Land) People Areas of Compensated Activities we must understand and implement the following to reach Maat.

*Land/Environment/Earth (Context): We have been sent to earth as caretakers of the Land. Our sacred inheritance provides the basic resources for all life and is protected in a manner to transfer this inheritance for seven generations and we, accept the guardianship of the land, of the water, of the air and of the sky. We, the spiritual beings having a human experience, we are the land/earth walking beings, acknowledging that all we are on the physical plane is that which the land is, terra firma, we are. This requires an utmost respect for Mother Earth and respect for the earth that covers our souls and should be treated with divine care.

1. Religion/Spirituality: We adhere to and are experiencing the fulfillment spiritual laws of the universe by acknowledging the divinity in ones' self and others for the purpose order, balance, harmony, justice, truth and reciprocity, otherwise known as the principles of Maat. Each survival unit must have some spiritual grounding. The dogma of many religions claims itself as the supreme, and only that religion

should be followed. This means that those persons blinded by such restrictions will not move out of that restrain and therefore we cannot expect all of earth beings to see nor acknowledge the universe, the one word of divine harmony. We should not be disheartened to the point where it stops the natural uniting of beings wanting peace. This is so because all dying systems must atrophy, give off that which is not supportive of the wholeness of life. The choice to live in the past or move forward is each person's choice. Our compassion must be for the world that is coming and purify ourselves for the vibration that will support it.

2. Politics: We realize and use power naturally in a manner that purposefully acquires the means for the people to secure the resources for our survival and to fulfill the highest aspiration of the survival unit (moving to become a family), community and nation. The re-education of the people must be rooted in human rights. The absence of consent is violence. The highest form of social living is consensus.

3. Law: We assert that law can only come from informed consent, to establish order and justice by raising community and family as more important than any individual and that all individuals, families and communities must act in agreement with communal aims for optimal well-being. We join with the human rights cities movement to organize on a local level and bring international covenants into play, starting with the Convention on the Child.

4. Labor: All persons, families and communities are to provide and invest in intellectual, physical, labor for the benefit of community well-being. Here, the goal of self-reliance for conscious people is a must. We must create institutions which can support our children, so they don't want to or choose to give themselves to the machine.

5. Education: We use education to produce systems of mental, physical, spiritual and social development to establish higher levels of order, balance, harmony, justice, truth and reciprocity. It isn't easy, but we must create our own education systems. Each survival unit must have an education agenda that they create for their unit. As we share these education plans, we are moving toward liberation.

6. Economics: All that we have on the planet from the earth is to be shared in a manner to support life for all persons, families and communities. Education must be tied to self-reliance economics.

7. Sex: Sex is considered a medium of communication for love, affection, companionship, affirmation of bonding and release of stress and isolation. Sex is a by-product and benefit of healthy relationships for the continuation of our people and community; not as a recreational

enjoyment for fun exclusively.
8. Entertainment: Our cultural entertainment is the assortment of arts, including music, visual arts, media arts, dance, theater and relaxation that uplifts the spirit, soothes and invigorates the mind, and comforts, as well, as strengthens the body.
9. War/Counter-War: We assert the right to self- defense for the purpose: survival of all peoples. We will always seek to create consent, relationship, empowerment and abundance first.

Planet Heal is a way to be directed to heal ourselves, our earth selves. How? By mending the sacred hoop in its many wo/manifestations: the individual; the survival unit (striving to become a family); the extended unit (extended family); the neighborhood, the community; the nation; the multi-nations; the world.

Let us affirm, "I am healing, you are healing, we are healing, our world is healing."

WHOLISTIC ACADEMICS 101: "WHOLISTIC HEALTH"

Winston "Kokayi" Patterson, Acupuncturist/ Educator

A COMMUNITY PERSPECTIVE
USING WHOLISITIC HEALTH PRINCIPLES
AS A FOUNDATION FOR SPIRIT, MIND, BODY, AND
ENVIRONMENT/COMMUNITY HEALING AND PUBLIC HEALTH

Question: What is wholistic health = spirit, mind, body, environment (community) approach? The word holistic comes from the word holism which is said to emphasize the importance of the entire whole and the interdependence of each section. The sections that function as fundamental and determining sections of existence also have an existence and being that is much more than the total of all the parts (creator induced). Therefore, wholistic health says that people are not just flesh, bones and blood, but a gathering of energies, electrical impulses, mind material, and so many other forces and processes, all of which come together to bring about dis-harmony(disease) or wellness (always loving one's self).

Designed & Developed
By Winston "Kokayi" Patterson
Healthy Wholistic Lifestyle Educator

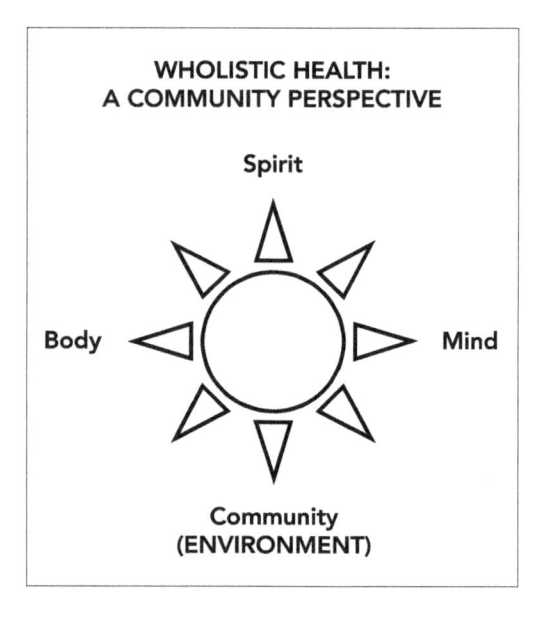

**WHOLISTIC HEALTH:
A COMMUNITY PERSPECTIVE**

Spirit

Body — Mind

Community
(ENVIRONMENT)

WHOLISTIC VIEW

- WHOLISTIC = a clear definition
- WHOLISTIC = (holi), holy, spiritual, creator induced, healing
- WHOLISTIC = (whol) whole. all parts, the whole thing, inclusive of all things associated with us(universe)

In contrast to conventional modern medicine, the wholistic perspective deals with processes of health separate from dis-harmony (dis-ease). In wholistic medicine the goal is to strengthen and maintain healthy systems (spirit, mind, body, environment/community) in totality, so one can be able to freely participate (live/experience) in the environment and prevent any crisis (illness/imbalance) from taking place. This is the self-empowerment that comes with the wholistic approach!

The concept of medical treatment consisting of specialists, impersonal facilities, and new-age treatments has been under attack for over half a century. There is a growing unease that is fueled by common sense (instinct) and reason, that this current healthcare system is missing the mark and that treatments often do more harm (continued suffering, side effects/sometimes death) rather than resolve the illness, and most patients don't fully recover to their vibrant selves.

The manner in which a society deals with these issues is directly connected to its vision (philosophy) of life (living). Wholistic processes have predated the modern scientific medical system by thousands of years, back to the beginnings of man, and have been *pro-productive* through the test of time. These processes have resolved unmentioned numbers of health problems and as a side effect have returned people to radiant health and happiness. Wholistic health goes beyond just working on the imbalance (illness).

From the wholistic perspective, medicine becomes more educational than treatment, and the doctors would be more educators, who would direct their clients towards maintaining the wholistic principles of life and wellness. It is based on an innate fact that our knowledge about health principles, daily food and drink intake, lifestyle, community (environment) and your thoughts and emotions, all contribute to your overall health. Valid research and common sense have shown that our health conditions are directly related to our decisions we make daily pertaining to our diet, exercise, substance abuse, sugar addiction, relationships, where you live, family and outside environment. Several other conditions are looked at as major contributors, not only to one's state of health and life, but to one's own quality of how their life is lived. Wholistic healing is connected to the entire social (community) and natural environment where we manifest and unfold!

REMEMBER, "TO HEAL A PEOPLE IS TO HELP HEAL A WORLD" kp STRAIGHT AHEAD!

DOCTAH WINSTON "KOKAYI" PATTERSON

(EXCERPT FROM SANKOFA-EL'S BOOK SACRED MAN)

D.A.D: DEDICATED AND DISTINGUISHED

Aundrieux "Khonsu" Sankofa-El, Manhood Coach

There is a difference between a father and a dad. Any man can father children; it takes a moment of passion and nine months of biology! A dad on the other hand, is dedicated in his distinguished primordial role for the long run; committed to nurturing his child from birth. The acronym for 'Dedicated and Distinguished' is, D.A.D. A dad learns the skills he needs to feed, bathe, clothe, stimulate and educate his children. He does his part in the home alongside mum (mom), or independently.

What does it take for a father to become a D.A.D.? There is no manual with all the answers, but much can be gained by being innovative and serving as a role model for your children to become a positive contribution to humanity. For one day your child may have children and will probably raise them based on the values you have instilled. When does being a D.A.D. begin? Well, it begins in the womb during pregnancy. Furthermore, it should begin with conscious conception; concentrated thought on you and your partner's synchronized intention to create a new soul.

Pregnancy can be beautiful moments to cherish or a time of challenge with hormones and emotional highs and lows from both parents. Holistically speaking, when the mother is pregnant, the father is 'spiritually pregnant'. Mum's super-enhanced senses can even pick up the father's mind state. From the womb, the child is emotionally attached to the father and will recognize the unique tone mum uses to communicate with the father. Therefore, be attentive and attuned to your partner's physical and emotional needs. Nine months of growing and forming a new soul is no easy task, incomprehensible to men. It's of upmost importance not to mess up with the honor and care of your mate. Emotional intelligence is key to creating a stable environment for mother and baby.

It may be wise to seek council from elder men who have the experience, and a failure to do so may be a great price to pay in your future relationship. Statistics to be aware of are:

- Half of all family breakdowns take place during the first two years of a child being born.
- Amongst parents who remain intact, 93 per cent are married.

(from The Marriage Foundation, 2013)

1. BE THERE

Be there during pregnancy. Escort your mate on errands and ease her increasingly heavy load. Prepare nutritious meals; be ready for unusual cravings. Hone-in on her positive and negative feelings with emotional intelligence and empathy. Tune into whatever may surface. Consult with your mate about home birth. The old-fashioned stereotype of father pacing outside the delivery room while mum goes through labor is outdated. Be proactive in birth planning and present in delivery. For centuries mothers birthed at home. Babies aren't naturally supposed to be born under fluorescent lights. Electronic technology and the medicalization of birth are modern protocol.

Natural birth should take place in comfort and safety, ideally at home. Know your options. Your home is a valid setting. A home birth can be arranged by your doctor, who is legally obligated to accommodate your choice, including providing you with a midwife who can facilitate a safe home birth. An alternative can be a birth centre which includes provision of a warm birth pool and is an environment more conducive than a hospital. Another option is hiring a Doula: a professional birth partner who supports mother, child and you throughout the pregnancy, at birth and beyond.

2. PROVIDE AND PREPARE

Organize a budget and shopping schedules in advance. Set aside for some nesting therapy for mother so she is settled in knowing all is prepared before labor.

3. PROTECT

Take the role of defender, protecting mother mentally physically and emotionally from any stress. Obstacles that may penetrate the well-being of mother and child should be buffered. Your goal for your future family is optimum comfort. The statistics for children of African origin raised in separated one-parent households are not healthy. We must reverse the negative unpreparedness regarding the way dads bring children into the world. May these words serve to contribute to consciousness for a better future for the black family.

4. HOLISTIC CHILDREN

A sacred man knows that the upbringing of his children isn't the sole role of mother. It is perhaps easier to feed your children food out of a packet, but any food processed in a factory is devitalized to some extent. Manufactured foods are usually treated with preservatives for long shelf life and/or flavor enhancers. It is challenging to steer children away from junk food, but your role is to be aware of keeping your children nourished naturally.

5. SPIRITUAL CHILD

Teaching your children spirituality can never begin early enough. Whatever your religious belief, a solid foundation in the acknowledgment of a higher force may help your children overcome obstacles in later life and keep them on a righteous path. Rituals and family traditions connect the family and set the foundations for future value systems. There is a wise saying, 'The family who prays together, stays together'. Simple family traditions like praying before you eat ground your children in spirituality.

Meditation, an alternative form of spirituality is not bound to a religion. Learning to still the mind, especially in this fast-paced technological world, can and should be taught to your children. A good method for teaching children meditation is have them be still for the number of minutes matching their age; for example, a five-year-old would practice meditation for five minutes, maybe in the morning and evening. It is said prayer is having a conversation with God, and meditation is listening for the answers. A holistic dad who cultivates prayer and meditation in his children knows applying the two equates to spiritual balance for your child's future life.

6. THE VIRTUOUS CHILD

It's easy to overindulge your children due to circumstances such as being a "weekend dad", or one who doesn't want their children to suffer the poverty they did growing up. It takes discipline not to over-spoil children by attempting to compensate for such issues. Children who get everything they want, do not learn that they will not always be ABLED to get what they want instantly. In this age of instant gratification such entitlement can have an adverse effect on a child. Spoiling a child may reduce their self-reliance and ability to overcome challenges. It is important that they learn that the protection of their parents in childhood isn't how life continues into adulthood.

Instill in your children the rules of earning from virtuous work. Earning material rewards at an early age builds character and ambition. Values such as working hard for the things they want, distinguishes sacrificing in the present for the things they want later.

7. VIRTUAL REALITY KIDS

T.V. and digital games can be a fun way to unwind but should be used moderately and filtered by the parent. These forms of recreation are passive activities that can overstimulate a young mind, but hamper brain work. Children of African origin interact with such technology much more than children of other cultures. Statistics show constant technological stimulation is having an adverse effect on the social skills and the attention spans of a generation of black children. Traditional games, such as chess and Scrabble can easily be incorporated alongside technology for balanced development. Traveling, as well as attending theatre events is excellent for cultivating a broadened view of the world. Free activities, such as museum trips can be organized with a little online research. Engage children with creative arts projects. Schedule nature trips to city parks or to the countryside.

Team sports build a child's character, health and social skills. Television, video games and internet in the bedroom should be avoided, as it is harder to monitor children being prematurely exposed to sex and violence. Statistics show that toddlers who watch more than two hours of T.V. a day can develop Attention Deficit Hyperactivity Disorder (ADHD). The 3D hyper-reality of modern digital devices can become very addictive. They tend to make slower more focus-orientated activities in the real world seem mundane and boring by comparison. A child addicted to technology can show signs of arrested development in social skills and impatience with doing slower tasks.

Look out for signs of a child wanting to engage only on their phone instead of interacting in social environments and oral tasks that don't involve technology. A sacred man is aware of the benefits of technology, yet aware of the virtues of low-technology, and having his children connect with nature. He develops his parenting skills to holistically raise socially aware, emotionally intelligent, cultured and loving children.

NATURAL TIME & GLOBAL PEACE THROUGH CULTURE

Wanique Khemi-Tehuti Shabazz, Scholar/Ambassador

In order to enter the 13-moon path which is a world of waves-pells, pulsars and overtone pulsars, of harmonics, chromatics, and galactic spins huemans must change their perception and projections of how to "tell time". The 13-moon calendar is the day-by-day approach to learning and living the different holon simultaneities of the fourth dimension. Following the 13 moons of the indigenous, every hueman has the opportunity of becoming a planetary kin.

Sounds cryptic? Most of us cannot even fathom a different way of perceiving time or our connection to Mother Earth and her natural cycles. The activation of the 13 moons of 28 days is a chance to experience the power of the newly evolving consciousness, it is what can be described as a 'pulsing' or 'activation'. This activation allows the individual a brief glimpse into the coming spiritual transformation. This glimpse also allows for the transformation of various concepts, because it deeply affects each incarnated entity more commonly known as "human" in a most profound way.

Each person will sense that their changes are part of a greater hueman and planetary transformation. Learning to navigate with a GPS© (Galactic Purpose Signature) is a major highlight for the synergizing of their 5 bodies-yes, **5** bodies. Having an awareness that we have more than just one sentient body or avatar allows for a more insipid healing that is not just limited or relegated to the physical 3rd-dimensional aspect of existence-one we use to merely navigate on this 3rd dimensional plane of mundanity. We are edified with this reminder as 4th-dimensional intangible mental, emotional, spiritual and soul bodies which are exacted and animated by the barometer of the Physical body.

We have coined these intangible "bodies" with the acronym "m.e.s.s." It is indeed a planetary "mess" where our physical incarnation in this matrix of "3d" (disease, deterioration, death) currently finds itself. Once one experiences this glitch in the matrix it becomes almost impossible for them to ever be the same again and thereby enter into the realm of immortality. One of the first things that occur is that our physical-mental emotional and spiritual changes become vastly accelerated. A new collection of spiritual realities began to set in. Sentient beings of such a high level of spirituality in time travel are able to embrace these newly formed realities and don't have to "dodge bullets" or fear alphabet "agents" in the 12:60 (12 months 60 minutes) matrix.

As this process of transformation increases, they also develop a great need to share this experience and to learn the meaning of the changes now happening around us. They also begin to observe the behavior and traits of nature's species who appear to have no natural lifespan cycles that one can trace nor identify. As they live by and obey the "law of time" and the harmonics that govern it and thereby gain immortality-yes eternal life on this 3rd dimension, not only through generational offspring or inanimate monuments or mission legacies…if this be not true show evidence of the cemeteries or final resting places for squirrels, birds, lizards, turtles etc. other than the unnatural road-kill by encounters with callous humans in their overweight metal machines *aka* motor vehicles. This is not to negate the predator-prey arrangements that some species are programmed to in order to maintain an ecological balance of populations in geographical locations around the globe.

Returning our focus to the natural cycles of Time through the "Dream Spell" count of 13 Moons-28 days helps to remove the belief system (bs) of the 12:60 mental field which has created an artificial, yet totally illusory, mental shield around the planet. The rigidity of this bs is all that keeps humanity not only from realizing that the chronosphere exists but also from receiving the enormous benefits of its presence. In our dissemination of 13 moons and 28 days, we are able to show that the 12:60 (12 months–60minutes) planetary shield is sustained by an artificial feedback loop which is a self-reinforcing system. At the root of this artificial 12:60 system is the belief that time is linear. To accept this belief is to surrender one's free will, for the belief that time is linear consigns the believer into a mental trap that says there is no choice but to go ahead according to the available options, which have all been conditioned by a linear development that can have only one foregone conclusion. In additional to contradicting the facts of the Earth's rotational momentum, spin and orbital circulation, the fatalism of the belief that time is linear generates a mental *disease* that afflicts all of humanity and the planet without exception.

Our mission is a jovial exploration into the unknown and yet it is very familiar territory as we are all innately born with cycles that are bio-rhythmic especially the bodies of the feminine species which has been suppressed and oppressed with the interruption of the Gregorian calendar of colonial imperial conquests.

There are no natural cycles corresponding to the number twelve. The natural human cycle is governed by the *female* biological rhythm of 28 days.

Thirteen of these 28-day cycles is 364 days, one day short of the 365-day orbital cycle of the Earth. The relation between the female biological rhythm and the cycles of the moon was known and understood by all of humanity prior to the rise of historic civilization in the Middle East, and memories of the thirteen- moon-28-day calendar persist to this day in many parts of the world

As previously stated our bodies were not created to keep up with such a crooked standard of time. Our bodies were created to live in sync with nature as multidimensional beings, resulting in a harmony and peace of mind, body, and environment. This has unlimited benefits for our health while offering a deeper understanding of the cosmos and our very unique and purposeful place in it. The lack thereof results in our bodies and minds exhibiting the stress of an inexplicable continuous discordance and unsustainable living."

Our consumption of Earth's produce will be within the natural harvesting cycles and will adhere to the adequate nutritional values without any artificial or genetic modifications. We will be in synch with all other species and have access to the immortal lifestyle they currently indulge and partake in for honoring the natural time cycles and not mechanical clock cycles. Changing calendars is the first and most important step to stop us from the path of destruction we are now following. There is no other solution.

Time is and always has been a mystery—the great mystery of our existence. It is inarguably the most familiar element of our lives. We are born into time, live in it, measure it, pass it, spend it, save it, waste it, die out of it, don't have enough of it, and talk and act as though we understand it. But if we step away from this "understanding" for a moment and ask the simplest questions about time, it quickly becomes apparent that we understand nothing at all.

We have crossed the threshold of the Mayan end cycle of "12-21-2012", with the added assurance that a return to 13 moons is a return to a harmony not experienced by humans since the inception of the Julian-Gregorian hijack of the indigenous natural cycles and ways of life.

According to Jose Arguelles—"...*the Gregorian calendar is a crooked standard of time. Every day that we use it, our bodies' natural biorhythms attempt to assimilate into it. This speeds up our biorhythms exponentially in an attempt to keep up with the machine...*"

Natural Time offers an alternative way of thinking and being. Once understood, it creates a more synchronistic or harmonic order within one's life and perception of life experiences. All healers are subject to the laws of what they convey—they come to us to show our fragilities and undisciplined proclivities and when they depart or ascend they remind us of our resistance to their lessons and the immutable laws of nature.

WEALTH IS OUR LEGACY, PASS IT ON!

Ellis Liddell, Wealth Manager

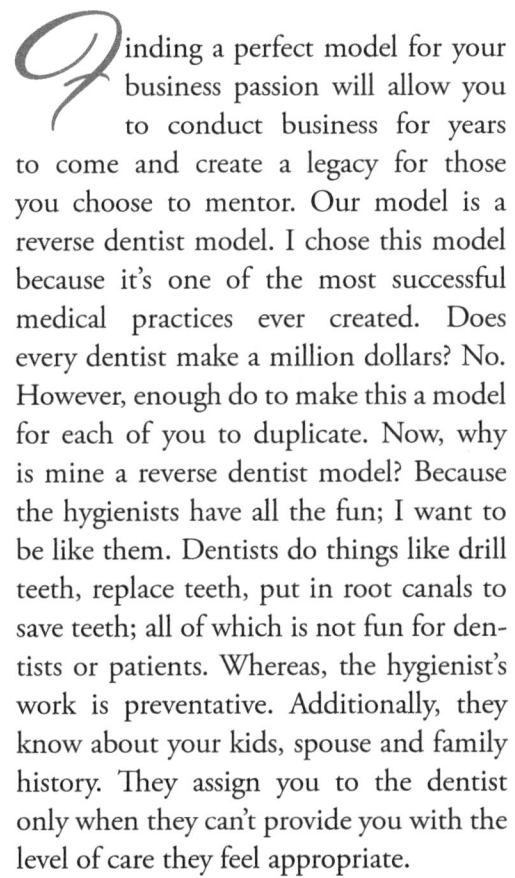

Finding a perfect model for your business passion will allow you to conduct business for years to come and create a legacy for those you choose to mentor. Our model is a reverse dentist model. I chose this model because it's one of the most successful medical practices ever created. Does every dentist make a million dollars? No. However, enough do to make this a model for each of you to duplicate. Now, why is mine a reverse dentist model? Because the hygienists have all the fun; I want to be like them. Dentists do things like drill teeth, replace teeth, put in root canals to save teeth; all of which is not fun for dentists or patients. Whereas, the hygienist's work is preventative. Additionally, they know about your kids, spouse and family history. They assign you to the dentist only when they can't provide you with the level of care they feel appropriate.

So, who really works for whom? If there's no dental referral the dentist sits around with not much to do. Now, some people are controlling individuals and will not allow the assistant to assist, creating a stressful environment in the work place. That's a formula for failure and lots of turn over (a little-known secret, a patient will follow a hygienist to their new location). My staff and I have been together for over 15 years. Each staff member has varying roles and the lines of our roles do cross each other to form a stronger bond. We respect each other's line but, we also have learned each other's job so when vacation, leave of absence or sick days occur we don't miss a beat.

I have also been the encourager, offered incentives, and yes, sometimes strong armed my staff into becoming the self-supportive team we need to take care of our clients while taking care of ourselves and our families. Our income has increased over the years, although there have been slow periods in which I debated on laying off members of our team. Like family, I've gone to the team discussed our challenges and we as a team tackle the problem head-on. You are not alone in your quest to heal the planet, we all have a role to serve, and we were born for times such as these.

HERE ARE A FEW THOUGHTS TO HELP WITH YOUR FINANCIAL QUEST (JOURNEY):

Saving: Do it often, choose a percentage to save (i.e. 10%)
Establish a checking and savings account: Checking to pay bills and saving to place your percentage in each month.

Introduce yourself to the branch manager at your bank: Form a relationship before you need them.
Purchase certificates of deposit (CD's) with 90-day staggered maturities: They don't pay much but you do this for the relationship.

Acquire enough savings to pay your recurring bills for 6 months: It can be deposited in your checking or savings account, 90-day CD's or a combination thereof.

Buy Real-estate: Consider your county's tax auction which allows you to pick a parcel of land, homes or apartment buildings for pennies on a dollar.

Invest in the various Equity Markets, DOW, NASDQ, S&P: Wealth creation has taken place in what is known as the stock market as well as financial ruin. Consult a trusted advisor before investing. Cars are pretty; however, they lose value the moment you drive them out of the dealership, and you have to plan for repair expenses.

Your primary residence—old way: "Buy more home than you can actually afford, and your salary will catch up with your purchase in the near future". Not necessarily the case in today's economic climate.

Plan for retirement: We are born, there's a dash (-) to represent all the things we will accomplish and do throughout our life and a date of expiration. If life was only that simple…it's not. At some point due to factors beyond your control or because you decide to you stop working. You will need assets to live on, as well as leave a financial legacy for those individuals or causes you want to support.

When asked the question: "What's the largest amount of money you have given away in your work lifetime?", most individuals answer the question incompletely. If throughout your lifetime you earn $1,000,000.00 and you have $200,000.00 net worth, then you have 20% of your earnings to show for it. Which means you gave away $800,000.00, hopefully, to people or causes that will be there for you in your time of need.

Money, resources, talents, gifts and the likes are values you can leverage to greater heights. It is our responsibility to take full advantage of every opportunity we are given to enhance our lives and the lives of those we can serve. Let's heal the planet one person at a time starting with ourselves.

HEALING YOUR MONEY MINDSET

Prophetess Afraka Sankofa, Financial Healer

So, the question asked to me by The Most Beautiful Spirit named Queen Afua, was, "What would you do to heal the planet?"

I felt blissed (full of joy) and honored, when Queen Afua, my wholistic mentor and spiritual health guide asked me to add my words on financial healing to this book, **Planet Heal**. I knew in that moment, that this was the Hand of The Most High Almighty Divine Creator moving and doing a great work in me to be of service to the Planet. Amun Rah. Twa Ntr.

Queen Afua asked me to answer the question from a Financial Healing perspective. I would like to start off by addressing what the Biblical Text says about financial healing and money and the mindsets around money and finance. I will also speak about how even the Biblical Text can be used as a guide, a flashlight in the dark so to speak to assist anyone on how to develop a healthy mindset on money.

My mantra is **"Basic Instructions To Begin Living On Earth."** I decided to really look at what the Bible had to say about Money. I discovered that Yeshua De Cristos, spoke over 2000 verses on money, more than he spoke on heaven, hell or faith. How Interesting, I thought. Well let's look at why Yeshua D. Cristos focused so much of his attention on Money.

In Ecclesiastes 10:19, it says, "A feast is made for laughter, and wine maketh merry: but money answereth all *things.*" So here is a Biblical verse that tells us that Money is the Answer to All Things, Not somethings, but All things. Yeshua D. Cristos was a mathematician and a scientist, he Innerstood that Money is multiplication, that is why he could raise 5 loaves and 2 fishes and multiplied them to an Infinite supply for a multitude.

In another verse of Scripture, 1 Timothy 6:10, it says, "For the love of money is the root of all evil: which while some coveted after, they have erred from the faith, and pierced themselves through with many sorrows." This verse, clear and distinct in its meaning specifically says, **"For the love of money…"** It **did not say** money is the root of all evil.

These two Biblical texts may seem conflicting in nature, but simply, they say, Money is something that helps you to live a life of service, to accomplish your goals and your success. However, *do not love* money to the point of creating an unhealthy mindset by worshiping and replacing (with money) The God within You, who has created you and given you life to live.

Let's talk about what money truly is. What is Money? Money is many things. First and foremost, "Money Is You." That's right, it is the Electromagnetic Currency that runs through your life blood. That gives you energy, so you can be the energetic transmitting utility to conduct business in the marketplace that you choose of your own freewill. Money is not the actual colored paper with a number on it. The paper is just a reflection of who you are and the level of energy field that you create and magnetize to your outside world to create a currency exchange in the market place. You are the Original Money and Currency Market that is leveraged in the outer realm of your world.

Money is a Unit of exchange in the market place. Money is love in its higher state of being. Money is patience, compassion, feelings, emotions, a gift, a blessing. It can represent and unfold great personal and business relationships, and most of all financial healing. Yet most people on planet Earth, have such conflicting, confusing and contradictory and negative feelings and relationships with this magnificent energy called Money, which is truly themselves within.

When a person says, "I have no money." or "I am poor." or "This item costs too much.", they are expressing outwardly the lack of their own personal internal currency flow. They are assessing their view of their electromagnetic charge that runs through their body; they are saying that there is a corruption in their circuitry. This is the time for them do the work of cleaning up their circuitry, so their electromagnetic currency can flow freely again. They must go within or do without, to activate their money and currency field from within themselves, so it can be reflected *outside* themselves. This will give them the opportunity to create mutual exchanges and interchanges in the marketplace of their freewill choice.

WHAT WOULD I DO TO HEAL THE PLANET?

Our students are taught about the Mindset one needs to have to create a healthy and healing relationship with money. The teachings ultimately lead the students to creating a personal relationship with themselves and their own sacred electromagnetic frequency. We focus on activating and practicing the Principles and Laws around Money. Our students learn to become those principles and laws in order that their lives become much more **Fruit Full, substantive, creative and happy.** This specialized information keeps them from being financial victims in the exchange and currency markets of today. They can obtain the much-needed specialized knowledge and learn what is eroding their monies daily and what has kept debt and poverty a reality in their lives. They learn how to acquire the righteous (right consciousness) mindset that will steer them on the right road to their own intimate and personal success. They learn how not to be a financial victim as, unfortunately, most of society has been subjected to being. They learn how to find, actualize and activate their own sacred purpose in their lives.

Our community platform is **Free** for those who are of **like mind** and desire to participate in their own financial healing and deliverance. Those who choose to join our community are able to form relationships with others who share the same goals and desires for financial freedom through knowledge of themselves regarding who they truly. They learn how to utilize and transform what is in them. Here they can decide to make a personal choice about shedding old negative thoughts, beliefs and patterns around money. Those who participate in our Free Community Platform can later decide to apply and through an approval process become a paying student for advanced education on money principles in our Mastermind Group. As such they are required to activate what they have learned in our educational platform.

In our Mastermind Group of Higher Learning, our students learn how not to be a slave to debt. Instead, they learn how to increase by planting seeds to bring about a harvest and actualize themselves as the principles and principals of their own magnetic frequency and currency. In addition, they learn how to be an increase to themselves and their loved ones, how to live a life of multiplication, like Yeshua did. This has been a blessing to me personally and to others who choosing to participate in their personal currency in this way. This money movement is transforming and shifting their mindsets, so they can feel and see the true intrinsic value in themselves and others.

I extend an invitation to those who would like to join our community and be an integral part of learning who they truly are. Equally invited are those who desire to learn how to create and elevate passive income into enjoying more control of the money decisions in their lives. They can learn to lower the risks to their monies becoming of lesser value in the marketplace. They can learn to accomplish an above average returns and increases to their monies; more so than they are currently receiving and experiencing in their financial lives. More importantly, they will learn the truth of money and how to increase it in a more passive way. In addition, with this new-found knowledge, they can truly bring a revolution and a paradigm shift to themselves and to their whole family story. They can leave a proven financial legacy for their children's children to InJoy. They and their families can have a plethora of purpose-filled free-will choices to actualize in their lives.

Best Regards,
Prophetess Afraka Sankofa

THE ESSENTIAL ENTREPRENEUR

Jeanne "Majestic" Taylor

IN the holy and righteous name of the MOST HIGH Creator, I greet all of you in the universal names of peace: Salaam Alaikum, Hotep, Shalom, Tashi Dalek, To-hi-du-lit, Namaste, Peace and blessings be upon you.

I am grateful for this divine opportunity to share this essay, *"The Essential Entrepreneur"* with you. I am humbled and want to express my gratitude to our Divine Creator, all the ancestors, those who love and serve humanity, the first family of wellness, Brother Ali Torain and our dearest Mother Queen Afua herself, for this opportunity to share with the people of the world.

For I AM the temple, I AM here to serve and strive to "FULL-fill" a greater purpose on our planet.

Some of the most Powerful people in our world today are entrepreneurs. Entrepreneurs are impactful, and they are leaders who bring ideas to the forefront of our society. Entrepreneurs are able to identify existing problems and understand the needs of the community. Through creativity and innovation entrepreneurs create businesses to solve problems, and supply needs. Perhaps we can agree that many people need a better quality of life and some type of self-healing. Whether it is on a mental level, physical level, or a spiritual level both the people and the planet can use some healing.

In many occasions the entrepreneur is a contributing factor to the success of a community and to that healthier quality of life. It might be wise to turn to the entrepreneur who most likely will have the answers on HOW to heal. In this article I will share some of the lessons I've learned that have contributed to my becoming of a successful businesswoman. Secondly, I will prove that the entrepreneur is an essential component in the global healing process, and in fact is one of the most influential members of society. Lastly, I will demonstrate that through entrepreneurship we can build a healthier community and heal our people and the planet on a large scale.

With over 15 years of entrepreneurial experience I have made tremendous gains on many levels. One of the most rewarding things about these gains is that others have benefited from my hard work and sacrifices. Growing up in a family of 9 we learned the importance of family and community. My parents taught us how to maneuver, how to grind and they did what it took to provide for us.

Lesson: I learned very young that we have to depend upon our own efforts to change our own conditions. This was a healthy state of mind. Watching my parents make ends meet, I knew that I could use that same strategic mentality to make money for myself. My brothers and I started to work for ourselves. At that time, I became the top sales girl in the company that I worked for. I made a lot of money selling chocolate bars, and the success motivated me. The money was sweeter than the candy. I grew more ambitious and it brought me joy to be able to help others when they needed it.

Lesson: Making money helped my family, even with paying the bills. When the bills were paid the stress was less. I stayed in sales into my mid 20s and eventually became a master saleswoman. I loved selling. When I was about 13 years of age selling chocolates in the streets of Toronto frequently I was told the word NO, but through persistence I turned N+O into a New Opportunity. Eventually, the reward of persistence was turning "No" into "Yes."

Lesson: I knew that IT depended on ME, IT would take me to make IT happen, whatever IT was. If there wasn't an IT, I would create one. Persistency and determination became my foundation. From my experiences came the birth of a new mindset, which prepared me for my future business. Flashback: I stared out as gritty chocolate "hustler" on the street corners of Toronto. This strong entrepreneurial mindset was the valuable assist that led to my development as a refined corporate owner of one of Toronto's finest Vending Companies. According to the Financial Times' definition: Entrepreneurial mindset "refers to a specific state of mind which orientates human conduct towards entrepreneurial activities and outcomes. Individuals with entrepreneurial mindsets are often drawn to opportunities, innovation and new value creation." With this mindset I will continue to assist with healing our planet.

Entrepreneurs lead the way in healing our planet by building businesses that promote products and services, which assist with the health and wellness of the community. Starting a business often creates employment and builds wealth. Wealth building creates a healthy culture of independence and self-confidence. When families own productive assets such as a business this serves the community, it minimizes debt and helps to alleviate poverty. Less poverty creates a healthier environment for the community and the person. Entrepreneurs are found in practically every field of business. The entrepreneur is essential, meaning absolutely necessary when it comes to healing planet Earth and the people. Entrepreneurs create businesses and services that make real change. Many great businesses began with an entrepreneur who had visions to change the way people think and live and even influence the way people behave. This is the kind of power that is needed to heal the planet on an immense scale.

Starting a business that can influence the way people think can lead them to making better health choices and even prevent them from destructive behaviors. For example, opening up a gym or a health and wellness business can encourage customers to exercise. A wellness business can promote maintenance for a healthy lifestyle. Many entrepreneurs today are getting into the health and wellness industry, including manufacturing natural and organic products or providing yoga and meditation services for cleansing the soul. With many opportunities in the market, large and small, it is the quality that matters not the size. Regardless, it stands, it takes many hands to heal our world and becoming an entrepreneur is just one way.

Through excellence, sacrifices and brilliance some of the world's most impactful entrepreneurs have demonstrated various ways to aid in the healing process of our world. Hence proving that the Entrepreneur is an essential component within our society. Not only have entrepreneurs demonstrated that we have the power to build healthier communities, but we have shown that through business we can have a positive impact on the quality of life for others.

Let me offer two prime examples. First, is the inspirational, Aliaume Thiam also known as Akon who is best known as an American singer, actor, songwriter, recording producer, entrepreneur and philanthropist. In 2014 Akon partnered with China and successfully launched the Light up Africa initiative that has provided millions of African people with electricity through solar power. To this day as he continues to light up Africa, he leads the way demonstrating that entrepreneurship is simultaneously financially rewarding for the entrepreneur and positively constructive for the communities.

The second example is a role model to many around the globe. A girl, who was born into poverty, learned valuable lessons used them to her advantage. She refused to become a product of her challenging upbringing. This is a woman of bravery, courage and tenacity worked her way into great wealth and influenced many along the way. This phenomenal woman holds many titles including entrepreneur, businesswoman, personality, philanthropist, and former talk show host. Yes, indeed, Miss Oprah Winfrey has truly defined excellence.

In 2011 Oprah made an impact on the world when she debuted the Oprah Winfrey Network (OWN). OWN is a media stream in approximately 80 million homes particularly targeting the African American audience. To date Oprah continues to inspire, change the lives of others and influence the world through media. Her Network is a healing tool that promotes positive and healthy lifestyles.

The opportunities for entrepreneurship and business to heal our planet are immeasurable. It is an open market of opportunities worth exploring. I've learned that it is important to do for self, create some type of independence, create a culture of ownership, and invest into building a strong community. Not everyone would have the interest in becoming a business owner, self-employed or even an entrepreneur, but I encourage those who are risk takers to give it a try.

I AM a healer. I am passionate in serving my community, self-development, nation building and the nurturing of life. It is imperative that others become educated and also advance into this understanding.

It is OUR mission as HEALERS to raise the consciousness levels in our communities by utilizing our skills and personal expertise within our fields of study. Our goals should include teaching others how to create healthier lifestyles and live a better quality of life. Among the many ways we can continue to HEAL planet Earth, becoming an entrepreneur and business builder is one of the ways I know best.

Give thanks.

Much Love, Light and Peace to the human family,

Majestic ~ the Element. ♥

PRESERVING THE LEGACY

Omar Hardy, President Of The Black Lady Theatre

Carrying on the legacy is imperative; we must not allow history to be forgotten. Our ancestors and elders within the community have laid down an amazing foundation, one which should not be erased. Historically, an entire race of people has already been stripped of their culture, and if we are not careful total destruction is imminent. We must remain conscious of this great struggle and strive to keep alive the mission for the best outcome. In fact, the community has been given the pillars on which to build and the blueprints for progression. It is our responsibility to carry on and continue to build.

As a child, I had been exposed to many varieties of Black leadership. The result of observing from drug dealers to church pastors, judges and business owners led me to understand the importance of entrepreneurship for the Black community. Although I am a Brooklyn native, my family relocated to the Poconos in Pennsylvania where I spent my pre-teen years. Growing up I was one of only a few Black kids in the neighborhood and in school, which came along with judgement, harassment and unapologetic racism. As I matured, I became more aware of my greatness not only as a Black man but also as a leader. Not only could I prove my former oppressors wrong, but also I had the power to change the fate of many young Black men and women who also had been affected by world views that were negative and destructive.

In order to avoid the pending ruin of today's Black community, especially the youth, we must initiate the process of healing. It is vital that this healing process happens with both vertical and horizontal alignment. Vertically, thoughts and habits are passed down from generation to generation while simultaneously the tech and information age provides us with a platform whereby (horizontally) we can influence peers and colleagues alike. Particularly within the African-American community, we must learn to support each other, learn from and teach one another and take an active role in seeking knowledge and practicing natural restorative techniques in order to heal mind, body and spirit.

Healing of the mind comes from knowledge of self. As a people we derive from Kings and Queens. We must first know and understand our worth and then acknowledge it. Included in our self-affirmation and meditation, we must activate peace and rid the self of the false thoughts implanted by others. If you understand your worth, you then understand the importance of surrounding yourself with high frequency vibrations, positive life-affirming thoughts and the essential foods necessary for nourishing the body.

Keeping the body healthy and active is another key ingredient to preserving the legacy of the ancestors. While it is easy to get caught up in the commercialized world of the food industry, it is a requirement that those wishing to progress in this society, become aware of the harmful additives often found in today's grocery stores. Implementing healthier eating habits, fuels leaders of today with the nourishment they need to continue fighting the war for those to come.

Engaging with the world from a spiritual point-of-view and with proper mind and strength of body, makes reaching the higher-self attainable. The achievement of unlocking one's higher self reveals the vast universe deep within the heart. The ability to take oneself out of the picture and begin seeing and affecting the needs of others is an attribute of this level of consciousness. My experience with this mission has given me understanding of this all too well. The entire reason I continue pushing forward with this endeavor is knowing that there are bigger forces at hand which will have a lasting effect on the work for future generations.

The Black Lady Theatre serves as the vessel to nurture these elements by providing a safe space for discussion, creativity and discovery. Supreme Civil Court Judge and visionary, Mr. Phillips took Brooklyn by storm during the early 1980s when he purchased two buildings and converted the sites into the Slave Theater and The Black Lady Theatre. My father, Clarence Hardy Jr. was a good friend and business partner of the late Judge John L. Phillips Jr. opening of The Slave Theater and The Black Lady Theatre ignited excitement and creativity in the Black communities especially among residents in Bed-Sty and Crown Heights. The theaters quickly became a headquarters for discussions on race, equality and forward progression.

Wisely, my father encouraged me to take the lead role of the family business in 2010. Since then, it has become my life's work to diligently and deliberately maintain the legacy. Thanks to my upbringing, my grandmother's no nonsense training, and my parents' grace, I have developed an unwavering desire for advancement, expansion and prosperity. The information and knowledge bestowed upon me by the elders in the business prior to my arrival has set me up to carry out the mission. The work of my father and Judge Phillips has created a solid ground for which the continued success of The Black Lady Theatre resides. My goal reaches far beyond having only a physical space to offer as a vessel, but I also aim to be the vessel myself. I aim to continue to set the precedent for others, much like my father set the example for me, and Judge Phillips Jr., set the bar for us, both.

Following in the footsteps of Judge Phillips Jr., is no easy task. When I began to craft the extended vision for the theaters, I knew that making old ideas new again would be one of the main ingredients for healing and success. I am in the present, but I am creating the space for the future. I am committed to preserving a legacy which honors the past, but I hope to propel future generations into new planes of existence.

PRESERVE PARADISE

Baratunde & Kayah Ma'at, Adventure Activists

In 2012, The Forgotten Foods… Remembered expanded its business and wellness ministry to the breath-taking country of Belize, Central America. We named the business, **The Forgotten Foods, International,** to embrace the new product herbal lines coming out of Belize and the Caribbean rainforests.

…Three years prior, we had created The Veggie Wellness Cruises. One of the first "healthy dining" cruises of its kind, it was hosted on one of the largest cruise lines in the world. A vegan/vegetarian chef catered to our guest's palates. We lectured on health and wellness and showed our world-wide guests, a wonderful time.

However, it was a cruise to Mexico and Belize that propelled us ***out*** of the cruise business. We discovered cruise ships were responsible for polluting the oceans and destroying the barrier reefs of the world! Belize has the 2nd largest barrier reef, (190 miles) and the largest "living" barrier reef in the world. However, over 24 miles of fragile Belizean barrier reef was being destroyed by cruise ships! Tropical Coral Reefs are the most diverse marine ecosystems on Earth, giving shelter to thousands of marine species. Many people depend on fisheries, tourism and coastal protection provided by healthy coral reefs. Yet, today, global coral reefs are dying at an alarming rate. The reef loss rate is about twice the rate of tropical rain forest loss.

Despite the promotional gains and the economic loss, we took the ethical high road, discontinued our Veggie Wellness Cruises and pulled away our support of the cruise industry. *This was our way of demonstrating.* We decided to redirect our captured audience to our "Paradise" in Belize, Central America, where the idea of **The Exotic Adventure Wellness Journey** was born.

At **EAWJ,** (pronounced EE-A-WAH'-JAY), instead of the more environmentally destructive cruise option, we offer our guests a new adventure wellness journey in Belize.

It is now imperative for us to discuss the Pink Elephant in our global waters… PLASTICS. This "out of sight, out of mind" colossal problem has grossly affected life on planet Earth. The world produces more than 300 million tons of plastic **every year**…including billions of plastic bottles and five billion plastic bags. **Plastic is wonderful because it is durable…but plastic is terrible because it is durable. Every piece of plastic ever made is still on the planet in one form or another**—half of which we use just once and then throw away! Single-use plastics are a human addiction that we must face head on.

This conversation cannot be ignored any longer, it's dangerously out of control.

Experts warn that plastic is one of the **biggest threats** facing the world's seas. By the year 2050, when the human population will explode to nearly 10 billion people, it is expected that plastic production will triple. The problem with that is that only a fraction of this plastic is recycled…the rest ends up in our environment, and its coating our land and our oceans like a disease. Researchers say if we don't clean up our act, **the oceans will have more plastics by weight than fish by 2050!**

Although some of the plastic comes from ships, most is washed from land into the seas via runoff, rivers and wind. Plastic pollution is not only impacting our waters and marine life, but also the human food chain and our overall health. When plastics break down into smaller pieces, they're more difficult to clean up, and marine animals often ingest the pieces, which is killing them in ever-increasing numbers. Larger pieces can entangle marine animals, and bigger animals often ingest those, too.

Also, when broken up into tiny pieces, plastic attracts toxic chemicals released over decades from industry and agriculture; the concentration of which increases as they move up the food chain. Exposures to these chemicals have been suggested to contribute to some cancers and infertility, as well as immune, metabolic, cognitive and behavioral disorders. The entry of plastic pieces into our food chain is of major concern to human health.

So, what can we do to heal Planet Earth? We would be part of the solution by **_RETHINKING PLASTICS!_** The reality is that the only way this problem can be addressed is by individuals and companies around the world agreeing to implement practices that reduce waste on every level. Our top tips for reducing plastic waste are:

Wean yourself off disposable plastics.
Ninety percent of the plastic items in our daily lives are used once and then chucked: grocery bags, plastic wrap, disposable cutlery, straws, coffee-cup lids, and so on. Take note of how often you rely on these products and replace them with reusable versions.

Shop Friendly.
Plastic bags can be efficiently replaced by reusable bags, many of which fold up compactly to be portable. Just think about how many bags you typically carry out of a grocery store and multiply that by the number of times you grocery shop. That's a lot of plastic! Carry a bag and always reuse plastic bags as much as possible.

Stop buying bottled water.
Carry a reusable bottle in your bag. Use water from your kitchen tap with a built-in filter.

Forget to-go Containers.
Plastic food containers, lids, and utensils are all easily replaced by reusable containers.

Recycle Everything.
Try to select items that come in non-plastic recycled and recyclable packaging, to do your best to properly handle items that can't be reused. Before trashing items, think RECYLCLING.

Cook more.
Not only is it healthier but making your own meals doesn't involve takeout containers or doggy bags.

Buy in bulk.
Select the bigger containers instead of buying several smaller ones over time.

Get Involved
Speak to lawmakers and get involved with government on any level and proposed alternatives when applicable.
Put pressure on manufacturers.
Though we can make a difference through our own habits, corporations obviously have the biggest footprint. They are at the heart of the problem. If you believe a company could be smarter about its packaging, make your voice heard. Hit them where it really hurts, support a more sustainable competitor.

It is indeed a new day and we must all find a new way to live and **PRESERVE** our **PARADISE**, Planet Earth.

MIND CLOSING

"Watch your thoughts; they become words.

Watch your words; they become actions.

Watch your actions; they become habit.

Watch your habits; they become character.

Watch your character; it becomes your destiny."

Credited to
LAO TZU
(ancient Chinese philosopher and poet)

SPIRIT

Would that you could live
 on the fragrance of the earth,
  and like an air plant
 be sustained by the light.

—Kahlil Gibran *(The Prophet)*

THE S.O.U.L. IN SOULMATING

Montsho & Nwasha Edu, Soul Mate Teachers

Do you believe in soulmates? Have you found your soulmate? How do you know? Maybe you want to believe in soulmates but feel uncertain about how. One thing most of us can agree on is that love is one of the most powerful motivators in the world. Believers spend billions of dollars on dating, weddings and love holidays. While cynics implore the current devotees to stop chasing waterfalls. There are thousands of websites, magazines, and experts sharing techniques for finding and keeping true love. Still, soulmates are an emotional impact concept that usually polarizes people into opposing camps.

We're here to affirm that soulmates are real and that the origin is the most ancient love story on earth. We are Montsho and Nwasha Edu and we help people remember how and why it is vital to love. And yes, as you probably guessed we are Sacred SoulMates Strategists. We use the ancient cultural wisdom and rituals of our ancestors to help create the space in the minds, bodies and environments of those who desire to cultivate empowering love.

A lot of the love advice that exists in the present world is lacking in understanding the spiritual art and cultural science of love. If you want the best relationship you can have, the one that inspires you and helps you develop into the best version of yourself, you'll need a SoulMate Strategy™. The key to true, fulfilling and empowering love is to keep the S.O.U.L. at the forefront of your SoulMate Strategy™. The S.O.U.L. in soulmate stands for Self, Others, Understanding and Love Systems and outlines the areas you'll need to perpetually work on to enjoy love.

The Science of SoulMating is the most glorious story of love and unification. The Divine creates soulmate pairs together in the spirit realm as one conjoined being. When a new life is conceived, one half separates from the whole to begin the process of physical creation that will ultimately become a newborn boy or girl.

Days, months or even years later, when the celestial environment complements the first half, the second half is sent at conception and will repeat the same complementary process as the first. An intricate system of divining the purpose of all newborns existed in ideal communities. A person called a Moamogedi, much like a shaman midwife, speaks to all the unborn children in the wombs of their mothers and is highly trained to divine and share the purpose that the forming child says they are coming to contribute. Moamogedi from neighboring communities keep track of each child's purpose in order to properly reunite soulmates in the terrestrial realm. They understand that soulmates are the perfect complement to each other and have a unified purpose that serves the greatest good.

The idea of complements is what we imply by saying "opposites attract". When you are looking for your soulmate, you're looking for your Divine complement. You need an understanding of your true Self to successfully select the right Other. There is initially an attraction to what is different. You're able to admire traits in someone that may not be as strong in you. One crucial difference to embodying a "complement" versus an "opposite" paradigm is that you are consciously seeking a level of completion and character perfection with your complement while opposite implies being intrinsically opposed to each other.

We also confuse the interconnectedness of all creation with Soulmate Science. All of our unions are sacred…and all serve to propel us to our greatest good. Certainly, the love we feel for nature, our family and friends is Divine. But your true soulmate represents a different love concept of completion of character. Your soulmate triggers places in you that no other relationship can reach. This is their Divine Responsibility. As your Understanding of this develops, the harmony of your relationship increases.

The composite of our thoughts, speech, actions, emotional response and symbolic creation and recognition is our collective soul. Creating Love Systems, or love rituals, empowers relationships and helps secure your desired love legacy.

The four Sacred Keys to understanding the intimate soulmate relationship are Influence, Belief, Purpose and Communication.

INFLUENCE

Early influences affect you more than you know. Most have made key decisions about what we find interesting and attractive in another person by the age of seven. We often don't even remember when or why we've decided what was attractive about height, body or style. What kind of relationships did you witness as a child? Were your influences full of love or did you see love as difficult or non-existent? Once you have a better understanding of your love influences, you'll need to find ways to learn and understand the love influences of others.

Montsho: I was born in 1970. The pro black natural imagery and self-determination language of the era became what I find most appealing, especially in women. I like naturalness in all people, determination and social honesty. I saw many married couples including my parents that appeared to be strong and happy. This stuck as an ideal model for me.

BELIEF

Our early influences set the stage for what our core beliefs on love will be. Beliefs usually are categorized as either a "generalization" (Love is positive) or an "if...then rule" (If you Love me you should show it). One of the most valuable skills we can develop is the ability to make new meaning of the past. The love lessons we learned as children follow us into adulthood...but as adults we can now make the decision to reframe the value of those lessons. EVERY relationship has taught us something. We often look at neglect and disappointment as "bad", but relationships are not good or bad. What we call "bad" often teaches us to hold our boundaries, love ourselves and know clearly what we deserve. If you have been abused, you probably have a sharp sense of people or spatial energy and can be a great protector. If you have spent a lot of time alone, you probably have the skills to know and love yourself well. If you've never been alone, you have surely developed skills in reading people, empathy or connection. Learn to look at hurts or love traumas with new eyes and new hearts to make your love stories useful for yourself, your family and your community now.

Nwasha: It's an ongoing process to let go of the beliefs that no longer serve you. I've made it a part of my life to check in with my beliefs. I ask myself, "What do I believe about love/marriage/parenthood, and so on?" Then I ask, "What would I need to believe for the outcome I want?" When what I believe doesn't correlate with what I say I want, I know I have a conflict and that I'm less likely to be successful.

COMMUNICATION

What we communicate to ourselves and others creates our reality. What is your internal love dialogue? If you've been less than nurturing to yourself, write yourself a love letter! Thank all of the unions you have had with yourself, your mates and the Creator. Thank them for what they've taught you. If what they taught is no longer necessary/useful, release the hurt, guilt, stress or embarrassment once and for all.

Our external dialogue can often seem complicated and full of drama. You must develop speaking and listening skills, know the right time to talk and understand the common differences between male and female communication styles. Communication can be drama-free if you learn these simple techniques. Do you ever avoid a conversation because you think there will be some drama?!? True intimacy can only exist when you can live and speak from the heart.

Montsho: I learned in my teens that honestly sharing my pain from dysfunctional relationships could free others who were having similar experiences. Subsequently, I became passionate and began a symbolic Harriet Tubman campaign to free the emotionally enslaved through heartfelt communication with myself and others. This ultimately has led to the work I do today.

PURPOSE

You have a divine purpose on the planet and there is someone perfectly created to complement that purpose as you complement theirs. Together your reach in the community is magnified. How you use your purpose at any given time may change, but it's important to stay present of the purpose of love and relationships in your life.

Nwasha: Personally, I've always believed in soulmates. Maybe it's because I'm a woman and I've had years of fairytale mythology? Maybe, on a subconscious level, I've always known the truth of the Science of SoulMating story. That doesn't mean reconnecting with my soulmate was "easy". In every fairytale or hero story there is always a challenge one must overcome. I had to understand my early influences, make peace with my beliefs about love and learn new ways to communicate to bloom in my purpose.

You have the power to create magnificent relationships in your life! We invite you to be empowered on your sacred soulmate journey.

HOW TO FIND LOVE AND KEEP IT ALIVE

Chris "Kazi" Rolle, Relationship Coach

I am Chris Kazi Rolle. I am a Matchmaker and a Relationship Coach, and I am the Founder of Together Apart: A Relationship Academy that provides courses, classes and matchmaking mediations. We help people find love and keep love alive. I have been doing this work since the year 2000. I started this work because of my own challenges and quest to understand why relationships fail.

Throughout history, you can find great leaders and entrepreneurs who went through a problem or saw a problem and sought to solve that problem. That became their purpose. As for me, I had many challenges as a young person. When I did the work on myself, I started asking the questions about why these things happened to me. It led me to examine my childhood and I started to explore my parents' relationship. The failure of that relationship was the catalyst for the things that happened to me. So, it got me started on a path of thinking about why my parents had challenges. That led me to my grandparents. Then I started to realize; the cycle of dysfunction was being handed down from generation to generation.

Sometimes we ask, "Why me?", but it is always so much bigger than we are. We are our parents. We are our grandparents. We are our ancestors. Within our community, specifically as the descendants of African people, there must be a lot of healing to recover from the traumatic experiences that we have dealt with as a race.

Dr. Joy Larry's work of Post Traumatic Syndrome teaches us that dysfunction (the same as our greatness) is handed down; both can be found in our DNA. I realized healing from generational dysfunction was critical. That is how I found myself in this healing work

I want to discuss the crux of my work for the last twenty years: what causes relationships to fail? How can we get on the front end of that as we seek love, and be sure that we are prepared to have a great relationship with our significant other?

Additionally, if we are already in a relationship, what can we do to prepare ourselves or transform ourselves to maintain a happy, loving, and healthy relationship?

I have pinpointed three specific things that I want to share with you as we fast, celebrate, pray and meditate on wellness:

The number one challenge that we face in relationships is **Unresolved Issues.** Let me tell you a story. I have these clients, a husband and wife who came into their relationship about ten years ago. When they came to me, they were in crisis. Crisis is when most people come for healing, which is why I emphasize that the best cure is prevention.

Anyway, they came to me. Their challenge was their communication. They shared many words that were not representative of a healthy-level relationship. I found out he was from foster care, and she grew up in a house with a tyrant for a father. Whenever there is a challenge, she walks away. She is not good at dealing with intense challenges within the relationship. Hence, he feels as if he has been abandoned and it reminds him of what happened when he was a child. They are both dealing with the yet challenges that existed even before they began their relationship.

When a traumatic or challenging experience comes up, we often reach back and pull up the memory of what happened to us even before the relationship we are currently in. What happened before now, becomes our present. That unresolved issue is causing a challenge in the present relationship. I see it in many of my clients when they come in for coaching or counseling. The crux of the present problem is something that has remained unresolved.

Challenge number two is **Ego.** I worked with a divorce lawyer and asked him, "What is the main reason why people come to you for help? What is causing them to end up in your office?" He said that it is Ego. Whenever he hears the term, "irreconcilable differences," that means that they have gotten to a place where it is "my way or no way." Thus, they are not willing to reconcile because they are so stuck on the "I." The Ego protects us and separates us. In any relationship, if you want to it to be successful it must be framed as about the "Us," not the "I." When it gets to "me against you," the relationship will fail. Ego is something we must look out for because it is like a termite that will eat away at the foundation of the relationship.

Lastly, challenge number three is **Poor Communication Skills.** Poor communication skills connect to the Ego and to unresolved issues because when we are dealing with something from our past, that makes us feel threatened, sad or hurt, our Ego comes up. Hence, to protect ourselves, we start communicating in a way that separates ourselves from our partner.

Back to the example of the husband and wife: She walks away, and he feels abandoned; so then, he follows her because he is defending himself or protecting himself from the feeling of abandonment. Then she gets angry because she is reminded of her tyrant father. Therefore, she starts responding to him through her Ego and saying words that are not healthy to her partner. He responds to her and she responds back to him in the same negative way. So much can happen from there; and then they end up in my office. Some people end up in a failed relationship or take the same unresolved issues into a new relationship.

In conclusion, I would like to present some practical steps to assist you with handling the fundamental issues that cause relationships to fail. These three things are helpful for both singles and couples for getting to a place where you can find love or keep love alive. If you are in a relationship, you should practice this. If you are looking for a relationship, you need to practice this.

1. **Be Proactive In Your Healing:** When I say healing I mean your mental, physical and spiritual healing, because our issues in ourselves show up in so many ways. I remember when I first met Queen Afua I had ulcers. I was a young man in my early twenties with ulcers. unresolved emotional and mental issues were showing up in my body. If you are proactive, you will learn self-healing must become your lifestyle; the issues will not be solved with an immediate "fix." If you make being proactive part of your lifestyle and are always seeking ways to increase your mental, physical and spiritual health, then you will end up finding and healing unresolved issues before they manifest in your relationships.

2. **Manage the Ego:** When considering the Ego, I think it really boils down to awareness. A great book you can check out is called *A Whole New Earth.* This awesome book expounds on the idea of how to manage the Ego. When the Ego has us in its grips, it affects how we see the world, and that affects our emotions and how we respond to the world—how we see everything.

3. **Learn To Communicate Effectively:** There are many things I can tell you about this topic that you can find out by following me on social media or on my website. There I post many free tools available for anybody who wants to improve their communication. Another great resource is the book *The Seven Habits of Highly Effective Families* by Steven R. Covey.

We can heal.
Be well.

SONGERVERSATION: I AM LIGHT

India Arie, Musician

SongVersations begin with a prayer: "May these words reach who they are meant, the way they are intended to be reached. May these words bring love, healing peace and Joy, and most of all, May God's perfect will be done."

My goal with Songversation is to speak spiritual truth and principles in very simple words. Numbing ourselves to our pain and blaming other people is always an option. But the world doesn't give you your power, you generate that from within. The most important part of the SongVersation: I Am Light essays, is the realization of that aspiration.

Through my own journey, of Breakdown, Break Through, Break the Shell, Elevate & Fly, I naturally began to yearn to understand self-care. And after the moment of embodiment on the mountain top, I began to live it. I PRAY! That this will assist you in your life.

BECOME A SEEKER AND FIND YOU:

Make "yourself-work" your hobby. My main avenues of exploration have been:

Praying: Prayer is just talking to God; whatever you believe God to be. This is not about religious affiliation, although it can be. I believe there is a God, and when I align myself with that higher power I am more clear about life. It's really that simple—Prayer has been a GREAT source of comfort for me. I don't pray because I think GOD needs that from me, I pray because it makes me FEEL connected to something meaningful, and it reminds me of what REALLY matters. Prayer helps me to focus my intention… EVERYTIME! No matter how scattered I am, when I pray, I am instantly calmed and focused.

Meditating: Meditation is listening to God. I see meditation much like religion, there are many paths to the same place. Find the way that works for you. I get quiet and still. I practice a few types of meditation. This is a part of MY daily spiritual work.

Journal: I journal, because I need to get things out of my head. My advice is to keep a journal no matter what. Even if you're not a writer, having a place to document your process is important. About 10 years ago I asked myself, "What are my weak points?" I thought, "NOBODY has read this, so let me be honest with myself." The things I admitted took me down a path of healing that shaped who I am today. Don't be afraid to look at yourself. Awareness is the first step to healing.

Create a Sacred Space: People think Sacred Space means Temples, Churches, Yoga studios…And, while these CAN be Sacred Spaces, none of that is necessary. Sacred Space is a PERSONAL space, dedicated to the intent of delving into your inner life. A place where you can go to be alone with, you, yourself, and God.

A SongVersation is co-created Sacred Space…Sacred Space is dreams…Sacred Space is where the synchronicities of life are seen, felt, and recognized as important… it is where you breathe, and when you breathe the body receives all that nature intended. Sacred Space is where you are still enough to drop into an altered state. Sacred Space is important because it is a foundation for exploration. Whether it is prayer, reading, meditating, writing, even making your daily schedule, your Sacred Space is for your spiritual work. It can be a prayer room, a chair in a corner, a closet; for me, it's MY windowsill. Make it YOUR style, use what is available to you, and GO there. It is the soil where "the work" you do is planted.

I AM Light

"The Truth of Who We Are"

I am light, I am light [x4]

I am not the things my family did

I am not the voices in my head

I am not the pieces of the brokenness inside

I am light, I am light [x4]

I'm not the mistakes that I have made or any of the things that caused me pain

I am not the pieces of the dream I left behind

I am light, I am light [x4]

I am not the color of my eyes

I am not the skin on the outside

I am not my age, I am not my race, my soul inside is all light

All light, all light [x2]

I am light, I am light [x2]

I am divinity defined

I am the God on the inside

I am a star, a piece of it all

I am light

At my windowsill I can sit in silence, look out on a beautiful natural vista, and write, and ponder, and pray out loud, and hear the whispers of inspiration in my ears. I can sit there for hours. All of my essays and blogs are signed from my windowsill *sill*. I'm sitting here now.

- I especially like being by the water.
- I like to hear soft colors.
- Deep in thought I like to drink warm drinks; but I find food distracting.
- I can have a life-changing epiphany, OR sometimes it can be a melody, or the perfect person calling at the perfect time…
- Singing all by myself at night time, in my prayer room, is Sacred Space.
- Counter to ALL of this, being on stage is Sacred Space for me. In the middle of a song, sometimes I forget the audience is there. For MUCH of my life it was the ONLY time, that I was thinking about anything else but that moment.
- Sing: This is my life's passion. I'm so blessed to have found my passion. Even when it's not for work, I sing. Everyone can't sing well, but everyone CAN sing. Affirmation: If you are not comfortable singing, you can also speak affirmations, or lyrics to your favorite songs. Read sacred text or poetry that is meaningful to you—whatever speaks to you. The intention is to use your voice.

Final Words about:
Worthy means deserving of effort, attention and respect. Learn to hear the voice of your soul, and let that truth guide you through your life. YOU ARE WORTHY!

DO WHATEVER YOU MUST TO HEAL and FORGIVE YOURSELF. Healing and forgiveness is not a destination, it is a journey. Never beat up on yourself for not being "perfect" because the TRUTH is, you already are, AND you never will be. Perfect is not the goal, WHOLE is the goal. And that is the definition of healing: *to be made whole.*

You, *as you are,* are WORTHY, every single part of you. As you walk through each day, make your wellness, your elevation. *YOU* are your hobby. As a truly unselfish act, the better YOU ARE, the better the WORLD AROUND YOU IS; we comprise the world. No one can do it for you. Trust that you will find your way. Even on the days when you have pain in your heart, *ESPECIALLY* in those days, MOVE FORWARD in the truth of who you are.

And when you inevitably fall down, and have to regroup, start the next journey knowing that THIS IS LIFE, –you are capable, and indeed WORTHY of starting again. And again. And again. Because there is always, another shell to break and another flight to take. Breakdown, Break

Through, Break the Shell, Elevate & Fly. We have the choice to truly be alive—This is your life—Child it's time. Life's gonna hurt, but it's meant to be felt; you cannot touch the sky from inside yourself. There is no place you'll arrive that will suddenly make your life perfect. Do the best you can…Keep living. Keep growing, and keep loving, *for that is the most powerful energy in the universe. All you have to do is use it; so, use it.*

This essay you are reading is a fly moment for me. Thank you for being a witness to my transformation. Now, go, celebrate your triumphs.

From My Windowsill
With Love, Strength, Courage, & Wisdom
India Arie

God Is Real
(excerpt) [Verse 1]

Sweetest honey to the brightest flower the largest plant

Into the smallest atom, snowflakes in the bird kingdom,

Smaller than the eye can see,

Bigger than the mind can conceive. (oh)

Heard a man on the radio today,

Must confess I disagreed with what he had to say.

[Bridge]

How can he not believe that God is real,

I don't understand how he could feel that way. When

There's earth, air, water and fire.

So many different flowers, sunshine and rain shower,

So many different crystals and hills and volcanos.

[Chorus]

That's how I know that God is real (all of this is not by chance) [x2]

That's how I know that God is real (I know this is not by chance)

That's how I know that God is real [x2]

THE PARADIGM OF JOY

Erykah Badu, Musician

There's this natural instinct we have as human beings. Regardless of our position, religion, color or kind, we all have a primal desire for immediate, and almost unwavering, JOY. Eventually, through the experience of events and circumstance, we learn that this desire just may be unreasonable and unnatural. We watch our emotions sway as we are affected and influenced by the energy around us. Our own resistance to "unpleasantness" restricts our movement.

In a self-medicated state, we start to become addicted to our pain. In some cases, it even starts to define us. We wear masks to protect ourselves and alas lose sight of who we are. Drained physically, spiritually and emotionally, we become ill and left with very little energy to cope. Our service to others becomes exhausting. Our breathing becomes shallow. JOY seems so far. Now we are stuck in our own minds, filled with random thoughts and collected fears. This place has become our world. We know we are imbalanced.

Something must change. How do we portion our busy lives to give the proper attention to our inner beings;…and vital wellness, the part of us that, at its core, regulates our mental, emotional self? Perhaps we change our state of being by looking inside and simply changing our perspective and perception.

BE STILL. OBSERVE. IDENTIFY. ACCEPT. ELIMINATE.

The wise woman knows instinctually that in order to truly realize herself, she must be still. She must give up things that no longer evolve her by first identifying what they are. She realizes that the ultimate human JOY we seek can only be found in the full acceptance of who we really are, and not in the avatars we've created to define ourselves. When she is fully present and can see her true self clearly, she realizes that the very need for JOY dissolves along with the need to resist pain. She replaces them with humility, for she now trusts the natural flow of life. She becomes one with the all.

It is in that very moment of complete acceptance where she is transformed. It is in that state of awareness that she expands and contracts and breathes life into her thoughts. She now knows that those thoughts become her reality. She has always known. She is…

THE SAGE.
THE MEDICINE WOMAN.
THE DOULA.
THE WITCH DOCTOR.
THE FORTUNE TELLER.
THE WISDOM KEEPER.
THE SANGOMA.
THE MGANGA.
THE MCHAUI.
THE HEALER.

We must remember that we are powerful beyond measure. Each obstacle we are faced with is another opportunity to use our power. It is a step toward our greatness. After all, we have asked to be great.

HEALING ART

Leroy Campbell, Artist

*Art is my saving grace; it is my center of power.
I don't know who I would be, or where I would be without art!*

My family dysfunction, poverty, and emotional childhood pain distracted me from its (art's) power. When I learned of its power; a power that was fighting for me all along, I joined the fight and started a healing force. A healing force that placed me on a path that led me to my passion and my life's purpose.

The healing power of art has been amazing for me. It is therapeutic, and spiritual!

When I paint, I am living in the present…a space where I feel secure, protected, and free. When I paint, I am free to heal, free to face my fears, free to learn from my mistakes, trust my instincts, tap into my potentials and more beautifully, be my authentic self.

I have grown so much, and I am steadily ascending. Because of art, I have befriended people who have helped strengthen my growth. Art has created opportunities for me that weren't there before. Art has invited me into academic and social circles not typical of a boy born poor and raised in the projects.

Because of art I am humanly sound, culturally solid, and spiritually rich.

Art has made clear to me that I am a huge component that makes up what the body of God truly is.

The remaining components are you, all things, life, the planet and the universe itself. Together, we are the body of God. We are all interconnected and supplying this awesome amount of energy that allows us to own our spirit, heal ourselves, find our center of power and our life's purpose.

I am telling you that the Spirit that lives in art lives in you; and in all things that live!

Spirit, because of you, I found me, in art.

A WORLD DECLARATION OF DIVINE LOVE

Nadi, Celestial Musician

May divine love be the centering, sustaining, stabilizing, true-heart connection of all peoples of the world, bridging every soul over the troubled waters of all that is ungodly, and unloving between us.

May the affectionately enveloping, activating presence of love divine be allowed to prove our integrated truth, irreplaceable shared value, and present all souls as necessary, essential participates in the precious body of humanity.

May the numinous, effulgent light of the Spirit of Love lift all veils, heal all that separates the depths of our real interconnection, proving the unmistakable beauty that we are as a planetary family lovingly united.

May our souls soar on the heavenly currents of universal love over the infertile feelings of uprooted yesterdays, ever galvanized, and empowered into the creative, unbounded spiritual intimacies of lovejoys revealed, worldwide respect sealed, and earth harmony fulfilled.

May divine love be given its rightful place in our lives, enthroned forever within each and every heart, wherefrom, now, and henceforth, we speak, fellowship, and have our being, righteously acting in loving relation with each, and everyone under the sun.

May the peace, and pristine presence of the Creator's love be breathed deeply between us, wherein the blossoming fragrances, and overflowing elixirs of ubiquitous happiness transforms all lovelessness into the exquisite harmonies of sweet loving oneness of sister-brotherhood—one-world joined together in fraternal unitary service.

May our essences emerge continually through our soul-eyes to embrace, and reveal the rich flowering bouquet of agape love, that sparkle of humanitarian vision we see as we look within the other, sending us straight to those lavish floral gardens of fruitful love, overspreading throughout mankind as an outgrowth of the oneness of our realized *inmost* divinest truth.

May we take wing and wed the wonders of infinite love in our lives, being, and becoming ascendant, kindred soul companions, unfolding into natures kiss, and cosmic bliss, our paths entwined toward that central shining beckoning us onward, and inward until we stand perfected in collective union within the glorious bosom of eternal love itself; of these times—presently—we live amicably, victoriously, and globally consecrated, triumphant of a Love Supreme, in a world of enlightened goodwill, spiritual light, and altruistic life without end, now, and forevermore.

"It's all about relationship, that supremely loving and joyous interaction with oneself and the heart and Spirit of other people. We are the living sound modules through which Spirit plays Its music, truth, beauty, and goodness upon our hearts."

"Love Triumphant—
Divine Love is now victorious in our lives throughout
the planet, with a faith of heart we begin to experience
the infinite resources and powers of this great gift of love
in every aspect of our lives."

-NADI (C)2015

HARLEM IS A DANCE DIVINE

Abdel R. Salaam, Master Choreographer

Harlem is a Dance Divine...

Harlem is the body motion sublime!

Harlem is the best, the worst, the light and the darkness
Of moving souls whose diverse destinies dance to the drums
Of dreams often deferred, but never destroyed as they
Dip, dart and dive into the endeavors of the divine...

Harlem is a Dance Divine...
The cultural symbol of wisdom through signs...

Harlem is dance to the infinitive power times one.
Harlem is the movement of God in an elliptical lean
nine degrees to right of being while balancing seven
degrees toward the left and center of creation...

Harlem is a Dance Divine...
The syncopated motion in time...

Harlem is the crown of Black energy through rhythmic feet;
a twentieth-century cool footprint that became
the hotstep of a world culture...

giving birth To the Planet Funk…
always hip as it hops toward the light…

**Harlem is a Dance Divine…
the healing fruit of rhythm dropping off the vine!**

Harlem is the S#@%!…The essence of a
People whose creative movement is so powerful that
Even their waste continues to fertilize not only a
Hungry society, but also a starving planet as she seeks
To enrich her global culture through the sacred and
Secular dances of the rhythms of life.

**Harlem is a Dance Divine…
…an urban cultural Mastermind!**

Harlem is the urban realization of your dreams
That dance their way into eternity…
Harlem is the urban plantation of the twentieth century
Whose crop of creativity fed an entire nation and then the world.
Harlem is the urban mojo of Black America with an African Soul and a hip-hop
beat…the fulfillment of an urban Prophecy of the global awakening of
never-ending dance with bangin' body feats.

Harlem was and is an urban prayer for American
Culture in the hopes of what it could be…
Harlem is hope In motion…people moving in praise
Of almighty God in his and her infinitive forms whose
60's anthem; "and we were dancin' in the streets",
became a vision realized in the next millennium as
an entire planet breaks, pops, and locks to a backbeat
…to the black beat…to the beat…

**Harlem is a Dance Divine…
A healer through dance and movements throughout time…
Harlem is a Dance Divine…**

©2004/2017

MUSIC MEDICINE

Katriel Wise, Metaphysical Musician

Since the dawn of time, music tones and rhythms have shaped our world. The ancients tell us that in fact our universe was created by sound. One of the definitions of the word uni-verse is "one song". Music as medicine comes from the metaphysical 'innerstanding' that harmonic tones directly affect the body's hormonal system positively or negatively. This is why a song can make you feel better or a song can vex your spirit. I always tell the story about a person who is depressed to the point of suicide, and a song comes on that completely changes their life.

When you look into the science of it, each note in the musical scale corresponds to a color and chakra (energy center in the body that channels life force energy to all the meridian points). So, you begin to see how using tones to heal makes sense. It gives new meaning to when someone says, "That song makes me feel good all over."

Some people take a very therapeutic and clinical approach to healing with music. Others intuitively create music from the depth of their heart and soul that causes radical healing in a natural way. We all have artists that "do it for us", ain't that right?

In reality everyone is their own healer and a major part of the work of global healers should be to create an international shift where people stop looking outside themselves for answers. Especially in this society, which is all about the external, it is time to go within and awaken your inner healer. Instead of being dependent on doctors to the point that we cannot think for ourselves or even more to the point "feel" for ourselves, we must go back to the ancient ways, to our ancestral wisdom.

As I've previously written [Excerpt from *Circles of Wellness* (2015)]:

"Western civilization has been in a linear, patriarchal and logic-oriented mode for several thousand years and thus has dominated the world through conquest. Now the return of the matriarch brings circular creativity and compassion.

The next level is SPIRAL which is reflected throughout nature and music. It is not enough to be circular because a circle can be caught in a loop that can't elevate to its fullest potential. When musical notes are played the pattern is circular, yes, but the harmonics of the overtones ascend in spiral patterns. Likewise, when we make the conscious choice to eat foods in their original whole form the spirals are visible to the eye. Try it yourself. Cut open an orange, okra, celery base…on & on to infinity…notice the spiral patterns…Heal thyself starting in a circle of wellness and daily as you do the work of wellness witness yourself holistically ascending into a spiral of profound transformation. The new Star Generation can also be called the Spiral Generation."

So, if you tie healing If you tie it back to music, it is all very simple. If we all sing more every day and even drum or play any instrument, we will become more "in tune" (pun intended) with the rhythm of life.

In love & oneness…
Katriel

ART GUIDES MY LIFE'S PURPOSE

Marilyn "Idaka" Worrell, Artist/Activist

Early in life, I learned to always stand in my power and speak my truth. What I was taught, I learned. What I learned, I live. What I live, I teach. I remain in the light. Keeping the spiritual, intellectual nkisi (medicine) content pure is a perpetual task.

I wrote one of my first poems inspired by the 'Tale of the Firebird,' read to my 6th grade class, by Miss Kane. One line of my poem impressed my father. **"Why has life just begun but nearly through? Why does the cow go moo?"** This was a manifestation of my childhood inquiry and investigation into the world around me.

The first Broadway production I saw as a child was Josephine Baker with Carmen de Lavallade and Geoffrey Holder, as the opening act. This set my standard for performance and production. All performance presentations are sacred ceremonial rituals.

I dedicate my art, to the advocacy, support and education of our youth and families, and in turn, our community in the holistic celebration of our societal improved healthy development. All storytelling, dance performances, performance art presentations, classes for youth, visual art projects are vehicles to disseminate historical, cultural and spiritual Nkisi (medicine). **OVO Productions** is my company committed to researching, writing, preserving and performing and teaching **O**ur **V**ery **O**wn African Diaspora cultural stories.

My signature literary performance art work is *'My Cells Are Awake and Remember',* for which I received a 1990 New York State Fellowship Artist Grant. This was my maiden voyage as a cultural lecturer through the arts. The work was a channeled, ancestral narrative. What has followed are a series of children stories connecting the elements of the universe to our human behavioral experiences. The series introduces; 'The Baale's Basket', 'Nimbus & Accaar', 'Lil Puff and 'Diamonte Love'. This soon to be published collection, will be a collaboration with visual artist illustrator.

What is most important to my artistic life is content and structural relevance to my humanitarian, ethnic, cultural being. My art was cultivated to be of valuable service to my world Kanda (community). hat training included alchemical, historical, physical, spiritual and health investigation, study, development and the dissemination of that knowledge. My cultural heritage Nganga (masters) have been: Baba Fu-Kiau, Dr. John Henrik Clarke, Dr. Leonard Jefferies, Dr. Frances Cress Welsing, Dr. Joy DeGruy Leary, Dr. Marimba Ani, Diana Pharr, Queen Afua, Dr. Ivan Van Sertima, Dr. Cheikh Anta Diop.

In addition to my cultural, artistic training and my Spiritual development, I researched and studied African Global history, art and natural healing. I continue to study Alchemy with Diana Pharr and acupuncturist, Lyndsay Flauntleroy. Nearly 30 years ago, I experienced my first 21 Day Fast was with the guidance of Queen Afua. The ritual of my body temple purification is a primal task. My divine creative instrument is my body and mind. My body houses my mind. My mind receives and delivers the thoughts of my spirit. My spirit is in commune with the universe. The ritual of purification keeps me clear, open and receptive to the positive light energy telegraphed through the universe.

With 50 years of a professional artistic career that has taken me around the globe, I continue to evolve. Now more than ever, I am committed to the elevation and celebration of educating and healing the ignorance and hurts in our society. We must keep our existing African Diaspora classical literature alive. These are the stories that tell the events of our survival successes.

Music is an important part of our cultural history. Musicians, composers, visual artists, filmmakers, directors, dancers, writers, poets and Spoken wordsmiths are all members of the sacred temples of creativity and become the initiated priests and priestesses of our culture.

Every performance I present is a sacred ceremony. I do not intend to preach a sermon. I only intend to present pure thought to honor and serve the attendees with shared blessed messaging from the universe to preserve and cultivate the purity and elevation of our kanda (community).

Each movement, sound, object, color and thought is deliberately chosen to add to the composition of the ceremony and is intended to transmit a message of enlightenment. CAUTION: All of the messaging is not going to be hypnotic pleasure. Some of the information coming through will be urgent alert warnings. There is need for serious attention to be paid to all information delivered to the kanda (community).

Our collective assignment is to be informed, trained and prepared to build, protect and strengthen ourselves, our children, our community, our nation and our world. We must remain vigilant in the guardianship of our children and elders by keeping a 'laser watch' on the institutions that have access to their minds and bodies. We must protect them, ourselves and each other.

My resource and recommended reference on the art of self-healing from the African prospective is the book: ***Self-Healing Power and Therapy–Old Teachings from Africa by Kimbwandende Kia Bunseki Fu-Kiau,*** *introduction by Nana Marimba Ani.*

Baba Fu-Kiau is the main founding resource for the structuring of the one cultural organization conceived and founded by the visionary, Kwayera Archer Cunningham. I am aligned with and have pledged commitment to this cultural arts institution, Ifetayo Cultural Arts Academy, which is an exceptional example of the African based institution truly dedicated to the principles of the Nzugo Saba, honoring, supporting and nurturing the children and families of African descent.

Finally, I share with you my creative ancestral collaborator, my beloved ancestor sister, Faybiene Miranda, who dedicated her art and her life to the service of the Kanda as the divine celestial Empress wordsmith. Her gifted words to the children, speak to us all:

"I am focused. I am centered. I am disciplined. I have pride in myself. Yes, pride in myself. I have a body and a mind, and i am connected. I am connected to myself."

FAYBIENE MIRANDA

"We are as strong as the baobab tree."

FAYBIENE MIRANDA

For healing the planet Earth, I offer:

"We are strong enough to be…" and *"my cells are awake and remember."*

Ashe!

LOVE IS THE LAW

Snt Urt Kaitha Het Heru

These Ancient Afrakan Khamit Nubian Beauty Wisdom Teachings are humbly offered by High Priestess of Sacred Beauty from The Temple Beautiful. BEAUTY IS THE OUTPOURING OF THE LAW OF LOVE.

There is a way. Not the only way. It is a path; not the only path. It is Wat Het Heru: Way of The Heart. This path teaches Love and Compassion for ourselves, each other and The Great Earth Mother, Ta-Urt. It teaches respect for the Ancestors, to look up at the sun, the moon, the stars, and send blessings to the Universe. It teaches that Beauty unfolds from within through setting an intention to be attentive to the ways of the Law of Love, the Law of The Source-Eress, the Divine Feminine Principle known in the ancient of days as Mut HET HERU; The Great SHE of Divine Love, Sacred Beauty, Wealth, Joy, Peace, Wholeness.

"…love thy neighbor as thyself." These words are engraved on our memory chips. We recognize them to be part of the commandments given to us by the Afrakan Master Yeshua, known as Jesus, the Christ.

How many of us actually live the truth of these words? How do we love our neighbors if we not first love ourselves?

Thousands of years ago before the birth of Christianity, our Afrakan ancestors, masters of the universal laws and science of mind were aware of the knowledge of the body's cosmic connection to the Divine Feminine and Masculine Principle, NTR.

Our Afrakan Masters taught ALL IS MIND, the universe is mental. They taught the law of vibration. Your entire body, all things, vibrates with thinking cells. There are millions of these tiny thinking cells in your body having the consciousness of Perfection, and intelligence.

Imagine! And, they are subservient to You—Consciousness.

The Afrakan Master Teachers knew of the effects of the mind and feelings, your emotions, on the body, and the incredible healing power of words.

It is our ignorance and misapplication of the laws of Mind, The Law of Love; Beauty; Forgiveness; that is responsible for the imbalances and *inharmonies* we suffer today.

More importantly, we do not LOVE OURSELVES. For the next seven days, morning, noon, at night, look in a mirror, into your eyes: Say, "I Love You." You have stepped onto the path: Wat Het Heru: Way of The Heart. Now, say to your neighbor, "I Love You."

The loss of and or forgetfulness of our spiritual and cultural traditions, rituals, family life, in addition to the psychological effects of slavery of all kinds, have been devastating. We have been deeply scarred by these experiences.

We do not love ourselves because we do not know who or what we are. We are ALL born of NTR, The One LoveSpirit.

We are the individualizations of the Infinite LoveSpirit. You are not a little bit or a spark. You are actually the creation and manifestation of the One Divine Ankh (Life). "We have been created and come forth from the limbs of NTR." We live and more and have our Being in Divine Ankh (Life). The true Temple is your Beautiful Body Temple.

Beautiful Star Lights! Dare To Sparkle! Stand In Love! The greater the awareness of the truth of your own being the greater is your power.

Master Peace. Simply Divine.

RITUALIZE, COME ALIVE

Prema

RITUALIZE COME ALIVE

Align with the Divine

Clarify your mind

Seize the time

Rise with the sun

Invoke the one

Chant, sing, beat on your drum

RITUALIZE COME ALIVE

Build a sanctuary in your home

Take a moment to weep and moan

Listen to the elders release your rage

Burn copal, cedar and sage

RITUALIZE COME ALIVE

Be silent hear the voice within

Blend with your most sacred friend

Prepare your soul to ascend

Testify to life and its worth
Celebrate each day since your birth
Plant seeds that will nourish the earth
RITUALIZE COME ALIVE

Breathe a full breath in the open air
Commune with nature while you are there
Exercise your body as a form of prayer
Protect your space, internalize truth and grace
Forgive someone, then embrace
Neutralize the forces that traumatize
RITUALIZE COME ALIVE

Visualize your plan when the new moon beams
Purify, fast, sweat, steam
Drink from a pure mountain stream
Observe the stars at night
analyze the depth of your plight
focus your gaze on the inner light
RITUALIZE COME ALIVE

Cultivate your most inspired gift
Dance, paint, energize, uplift
Be disciplined, be swift
Activate, meditate, create
Alternate your state, validate
Spiritualize, organize, strategize, actualize
RITUALIZE COME ALIVE

©Prema2006 (From CD—RITUALIZE/Prema)

WOMEN NEED TO HEAL

Reverend Hasifa A. Rahman, Awakening

For too long now, women have been subjugated by men and not allowed to be their fully sacred selves. Women have been abused and even killed for being themselves. It is historical that for centuries in some cultures, thousands of babies and women were abused and killed every day simply because they were born females and were thought to be of little value. Women have always known that this was wrong but were often too powerless to do anything about it.

Although women have suffered various forms of abuse for centuries, we sometimes don't even recognize it, especially in today's fast-paced, high-tech, globally-connected, sophisticated world. Recently, I saw hundreds of thousands of women come out politically to demonstrate against Donald Trump because of the way he views women, and the terrible things he said publicly about them. This said something to me: this is the time to start a new Women's Movement to build the kind of self-esteem and empowerment that will get us what we want and need.

There were more than 250,000 women who organized themselves in Washington, DC to send Donald Trump a very strong message, on the day after his inauguration. They organized and presented themselves in peaceful protest, as simultaneous demonstrations took place all over the world. What I learned, is that we must have faith in ourselves.

Organizing and presenting ourselves with courage and conviction, represents power. Remembering the past and judging how it could have been, I see the future, and how it can be. The time has come that we've all been waiting for—the time of change when the female comes into her full power. We almost had a woman President, but the powers that be did not allow that to happen in US politics in 2016.

In my opinion, although Hillary was, in many ways, the perfect candidate, with an exceptional record of decades of service, global experience, courage and personal fortitude in the face of many adversaries, there was a long-time war on her, and in the end, she was the victim of abuses by the political system based on her gender. It's time for a change.

Women must be respected as equal to men and will not remain in second place due to culture, religion, economics or politics. We've come to the place where we must heal from the pain of the past. We must cleanse our minds and bodies, and we must not allow any more abuse from any part of society. Men who hurt us physically, mentally, spiritually, economically and politically, will have to be removed from power over our lives.

As women, we should turn to each other for love, comfort and healing help. We must continue to join together and bond in new and creative ways. We can put our monies together, so that we have the economic leverage and financial independence to let go of the men who hurt us. We must continually educate our children about the power of women, so we can begin a new world, a bright world, where women are respected, and rightly understood. We must move on to God head.

Be The Light!

Reverend Nafisa Sharriff, Meditation & Dance

I like to say, "My mother gave life to me twice: once in my birth and once in her death." For the past thirty (30) years, since my mother's death in 1987 I have been on my personal journey to heal my heart and to know my Self—the Divine Love and Light that resides within the Holy of Holies of my own heart. It has been and continues to be a path of purification, meditation, reflection, contemplation and complete transformation.

Who knew that the more I anchored myself on my Spiritual path the more disruptive the path would become: my marriage would fall apart, money would become illusive, I would spend a complete year in prayer, meditation and isolation? And, who knew that I would spend nine years of my life journeying from one home to another dismantling belief systems, thought patterns, habits and ways of being that once so perfectly defined my life? All necessary—if I was to develop a deeper, more profound relationship with God within ME!

One day while in meditation, I received a message to start wearing all white. No problem. I thought that in a few days or weeks I would go back to wearing my wonderful, colorful wardrobe. Wrong! For the past 16 years I have been wearing all white, all the time - even in New York City in the winter time! Needless to say, I have very interesting conversations with strangers who are intrigued, perplexed and even inspired by me wearing all white—all the time.

One of the most interesting and thought-provoking questions from a stranger was, "Are you as pure inside as you look outside?" Without missing a beat, I said, "I try to be." We both smiled, and she walked away.

This stranger got me thinking. Am I as pure inside as I look outside? Am I walking my talk? Have I truly integrated all of the esoteric teachings I learned from my various teachers in Egypt, India and especially from the Brotherhood of Light, the Masters of the Dimensions who gifted humanity with a complete system of Spiritual Tools for Transformation? I live my life by these teachings; they are the foundation and Hallmark of Entering the Holy of Holies, An Institute of Learning and Healing, Inc., my not-for-profit 501(c)(3) organization I founded in 2004. I decided then, and there, right on a train platform in NYC, to raise my Spiritual bar and commit to paying more attention to the Spiritual unfoldment of my own life.

I decided to meditate more, chant the name of God more, place myself in spiritual environments where people were praising God more and be more kind to strangers, the homeless and the downtrodden – all with the intention of laying down my judgments and seeing God in everyone and everything—all the time.

If this sounds like "work", it is. The Spiritual journey demands all of you, all the time. It requires a vigilance to every thought, word and deed that you express as well as a willingness to always choose Truth and Love over Fear and Hate – no matter what.

For many people the idea of deconstructing their reality and reconstructing a new one is daunting. The very thought of diving deep into your own mind, body and spirit and dismantling most of what you discover about yourself and then taking full responsibility for assembling and assimilating the life of your dreams into your every-day reality is overwhelming.

But when your spiritual alarm clock goes off—and one day it will—nothing and no one can keep you from embarking upon what will eventually become the greatest gift you will ever give to yourself.

You don't have to change your religion, go live in a cave or wear white. But you do have to commit to Being The Light with every breath and every step that you take; for to find your Life - the essence of Love and Light that you are - you must first lose your life, as you know it.

This path has been prepared by the many—Masters, Ancestors and Ancient Ones—who walked it before you. They are just waiting for you to join them on the journey. Remember, although it may sometimes feel like it, you never walk this path alone. Be encouraged and find faith in even your small victories. Allow your heart to open and your mind to come unto peace. Learn to love yourself, each other and the world. You will be amazed at whom you will meet and what you will be able to accomplish along the way!

With Great Respect and Love, I wish you Benevolent Blessings, as you become the Light.

With Every Breath…Breathe Love!
Copyright 2017

THE POWER OF L-O-V-E... NUMERICALLY SPEAKING

Lloyd Strayhorn, Astro-Numerologist

Healing the planet and the urgency to do so is stronger now than ever. So, going "green" and/or being conscious of global warming, carbon emission and man's insatiable desire to blow the planet to kingdom come, is now front and center. With growing concern! That's because toxic air, polluted water, greed, political ignorance and other negative effects are causes that can no longer be denied. For example, on the big island of Hilo in Hawaii, in the 1980's, rainfall was a very frequent occurrence. Fast forward to the present, rainfall isn't as frequent now as it was then and it's not only in Hilo. There are ecological changes affecting this entire planet earth, be it North, East, West or South. Part of the process leading to a healthier, happier, healing planet is to work in harmony with Mother Nature, rather than trying to control it. Controlling the earth in a man-made way will never be as beneficial as man working in a spirit of harmony, teamwork, cooperation, and understanding with nature.

There's another way of being in accord with healing the planet. That is Numerology. I can imagine someone saying, "Umm what do you mean?" I'm glad you asked questions. Numbers, in this case, Numerology, act as a guide to the best time to be on the best of terms with Mother Earth. For example, this healing earth knows the best time and location for vegetation and fruits to come to the surface! This healing earth also knows when to signal for fish to swim upstream, birds to fly South and other species to migrate as well as other earthly phenomenon. If one were to look closer, there is an element of time (or numbers) for these processes to take place; from the time a seed is planted to the time it bears fruit and from the time a fish or bird is signaled to start their journey, to the time they finally reach their destination. There is a numerical order or sequence that guides this awesome force of nature.

Numerology, therefore, is an esoteric

outreach to this healing earth by knowing the best time for activities and decisions that are in alignment with the earth itself. For example, let's say you're a Leo. Well in astrology, Sunday is the best day of the week for this sign to carry out their plans. Well, in numerology, Sunday is the best day of the week for anyone born on the 1st, 10th, 19th or 28th of any month. This cosmic law works for everyday in the week, every sign in the zodiac and every birthday from the 1st to the 31st. You may be asking what is my point regarding Numerology and its relationship to this healing earth?

The point is simple, really. The more aware we are of our cosmic make-up by way of Numerology and other cosmic branches, the better off the world will be, the faster it's healing process and the happier and healthier we'll be as Mother Nature continually heals herself.

When asked the question, "How I would heal the planet, there're likely to be a million and one ways; and then some, how to do it. Someone would suggest an end to pollution; another, say this, or another, say that. And each one would be entitled to their opinion. I have my opinion, too! My opinion is L-O-V-E, and the power behind when its intentions are properly applied.

The word, LOVE, sounds so simplistic. But, LOVE is magic. LOVE is eternal. LOVE has the power to heal! And, if no one else, at this point in time, who needs healing? Mother Earth; Mother Nature, herself! But it all starts with us, which begins with YOU. Seeds planted with the right intension (LOVE), especially in 2017, should bear fruit in ways you couldn't possibly imagine up the road ahead. When you truly LOVE yourself, it begins the process of healing the earth.

One, hopefully, realizes that they too, have a place on this planet, but with a measure of time. It's within this measure of time, when the process of LOVE begins. To LOVE and love selflessly! That, the intentions be without thought of what is to gain…personally or otherwise.

Universally, it sets into motion, like a rock thrown into a middle of a pond, to send out ripple waves along the water, returning to shore. Imagine, a simple act of kindness (LOVE) towards one another each day and its "ripple" effect of LOVE, will set your "pond" into motion.

At the moment, HATE, seems to permeate the earth by its conflicts of war, and the ugliness by way of words and deeds to others. HATE, at the moment, with its divisions on far too many levels, would appear to be the new normal. Not True! When it comes to that fine line between LOVE & HATE…LOVE will always rule!

Don't take my word for it…Google it! Check out the history of any individual, country or nation, where HATE and ugliness prevailed. What were the results?

Mother Nature's LOVE, despite it all, will heal planet Earth.

When asked the question, "How I would heal the planet, there're likely to be a million and one ways; and then some, how to do it. Someone would suggest an end to pollution; another, say this, or another, say that. And each one would be entitled to their opinion. I have my opinion, too! My opinion is L-O-V-E, and the power behind when its intentions are properly applied.

The word, LOVE, sounds so simplistic. But, LOVE is magic. LOVE is eternal. LOVE has the power to heal! And, if no one else, at this point in time, who is in need of healing? Mother Earth; Mother Nature, herself! But it all starts with us, which begins with YOU. Seeds planted with the right intension (LOVE), especially in 2017, should bear fruit in ways you couldn't possibly imagine up the road ahead. When you truly LOVE yourself, it begins the process of healing the earth.

One, hopefully, realizes that they too, have a place on this planet, but with a measure of time. It's within this measure of time, when the process of LOVE begins. To LOVE and love selflessly! That, the intentions be without thought of what is to gain…personally or otherwise.

Universally, it sets into motion, like a rock thrown into a middle of a pond, to send out ripple waves along the water, returning to shore. Imagine, a simple act of kindness (LOVE) towards one another each day and its "ripple" effect of LOVE, will set your "pond" into motion.

At the moment, HATE, seems to permeate the earth by its conflicts of war, and the ugliness by way of words and deeds to others. HATE, at the moment, with its divisions on far too many levels, would appear to be the new normal. Not True! When it comes to that fine line between LOVE & HATE…LOVE will always rule!

Don't take my word for it…Google it! Check out the history of any individual, country or nation, where HATE and ugliness prevailed. What were the results?

Mother Nature's LOVE, despite it all, will heal planet Earth.

CHANGE STARTS WITHIN

Un Nefer Hetep Rā "Jawanza!", Holistic Dialogue

---

*L*et us take a few moments to talk about change. According to the dictionary, "change" is defined as, "…to make radically different…transform…replace with another…become different…undergo transformation…" So, in the context of the questions: "How do we change the world?" (in the macrocosm) and, "How do we change ourselves?" (in the microcosm), it is very important that we agree on several points. First, we must understand what needs to be changed and secondly, we must learn why we need to change it. Let us explore these questions in depth.

The negative state of affairs in the world is sadly alarming. Things could and should be better. Statistics relating to criminal behavior, failed marriages, infant mortality, pollution, starvation, domestic violence and so on, paint a vivid picture that something is desperately wrong. How did we get here? Shekhem Ur Shekhem Ra Un Nefer Amen provides us with ancient Kamitic teachings which say: It is Man's (Woman's) identification with the *human* aspect of our being as opposed to the *Divine* aspect of our being that is the source of all of our problems in the world. We must do the work to awaken the dormant faculties within us. As the human race, we can rise above greed, anger, stress, jealousy and selfishness, which manifest in the world as wars, crime, divorce, sickness, and unjust profit over people. When we realize that, our humanity is an evolutionary stage and not the end goal, only then will we seek to transcend the human identification with its flaws and embrace a higher self-image. Such a Divine self-image is consistent with the purpose for Woman's (Man) creation, which is to allow God the use of our person to come into the world. Yes, God needs us!

Now the question becomes: How do we make this shift in consciousness, which is to become the foundation for change? I am so glad you asked. Meditation is the vehicle that many on the "enlightened path" have used to transform their individual lives. It is clear that very well meaning "Spiritual Leaders" have given techniques that have done little to affect the state of the world on a large scale. That is where the ancient Kamitic teachings under the guidance of Dr. Ra Un Nefer Amen come in. The Kamitic Tree of Life, the Metu Neter Volumes, and other of his works provide Man (Woman) a framework within which to start the process of going within to make the necessary changes, using meditation, words of power (e.g. hekau), visualization and other tools to aid in the transformation process. Dr. Amen teaches, "Anything that is harmful to you can't be natural to you." Toxic expressions such as anger, fear, worry, grieving and jealousy, ultimately release harmful, toxic emissions into the bloodstream causing a host of medical problems. The answer lies in knowing that your "nature is an unconquerable peace that nothing can disturb."

The change we are seeking will occur only when it is understood that the harmful manifestations of the human identity, as well as, the animal and reptilian brain, not only can, but must be transcended. If we look at the very well-meaning attempts to enact change in the human condition by humans, they have mostly been external in nature. We have marched, prayed, lobbied, rioted and passed laws. Yet the negative conditions still exist and in many cases worsen. Here's why. Change cannot start from without. For example, I cannot pass a law to make you love me or see me as your equal. That is an inner job that each of us must make a priority if we are going to peacefully co-exist on this planet we call home. Will we actually live to see the result of our individual/collective efforts? Time will tell, regardless, we must start the process. Our children's future is literally in our hands. As with any endeavor, after goals are set, there must be barometers in place to measure whether or not we are on course.

The desired goal is the changing from identifying with the "human" part to the Divine part of our being. This new identity is not to be a hit and miss, occasional occurrence, but an everyday, minute by minute, all the time transformation. This is more than a name change; this takes work. It will be more than a change in wardrobe. It will take more than "going natural" or wearing the Ankh. Change starts within. Accompanying this new shift in awareness, there will need to be a shift in your attitude. There will be no need to argue, debate, ridicule, or in any way demean those of our co-earth inhabitants for their level of awareness. We all have room to grow; that is part of the reason that we are here. We all know people who have gotten a little information and embarrass themselves trying to prove what they know. Of course, it feels good when the "light" inside starts to illuminate the chambers in our minds. But do not judge others. Let your new light shine through you peacefully, patiently, and lovingly. Remember, "One man plants, another waters, but God gives the increase."

Your Sheps, your Enlightened Ancestors have brought you to these pages for a reason. It is no accident that you are here. You had an appointment with these words and you are on time, as I knew you would be…We are One. Not only are you reading these words, you wrote them. The Divine that is your Consciousness (and mine) has just introduced us to Ourselves. What an honor to meet you (me). As you turn these pages and move on to the next, remember why you came to this work in the first place. Remember why you picked up this book, and more importantly, why you wrote it. You have been chosen. Did you think you were called here by accident? Everyone in the world will not read these words, but you did.

Next question: What now? How do I fulfill my purpose? The answer is: "Change starts within." Let's start right here, right now. Close your eyes for a moment and take a slow, deep breath, inhale and release your breath through your nostrils very slowly. It is time to connect with your own breath. It is time to connect with your ancestors. Do you know who you are? You are Divine. Embrace your Divinity. Cultivate and charge your Life force. God needs you to come into this world! Are you ready to surrender everything to become the change, so that others actually may see your transformation and be inspired to join you on this path of healing? Are you ready to let go of anger, guilt, fear, jealousy, sickness, grief, stress, judgments and hate? Are you ready to live a life filled with, peace, joy, success, love, justice, health and wealth? If your answer is "Yes" to these questions, then get ready to go inside because change starts with you and change starts within.

Until we meet again, I want you to start the practice of journaling because you will need to monitor your progress. Remember, change must be measurable; otherwise you are just talking to be talking. You need to see if you are indeed making strides. Also, remember not to be hard on yourself. If you are not careful, you can become frustrated when you encounter someone else who appears to be ahead of where you currently are. Don't get caught up in that trap, you are where you need to be: right here, right now!

The challenge...

I, Jawanza, challenge everyone reading these words to read several books: *MAAT: The 11 Laws of God* by Ra Un Nefer Amen; *Metu Neter* Series by Ra Un Nefer Amen; *Sacred Woman* by Queen Afua; *Heal Thyself* by Queen Afua.

These authors have given us groundbreaking information that we can use to help enhance our Spiritual walk by providing guidance that is unparalleled. As you continue with your journey, it will be of utmost importance to feed your mind, and not just for intellectual stimulation. The ancient Kamitians have left with us with this saying: "To know truth, you must live it."

I humbly bow to your Presence acknowledging the Divinity that you are. Now it is time to manifest that Sacred Divinity in every word, thought, and deed. That change, needed to manifest God will have to start within.

Are you ready? I thought so...Change Starts Within!!

Peace and Blessings,
The Shepsu, the Enlightened Ancestors are speaking...are you listening?"
Jawanza!

HEALING THE SOUL

Memnon Uzan, Mathemetician

Spirit has never been correctly taught in this world. All things must start with Spirit, first. When we graffiti the soul, the spirit loses its head; behavior then becomes polluted through the flesh and moves in only the animal state.

Man and woman have defined this reality. In metaphysics, man is the Sun and woman is the Earth. The Sun nourishes the Earth. In its lead and radiance, the Sun cultivates a seeds of growth, benevolence, charity, tolerance, health, wellness, omnipresence, omnipotence and omniscience. what is in that Sunlight determines what will be fed to the Earth. The Woman is everything, she is the celestial grounding and grounding spirit of what rises anew. If that is polluted it destroys a world. Indeed, it is VITAL that the Sun shines an optimal nutrition and responsible light to the Earth. This world is suffering from a from the gluttony of foul.

Man and Woman have no true alignment of what is man or what is woman. Healing starts with psychiatry. Etymologically, psychiatry means "healing the soul." The world must go through a series of questions: What is soul? What is spirit? What is pure to the soul? What is food to the spirit? What is the diet to the Being. These questions answered develops an idealism of what is upright, what is the law to character, what is identity, what is genius, what is God; how am I connected?

We are here to master the Being and to live it as human. Instead, we have flipped this and become more of the flesh and less of the Spirit. This academic brings a new consciousness; we are consciously and subconsciously illiterate to the greatness that is the true form of the self-identity. To heal the planet, we must heal our worlds. We must begin by going in on what makes us GOD!

THOUGHTS FOR PLANET HEAL

Lauren Von Der Pool, Chef

When I think about the word healing, my mind immediately goes into the jungle. I understand the synchronicity between healing and the environment. From the oxygen levels, to the frequencies and the foods that grow in it, to the animals and plants that live there, all are adding to life's symphony. We are spiritual magnets that attract magical vibrations that go beyond food, made more accessible in a natural setting. That includes for Instance, our ability to express ourselves through positive actions. I believe the reason why there is so much healing needed in our world is because there are so many cities and far too few jungles. Either way, we must do our best where we are, knowing that the healing is still very much possible within us and the land that we're on! I am an example of that, I was a little girl that had enough initiative and desire to want healing for myself and for all living beings around me.

That initiative energetically called me to a book called ***Heal Thyself*** which I am sure you're all familiar with. I was sixteen years old and it was my first introduction to understanding the value of eating foods that grow from the earth which was a miracle for me and served as an amazing foundation for so much more that I would discover. It is delicious to understand the energies of food, and the importance of it being organic and if possible, home grown. To me the bigger picture is understanding the miracles that we are and how we can impact the food with our presence, sound frequency, thoughts and affirmations. We are exuding this magic, this God presence so to speak, the essence of healing.

My greatest healing experiences come when I am spiritually, physically, and emotionally aligned. It is not enough to eat plant-based foods and rave about our vegan diets, especially when we know we ain't right within. It is more impressive to remember to be kind, loving, compassionate, courageous and grateful at the same time. This is true healing! You see, you can juice and eat organic all you want, and it will help, but if you don't clear the emotional and spiritual toxicity you are holding onto you could very well be worse off than someone eating a Standard American Diet (SAD). A positive spirit can transcend bad eating for a while, a negative spirit can poison everything you touch including the beautiful food you eat. Everything is energy! Everything! I believe you have to have love and what I like to call "feel good energy" in order to give real healing. It moves in a circular motion just like life, when you give healing you are the first to receive it, just like anything else. Understanding these basic principles are the foundation of healing.

As personal chef to the Williams sisters and many other icons of our day, I will tell you first hand that although healthy eating is a part of it, there is so much that goes into being a champion…..Being the greatest and being the healer. For an example, if you are sad, guilty, angry and/or feeling shameful about anything, even if it is justifiable, you close your valve to God's creative abundance because these are low frequency emotions also known as bad vibes. If you are not taking enough time to go within and love yourself you too will be out of balance and the same goes for food. If you aren't loving yourself enough to eat foods that will nourish and electrify the cells in your body, it does not matter how athletic or talented you are. Your physical body will begin to catch up with your low frequency eating habits. You are what you consume on every level.

The awareness of this gives me such a freedom to live life out loud from my expanded self. Knowing that I have access to all things, but I also have the wisdom to choose the juiciest experiences that are most abundant and in alignment with my purpose. The question of how consuming anything, from thoughts to food will add or subtract from me has been a constant life saver for me. As it does for me I hope this awareness gives you the freedom to be who you truly are. I wish for you to be fully, self-expressed in whatever you choose!

The self-realization that God is, was and always will seep through every part of me, was my first step to healing!

SPIRIT CLOSING

"Every great dream begins with a dreamer. Always remember, you have within you the strength, the patience, and the passion to reach for the stars to change the world."

HARRIET TUBMAN

HEALERS UNITE
We, The People

There are many healing strategies in this volume of work. This is a call to AWAKEN THE HEALER WITHIN you. Add your thoughts below. Share. UNIFY.

Date	What would you do to heal planet Earth?

> *We need more light about each other. Light creates understanding, understanding creates love, love creates patience, and patience creates unity.*
>
> MALCOLM X

> *Dr. King wants the same thing I want —freedom!*
>
> MALCOLM X

> *The hope of a secure and livable world lies with disciplined nonconformists who are dedicated to justice, peace and brotherhood.*
>
> MARTIN LUTHER KING JR.

QUEEN AFUA PRESENTS
24 HOUR GLOBAL FAST
SPRING EQUINOX TELECONFERENCE

Meet, greet and celebrate wellness as QUEEN AFUA and music maestro KATRIEL WISE host 35+ Healers, Naturopaths, Yoginis, Vegan Chefs, Community Activists, Wealth Advisors, Motivational speakers, Metaphysicians, Life Coaches, Musicians, Poets, Crystal Healers, Sacred Woman, Soul Sweat and Man Heal Thy Self Practitioners, Colon Therapists, Womb Workers, Reiki Practitioners, Massage Therapists, Numerologists, Authors, Holistic Medical Doctors & Spiritual Leaders that will help heal the people of the planet.

FRI. MARCH 20TH (6PM SUNSET - 12AM MIDNIGHT)
SAT, MARCH 21ST (6AM SUNRISE - 12AM NOON)

FOR MORE INFORMATION AND TO REGISTER VISIT
www.24HOURGLOBALFAST.com

AS THE HEALING CONTINUES

Citizens of planet Earth, followers and leaders of **Planet Heal**, may we live in collective holistic harmony with nature's elements—Air—Fire—Water—Earth. And so, thereby radiate peace in our families, friends, neighbors and communities.

May we citizens of planet Earth respect one another and follow nature's law so we may be made whole.

May **Planet Heal** inspire us to heal thyself daily in body, mind and spirit and cause humanity to reach a radiant optimal frequency of well-being.

Planet Heal is a call out to we, The People, to waken or reawaken the knowledge that the power to heal is within us. As was shouted out in the streets and across this planet during the Civil Rights Movement of the 1960s, may it always be remembered and acted upon, "All power to the people!"

To Shift, To Overcome , To Heal,

Queen Afua

WE STAND UPON THEIR SHOULDERS

———◦◦∞◦◦———

Honor and respect to our Cultural Healers; among them
ESTEEMED ELDERS and BELOVED ANCESTORS.
The teachings from these educators and/or artists have laid the
foundation for the restoration of our cultural well-being.
Many are acknowledged and quoted throughout this volume.

In appreciation we continue to affirm:
"We stand upon their shoulders."

Educational Cultural Healers:
Dr. Marimba Ani, Dr. Molefi Kete Asante, Dr. Yosef Ben Jochannan (Doc Ben),
Ida B. Wells-Barnett, Dr. Mary Mc Leod Bethune,
Dr. George Washington Carver, Thurgood Marshall,
Dr. John Henrik Clarke, Dr. Cheikh Anta Diop, W.E.B. DuBois,
Marcus Garvey, Professor William Leo Hansberry,
Heru Ankh Ra Semahj Se Ptah, Dr. Asa Hilliard,
John G. Jackson, Dr. George G.M. James,
Dr. Leonard Jeffries, Dr. Rosalind Jeffries,
Brother Bill Jones, Sister Kefa Nephthys (Jones),
Nana Amma Ansaa Atei, Dr. Maulana Karenga, Dr. Richard King,
Dr. Jawanza Kunjufu, Dr. Joy DeGruy Leary, Jitu & Angela Weusi,
Gil Noble, Arturo Alfonso Schomburg, Dr. Edward Scobie,
Shekhem Ur Shekhem Ra Un Nefer Amen, Professor James Smalls,
Dr. Frances Cress Welsing, Dr. Chancellor Williams, Booker T. Washington,
Dr. Amos Wilson, Dr. Carter G. Woodson, Dr. Ivan Van Sertima...

Artistic Cultural Healers:
Alvin Ailey, Marian Anderson, Dr. Maya Angelou, LaRocque Bey,
Marie Brooks, John Coltrane, Baba Chuck Davis, Ossie Davis & Ruby Dee,

PLANET HEAL™

Nana Opare Dinizulu, Katherine Dunham, Fela Kuti, Aretha Franklin,
Lorraine Hansberry, Zora Neale Hurston, Baba Kwame Ishangi,
The Last Poets, Abbey Lincoln, Bob Marley, Arthur Mitchell,
Charles & Ella Moore, James Baldwin, Babatunde Olatunji,
Marian Anderson, Miriam Makeba, Oscar Peterson, Pearl Primus,
Paul Robeson, Pharaoh Sanders, Nina Simone,
Nipsey Hussle (Ermias Asghedom)—too soon an ancestor.
Your healing work will continue…

…And we stand on the shoulders of Toni Morrison, Nikki Giovanni,
Sonia Sanchez, Stevie Wonder…

We are profoundly aware there are MANY more.
Indeed, write their names on these pages
and on your hearts.
Let us commit to pass on the legacies
that have been so generously passed on to us.

HEALERS DIRECTORY

AFRIKA, ND, LLAILA O., PHER ANKH: OUR HOMES AS MEDICINE

Teacher, Historian, Lecturer, Author, Health Consultant, Dr. Afrika is a world-renowned authority on health and nutrition. He has a doctorate in Naturopathy and is a degree Certified from The American College of Addictionology and Compulsive Disorders. He was a U.S. Army Social Worker Nurse and Psychotherapist. He is a Metaphysician, Massage Therapist, Herbalist, Medical Astrologist and a Certified Acupuncturist knowledgeable of Chinese Medicine. Dr. Afrika teaches therapeutic massage for stress reduction. Students who complete his Nutritional Counselor Certification course can graduate and be licensed as Naturopaths by Washington D.C.

Dr. Afrika has over 45 years' experience in ethno-medicine (disease diagnosis and subsequent remedies based upon the biochemistry of a race). He has lectured for The International African Holocaust Organization (death and disease caused by the slave trade). His topics include the effect of junk foods on health throughout the African Diaspora. Director of the International Healers section of the International Board of African Thinkers, Priests and Healers, Dr. Afrika contends that good health is a human right and product of nature.

CONTACT:
African Holistic Health Group
P.O. Box 1645
Grand Rapids, MI 49501
For certification courses, lectures and seminars:
Email: llailaafrika@juno.com
Call: 317-216-8088

AKIL, ADIO KUUMBA HEALING WITH FOODS AND HERBS

Adio Kuumba Akil is a natural food chef, cosmetologist, entrepreneur, naturalist, visionary, spiritualist, lover of life and lover of the life. She is the president of Praises Enterprises and the chief formulator of Praises All-Natural Hair and Skin Care products. Serving food at Namaskar in Brooklyn, NY. she says, "I like to focus on beauty from an internal aspect. As a person accepts and loves self and tunes into nature, a world of subtle, miraculous events takes place within. These feelings will soon 'out-picture' themselves as a radiant smile, a twinkle in the eye, a glowing complexion and a cheerful demeanor. I like to say, "What goes in, must come out!"

Adio's Topics include: The Connection Between Health and Beauty; Women's Natural Healing Remedies; Healing the Wounded You; Integrative Food Therapy; Natural Raw Food Preparation I & II; Food Shopping Strategies for Vegetarians and Vegans; Menu Planning/Food Management for Healing and Wellness

Adio presentation history (abridged): American Museum of Natural History; 'Adornment' Natural Hair Care Exhibition, London, England; Georgia Association of Realtors; Naturally and Curly Hair Meet-up; Bronner Bros International Hair Show; International Locks Conference

CONTACT:
Phone – 786-314-3692
Email – adio@praisesproducts.com
Website – http://praisesproducts.com
Facebook – praisesproducts
Twitter – @AdioAkil1
Youtube – praisesproducts

ALEEM, TAHARQA & TUNDE RA
HOW TO HEAL THE PLANET

Since the mid-1960s when they worked and recorded with Jimi Hendrix until today, the legendary twin brothers, Tunde Ra & TaharQa Aleem, (a.k.a., the Ghetto Fighters, Prana People, Us and Fantastic Aleems) have been making rock, blues, R&B, dance and rap music that has proven their musicianship, performance and production artistry. Their place in music history is well established as premier independent record label pioneers. Their status as collaborators with major music talent has propelled them to Hall of Fame attention and recognition in the world of black music, as well as in the world of popular music as a whole.

The Aleems are the authors of: *Jimi Hendrix & the Ghettofighters in Harlem World; Sacred Formulas to Raise the Royal Mind; Jimi & the World of Mu;* and *The 66 Attributes of the Niggar.* They are also the founders of Mind Tour Inc. an advisory agency for the entertainment and the sports industry. The Aleem brothers established Hip Hop for Humanity, a non-profit organization committed to assisting youth by helping them to understand their role as leaders and take responsibility and positive action in their community and in the world.

CONTACT:
aleement@hotmail.com

ARIE, INDIA
SONGERVERSATION: I AM LIGHT

A multi-Grammy award winning singer-songwriter, actress, musician, and record producer, India Arie has sold over ten million records. India went from being a teen in Atlanta, "singing under a tree in the park" to being nominated scores of times and receiving Grammy Awards for her outstanding work. "In 2009 I let go," recalls India. "I realized I had to seize the chance to make the career and life I wanted, not accepting what others wanted me to do. So, I decided to retire, asking God to show me where I am supposed to be." After an extended break, away from the frenzy of the music industry she completed SongVersation, her fifth studio album. India refers to her hiatus and the creation that followed as her time for, "…stepping into my power…being more me in both my life and career." She offers SongVersation: Medicine, an EP meant to encourage healing. SongVersation: Medicine was made to be listened to in a quiet time, during prayer, meditation, and/or Yoga. "My wish is that these songs bring softness, clarity, calm, and inspiration."

CONTACT:
Please visit India.Arie at:
@indiaarie
https://www.facebook.com/indiaarie

AWADU, CHEF KEIDI
SUPERCHARGING THE IMMUNE SYSTEM FOR THE SUPERBUGS OF THE FUTURE: THE 7 PRINCIPLES OF OPTIMAL HEALTH REVISITED

Chef Keidi Awadu is the author of *Living Superfood Longevity: Mastering the Possibilities of High Quality Life Extension.* He is a Las Vegas-based raw food chef who has developed a brand of nutritionally dense cuisine he calls Living Superfood ™. Chef Awadu has pioneered a healing modality called "full-spectrum hyper-nutrition" which uses gourmet raw food cuisine as the delivery vehicle for clinical nutrition (food for healing) and functional medicine (disease prevention). A few of Chef Keidi's biographical "Life-Lights":

- Award-winning raw food chef and longtime master of vegan & vegetarian cuisine
- Developer of the Living Superfood Full-Spectrum Hyper-Nutrition healing system
- Author of 28 books on health, economics, culture and the humanities
- Multi-media journalist for 39 years in print, broadcast and an Internet webcast pioneer
- Internationally featured lecturer on health, culture, global economics, conspiracy and progressive activism
- Life-long career musician and recording artist
- 3 Years of laboratory experience as a reproductive biology cryogenics technician
- Trilingual (English-Spanish-French); studied a total of 8 languages
- Life-long organic gardening expert horticulturalist

CONTACT:
Chef Keidi Awadu
323.902.2919 Las Vegas
702.580.0662 Mobile
Email: Keidi@ChefKeidi.com
Living Superfood
http://www.LivingSuperfood.com

BADU, ERYKAH
THE PARADIGM OF JOY

Self-described as a "mother first," Erykah Badu is a touring artist, DJ, teacher, community activist, three decades vegetarian, recycler, and conscious spirit. She is a Grammy- award winning American singer/songwriter best known for the unique style of her music. Producing iconic soul-hip-hop-jazz sounds, Erykah is regarded as the Queen of Neo Soul. Her celebrated debut album, **Baduizm,** went triple platinum and won Grammy Awards in 1998. Later, Badu released a two-part New Amerykah series, political in tone, it features live instrumentation and highlights Badu's emotional side.

On a personal note, Erykah (assisted by a midwife) gave birth to all three of her children at home. An advocate of natural childbirth and breastfeeding, she appropriately was the keynote speaker at the International Black Midwives and Healers Conference in 2010. Erykah has studied with masters: Queen Afua, holistic health practitioner and spiritual teacher; Dr. Jewel Pookrum, neurosurgeon, physicist and midwife; and Dr. Laila Afrika, scientist, health practitioner and theorist. In 2006, Erykah was certified as a holistic health practitioner through Dr. Afrika; and is a 3rd Degree Reiki Master-Teacher. She studies sound and vibration healing and apprenticed as a direct entry midwife. Erykah has served as doula for natural births.

CONTACT:
http://www.erykah-badu.com/

BEAN, DAAM, DANETT C., HEAL THE MOTHER, HEAL THE EARTH

Dr. Danett C. Bean (Doctor of Acupuncture and Asian Medicine) is a women's health specialist, who in 2018 marks her 15th year in private practice. She is the author of Yoni Box, a health-savvy women's blog and the online bestseller, *A Taste of Our Own Medicine: 3 Vital Keys to Ending Postnatal Depletion, Nurturing Mothers and Improving Our Communities.* Dr. Danett speaks on preventive women's healthcare emphasizing solutions to "increase vitality and decrease health disparities." Her signature Back To The Middle Method and natural remedies has helped women of all ages emphasizing fertility readiness, pre-birth acupuncture, postnatal care and healthy aging. In her private practice in Brooklyn, NY she utilizes meridian imaging to assist patients heal on a root level, as well as provides virtual consultations worldwide. She is a New York State licensed acupuncturist with certifications in Chinese herbology, Eastern Nutrition and Earth Qi Gong. A Clinical Instructor in the Department of Medicine at SUNY Downstate Medical Center, Dr. Danett is appointed to the medical board of the University Hospital of Brooklyn.

CONTACT:
website: drdanettbean.com
email: drdanett@drdanettbean.com
phone: 718 789 2289
Facebook, Twitter and Instagram: Dr. Danett Bean,
YouTube channel: Yoni Box

BLUEPILL (AKA PAUL MORELAND)
PURGE & PURIFY

KTLempowerment@gmail.com
bluepillar44@gmail.com,

You Are Now Rockin' Wit the Best!
www.facebook.com/paul.moreland
www.blogtalkradio.com/knowtheledgeradio
www.youtube.com/knowtheledgeTV
www.thetwinpillars.bandcamp.com

HEALERS DIRECTORY

BOYD, KIMBERLI
WE ARE AT OUR BEST WHEN WE ARE HEALING

Kimberli Boyd is a dancer, choreographer, master teaching artist, registered yoga teacher/yoga therapist (RYT-500) and founder of "Dancing Between the Lines," a movement arts organization based in the Detroit metropolitan area.

A graduate of the Midwest Brain and Learning Institute, Kimberli specializes in improving student learning and creativity through interactive lessons. Her curriculum uses movement and creative dance to teach concepts related to math, science, language arts and more. Through this dynamic fusion of dance, yoga, and learning, Kimberli holds a vision of transforming the educational experience of everyone she has the privilege to teach.

CONTACT:

For more information to reach Kimberli Boyd anytime:
Phone: 248-761-4547
www.DBTLonline.com
info@DBTLonline.com
boyd.kimberli@gmail.com
kboydinc@aol.com
Facebook@bestRKL

BROWN ND, JESSE R.,
A HEALER IN EVERY HOME

Growing up, Jesse Brown had seen family members suffer from heart disease, cancers and near-death experiences. Thus, in his teens, the native of Detroit, Michigan decided to convert to a healthier lifestyle. Once he obtained his undergraduate degree from Eastern Michigan University (1981), Jesse continued studying wholistic health methods. Dr. Brown has trained people from across the US, Canada, the Caribbean and Africa. He and his staff (therapists and consultants) have wholistically served over 50,000 people from all walks of life. A very popular speaker among professionals and laypersons, Dr. Brown has an easy and sometimes humorous way of converting complicated ideas into motivational objectives.

Dr. Brown's Lecture Topics (abridged):
- From the Garden of Eden to the Garden of Eatin'
- A Healer in Every Home
- Genius in your genes and Diamonds in your DNA!
- Discover the Healer in you
- The Wholistic Training Institute - Treatments and trainings (abridged):
- Eating from the Garden
- Colon Hydrotherapy and Digestive Health
- Herbs and Healing
- Iridology
- Reflexology
- Nutrition

CONTACT:

Learn, teach, write books, create health and wellness products.
Detroit Wholistic Center:
20944 Grand River Ave
Detroit, Michigan 48219
www.WholisticTrainingInstitute.com
Twitter @Wholisticguru
313-255-6155
Visit Facebook or LinkedIn pages.

BROWN BA, MA, PGC, SELINA, HEALER WITHIN

Selina Brown is a British-based Success and Soul Coach. Starting from bright beginnings as an elected Member of Youth Parliament at age 16, Selina excelled to gain a Masters in Media Enterprise at just 22 years old. Currently she now holds three educational degrees.

Following her calling as a Healer and Entrepreneur, Ms. Brown birthed Little Miss Creative, Creative High and TNF Mag. Brown's success has led to many opportunities including being featured on MTV and BBC. Through her coaching and empowerment programs, Selina Brown. a certified Holistic Wellness Practitioner is committed to supporting women to own their power and live in their greatness. In Summer 2015, Selina released her first book, ***Before Breath.*** To celebrate its launch, the book was toured in New York, Miami, Brazil and Jamaica.

Qualifications & Coaching Certifications:
BA (Hons): Media and Communication (2010)
MA: Media Enterprise (2011)
International Business Studies (2012)
Certified Womb Wellness Practitioner: Queen Afua (2012)
Holistic Health Practitioner: Queen Afua (2012)

CONTACT:
A: 321 Bradford Street, Digbeth, Birmingham B5 6ET
E: selina@selinabrown.com
W: www.selinabrown.com

CAMPBELL, LEROY, ARTIST HEALING ART

Simply put, Leroy Campbell is a quintessential artist. His work created in a variety of mixed media and
reflective of the African-American experience, evokes an unexpected range of emotions. He becomes a griot, telling stories of hard work, dignity, love and caring. The stories at times are haunting and painful, yet hopeful and inspiring. The stories bring to life folks who are proud, God-fearing and self-reliant.

"I am an artist who believes that art can influence, inspire, and encourage dialogue. I believe art heals, breaks down stereotypes and advocates diversity. My new works proclaim a spirit of universality that will hopefully open the lines of easy communication and promote peace."

CONTACT:
Campbells Fine Art, LLC
Leroy Campbell
1686 Hardin Ave
Atlanta, GA 30337
404.490.0779
www.leroycampbelloriginals.com/
Studio manager:
Patrice
404.441.8281
palexander429@msn.com

CHEATOM, MAKEDA DREAD
PERMACULTURE: HOLISTIC GARDENS AND HEIRLOOM SEEDS

Makeda Dread Cheatom
Executive Director, Founder
WorldBeat Cultural Center
2100 Park Blvd.
San Diego, CA 92101
Direct: (619) 723-8693
Office: (619) 230-1190
Fax: (619) 325-1337
makeda@worldbeatcenter.org
www.worldbeatcenter.org/childrensoutdoor-classroom

WORLDBEAT CENTER

"Your Passport to the World of Music, Art, Dance, and Culture."

CHEF AHKI, ACTIVIST
WHAT'S WRONG WITH HYBRIDS?

Chef Ahki, CEO of Delicious Indigenous Foods is a celebrity chef (Lenny Kravitz, Common, Lee Daniels) and natural foods activist. She says, "In an unfortunate series of events, we have gone from a diet of wildly grown fruits, vegetables and herbs to a diet of **blood** and **starch**." She has guided hundreds of clients through detox programs, colon therapy and overall wellness through a vegan foods lifestyle. Her message, "I'm not eating salad, I'm eating sunlight." has caught fire with mature health nuts and young foodies alike. Her social media presence caters to a highly interactive community as she provides real time, relevant content, practical tips, tools and recipes.

Chef Ahki teaches what she calls "Electric Foods 101" and is busting through health myths daily on her blog while teaching vegan and living food prep classes. The Electric Foods Diet consists of fresh, organic, non-hybrid whole foods, fruits, vegetables, nuts and seeds, sprouted, ground or whole and fresh or dried herbs that are combined for proper digestion. Natural foods are alkaline with a PH of 7 or higher.

CONTACT:
CHEF AHKI
CEO/Celebrity Chef Blogger
DELICIOUS. INDIGENOUS
800-987-1466
www.GoChefAhki.com
www.facebook.com/TheChefAhki
www.twitter.com/Chefahki
www.instagram.com/chefahki
Manager: @itsJonnelle

COLBY, BABA OSAYGEFO
THE CREATOR HAS A MASTER PLANET

Baba Osageyfo Colby returned home from Viet Nam determined to work for himself and to help uplift and empower Afrikan people. The former Philadelphia resident was drawn to the vendors and jewelers making and selling their wares on the sidewalks. By sharing ideas, techniques and expertise, he developed his skills as a master silversmith and entrepreneur. His clients include Wesley Snipes, India Arie and Keith David.

Currently residing in Atlanta, GA, Baba Osageyfo is the proud owner of Timbuktu Art Colony (established in 1971) described as, "A symbiotic system of cooperative economics and sharing of information through art."

CONTACT:
phone: 414-803-5033
email: timbuk2artcolony@gmail.com
website: www.timbuktuartcolony.com
Facebook: Baba Osageyfo

KARMA "SOUL DOCTOR"
THE CREATOR HAS A MASTER PLANET

Karma "Soul Doctor" Colby is a graduate of the Institute of Integrative Nutrition as a Certified IIN Health Coach. She is also certified with global master healer, Queen Afua, as a Sacred Woman (Womb Yoga Dance Practitioner and mentor). Karma has become well-known for her detox facilitation and performing arts healing work and plans to continue practicing from a global and holistic perspective. She attributes her work in the wellness field to being born into a health-conscious home and family business. Karma continues to hone her skills as a designer, jeweler and entrepreneur.

CONTACT:
phone: 832-452-5984
email: karmasouldoctor@gmail.com
website: www.karmasouldoctor.com
Facebook: Karma Anika Lea Colby
Instagram: karmasoul

EDU, MONTHSO & NWASHA
THE S.O.U.L. IN SOULMATING

Monthso and Nwasha Edu are a happily married SOUL MATE team. Together they are the Co-Founders and Co-Directors of The Akoma House Initiative, a culturally based Counseling and Consulting Firm. Their unified purpose is to initiate unity through loving service in ALL our relationships. The Edus are the creators of Akoma Day (The Cultural Alternative to Valentine's Day) currently celebrated in 11 countries around the world, the authors of 3 books and several social development curricula.

CONTACT:
Organization: The Akoma House Initiative
E-mail: akomahouseinitiative@gmail.com
Phone: 609-474-4203
Website: www.akomahouseinitiative.com

EVERETTE-HALE, SHEILA
NATURAL HAIR AND LOVE ON OUR PEOPLE

Sheila Everette-Hale is the CEO and Educational Director of Everette's Natural Beauty School/Salon. She started her business in Detroit, MI, in 1978. Sheila created a new license for the Natural Hair Culturist in the state of Michigan, signed into law in 1997. In 2000, she opened the first worldwide 400-hour Natural Hair Care School. In 2008 Sheila created the first online Natural Hair Care Webinar, teaching both theory and practical techniques. Everette's mission is to create a strong educational foundation in the Natural Hair Industry, worldwide.

Everette-Hale founded LEEP (Linking Everyday Extraordinary People), a community-oriented business incubation and collaboration project dedicated to promoting worldwide entrepreneurship in 2014. The mission is "To create the space and opportunities for people to express and experience their full self-expression (passion)…and get paid."

Sheila, the "Tambourine Queen" is a jazz entertainer and event planner.

CONTACT:
Everette's Natural Beauty School, Inc.
227 Iron Street, Loft 133
Detroit, MI 48207
313-527-2884
www.everettes.com
sheila@everettes.com

FORD, ERICA
HEALING THE COMMUNITY OF SELF

LIFE Camp Founder and CEO Erica Ford provides at risk inner city youth with valuable tools needed to stay in school and out of the criminal justice system. In the 1980s, crack use and gun violence were occurring daily in Jamaica, Queens. At York College (CUNY) Erica served as President of the Black Student Caucus and Vice President of the Evening Student Government. In 1994 she co-founded The Code Foundation with her friend, the late Tupac Shakur, and others. Their mission was to keep young people out of jail and to decrease "Black on Black" crime. In 1998-99, The Code co-coordinated the Million Youth March, when tens of thousands of youth from across the country rallied against injustices and strengthened their platforms. In 2002, the tragic murders of two local children inspired the creation of LIFE Camp (Love Ignites Freedom through Education). Her consistent dedication to reducing violence among young New Yorkers has garnered Erica awards and recognition from notable figures including, former NYC Mayor Michael Bloomberg, Reverend Al Sharpton, and hip-hop mogul, Russell Simmons. Ms. Ford's leadership is manifested by her extensive speaking engagements at prisons, community centers, schools, colleges and conferences, nationally and internationally.

CONTACT:
ericaford@peaceisalifestyle.com

GARRISON, KLARQUE
PHOENIX AFFECTS

Born in Los Angeles, Ca. and educated at Florida A&M University, Klarque Garrison's mantra is "I Love Media, I Am Media, I've Become Media. AND, I need you to help me DRIVE Media." For over 7 years Klarque's been hosting the award-winning show, "The Conversation" where he interviews mainstream and grassroots activists, artists, creators, coaches and entrepreneurs who are making a difference in their communities and the World. In 2012, he founded the Survival Radio Network with the aim at providing top notch programming that will inspire, motivate and educate listeners Worldwide. A Few, years later Survival Radio Christian Network would be born. In August of 2015, Tris Sicignano created Surge Television, a revolutionary new streaming network. Their goal was to support Indie Film Content Creators Worldwide.

CONTACT:
Klarque Garrison
404 447-8265
klarque@survivethenext365.com
www.klicks.us

GOSS, PAUL, ND
THE SENSE OF REASONING AND WILLPOWER

For 60 years Dr. Goss has shared his largely self-taught knowledge of herbs and holistic healing with a growing number of clients. In 1976, he established NEW BODY PRODUCTS in Compton, California. His holistic knowledge had by now earned him the formal title of Naturopathic Doctor.

Using iridology for diagnosis along with herbal remedied and vegetarian diets for treatment, Dr. Goss helped people achieve the NEW BODY they needed or wanted through his unique application of the ancient art of holistic healing.

Dr. Goss has lectured on holistic topics throughout the US state, in Mexico, Jamaica, as well as in countries in Africa and Europe. He has written four books, *Forever Young*, *The Natural Way*, *The Rebirth of God*, and *The Eyes of Forever Young* used in many universities today. His celebrity clientele includes actors Wesley Snipes, Niecy Nash, Stevie Wonder, John Sallie just to name a few.

Today, NEW BODY PRODUCTS are used by millions with over 20,000 distributors, experienced holistic practitioners, and wellness centers all over the United States and other parts of the world.

CONTACT:
Dr. Paul Goss of New Body Products
464 W. Compton Blvd
Compton, CA 90220
Phone: 1 800 638 4372
www.newbodyproducts.net

GRAY, ND, AKUA AND GRAY, ND CHENU
CONSISTENCY

Dr. Akua Gray and Dr. Chenu Gray are the founders of A Life of Peace Wellness Education Institute and have been working in wellness since 1990. Our philosophy in wellness is to be so in alignment with right living that perfect health is a daily occurrence and we have as a personal wellness goal to teach what is best about health and wellness until there is a healer in every home. As recent repatriates to Ghana, West Africa, we have pioneered Divine Life Sanctuary, a Pan-African community on the beautiful ocean front overlooking the Gulf of Guinea. In just a little under a decade, seven families are fully vested, and we have invested in a one-hundred-acre farm project to grow both local organic foods and export crops known as the Divine Life Farm Cooperative. Celebrating 30 years of marriage in March 2018, Dr. Akua and Dr. Chenu are the proud parents of three sons and two beautiful grandchildren.

CONTACT:
www.alifeofpeace.org

HANDY-KENDI, BREATHOLOGIST, AYO & JOHN DAVIES 3, SOUND HEALER
THE POWER OF THE BREATH AND SOUND TO TRANSFORM AND HEAL

The Breath Sekou, Ayo Handy-Kendi is a Sound Healer and Reiki Master. She is the Founder of Optimum Life Breathology ™ & Transcendence Breathwork™ , Founder/Director of African American Holiday Assoc (AAHA) and of the Feb. 13th BLACK LOVE DAY. A master teacher (Sekou) with over 40 years of breath work, Handy-Kendi, is one of a few African-Americans trained in transformative breath techniques. As a Certified Breathologist, Laughter Yoga Teacher, Transformational Facilitator, and Reiki Master Sekou Ayo has presented breathology to billions both on-line and in-person. She also provides "breath-shops", programs and certifications.

Ayo's husband, John Davies 3 a Certified Breathologist, has been a musician and sound and production technician since the 70s. An artisan who creates sacred geometries, orgones, and other crafts using sound patterns, John is also a sought-after photographer and video photographer.

Ayo and John collaborate as the CEO's of PositivEnergyWorks, LLC, a holistic health service focusing on relaxation and stress management. With their Earth Love Tune Up Crew (ELTUC) they co-produce books, CD's and DVD's about using Breathology practices. ELTUC delivers a unique relaxation experience in this stressed-out world. ELTUC provides "African-centered and natural sound, tune-up music" as the sacred balance for breath and sound healing, play, laughter, visualizations, relaxation, movement, lifestyle/health management, and racial/diversity healing.

Breathe deeply, calm down, and tune up to tune-in, in order to be in peace and balance to transform to your highest frequency.

CONTACT:
Emails: ayomeansjoy@yahoo.com
   jpdavies3@gmail.com
Phone: 202-667-2577
ayomeansjoy1@skype.com
Ayo Handy-Kendi@youtube.com
http://www.PositivEnergyWorks.com/
http://www.africanamericanholidays.org/
https://www.facebook.com/BreatheBetter-LiveBetter/
https://www.facebook.com/SBBShow/
https://www.linkedin.com/in/ayo-handy-kendi
https://www.instagram.com/kendiayo/
https://twitter.com/AyoHandyKendi

HARDY, OMAR
PRESERVING THE LEGACY

I have been gifted with the opportunity and the responsibility of preserving the legacy of my great ancestors and the elders who have paved the way before me. I am the son of Clarence Jr. 2X Hardy Shabazz, and co-owner of Brooklyn's legendary The Black Lady Theatre. My father was a good friend and business partner of the late Supreme Civil Court Judge John L. Phillips Jr., founder of The Slave Theater. During the early 1980s Mr. Phillips took Brooklyn by storm when he purchased two buildings and converted the sites into the Slave Theater and The Black Lady Theatre. Three decades later, my father wisely encouraged me to take the lead role of the family business. Since 2010, it has become my life's work to diligently and deliberately maintain the legacy Mr. Phillips and my father built. I am committed to honoring the visions of success, unity and continued growth for all of us affected by the mass division of African people during the Transatlantic Slave Trade. Graciously, in body, mind and spirit, I have accepted the torch handed down to me.

CONTACT:
The Black Lady Theatre
718-771-0900
theblackladytheatre@gmail.com

HENDERSON DC, ALISON F. PARKER
HEALING ACROSS THE CONTINENT

Dr. Alison F. Henderson is a Chiropractor, Nutritionist, Chiropractor, Rehabilitation Counselor practicing in Washington, DC and Ghana (West Africa)

CONTACT:

Office locations in Washington, DC - Maryland; Accra, Ghana
Washington, DC: 202-288-8354
Ghana: 0572043295
email aahdiva@yahoo.com
FACEBOOK: Alison Parker Henderson
Back to Fit, and Miracle Health Center

HERU, SNT URT KAITHA HET
LOVE IS THE LAW

Visionary entrepreneur, Snt Urt (Elder Sister) Kaitha Het Heru is the founder of The Temple Beautiful, (with Heru Ankh Ra Semahj Se Ptah, Sen Ur, Kera Ptah, Elder Brother, Shrine of Ptah of The Sacred and Most Ancient Afrakan Nubian Khamitic Order, Het Ptah Ka) An ordained Khamit minister, she is also High Priestess of Sacred Beauty, The Temple Beautiful, a spiritual and cultural arts institution. Author/publisher of *I Love My Beautiful Body Temple,* Kaitha is a recipient of Q Kingdom Ministries' Woman of Great Esteem Award for Religion and Culture.

Artistic director of the Living MUSEum (KHHLM), Kaitha's mission is to educate the public about Khamitika Art (a term she coined) through the promotion of her handwork: The Master Peace Collection, A Woman's Work: My Art & My Textiles. Khamitika, contemporary and functional textile, fiber, needle and ceramic art is influenced by Afrakan and Hapi (Nile Valley) heritage, spirituality, culture, Goddess themes, mythology, city life and nature. Visitors to the "living museum"/gallery, have the opportunity to purchase hand-woven crafts from the evolving collection. Selected pieces have been in national and juried exhibitions. "I create sacred things to grace the spaces you call home."

CONTACT:
E-mail: hetherukaitha@yahoo.com
Website: www.kaithahetheru.com

IBOMU, STIC & AFYA
EAT GOOD ON A HOOD BUDGET

Stic and Afya are a health and hip-hop power couple who have been together and inspiring others for over 25 years. This husband and wife team are founders of the holistic wellness brand RBG FIT CLUB.

Afya holds a bachelor's degree in nutrition, is certified in Holistic Health and is an author of two award winning cookbooks, *The Vegan Soulfood Guide to the Galaxy* and *The Vegan Remix (Named one of the best cookbooks of 2015 by Vegetarian Times Magazine)*

Stic (aka stic.man of renowned rap group Dead Prez) is an award-winning hip-hop artist and producer, author, certified long-distance running coach and creator of a new music genre dubbed "fit hop". Stic is also the CEO of the first ever music label dedicated to Healthy Living-RBG FIT RECORDS.

CONTACT:
Afya Ibomu B.S, CHHC
Holistic Nutritonist
President of RBG FIT CLUB ™
Web: www.RBGFITCLUB.com
Email: Afya@rbgfitclub.com

JANAY, TIFFANY
ORGANIC BLOOD

Crystal therapy is the use of elements of Earth to bring about balance. Around the world, crystal therapy is as old as the ages. Connecting with the power of the womb is liberating and can boost a woman's self-confidence. There are so many layers to be explored within the womb space and using crystals and semi-precious stones to assist on that journey has proven to be of major benefit to women, globally. Join Tiffany Janay of Organic Blood for a 10-minute download on how to activate the power of your womb by infusing it with the masterful energy of semi-precious stones.

Tiffany Janay is the co-owner of Organic Blood Yoni Eggs and creative director at Organic Blood. She is an entrepreneur, a motivational speaker, and holistic health advocate who spends her days building her sisterhood tribe. Tiffany educates women on the power of their womb and provides them with valuable tools for unleashing their inner Queen Goddess.

Janay's passion for Yoni Eggs, Yoni Wellness, Entrepreneurship, Social Media Marketing, Health & Wealth, Relationship Sustainability, Manifestation, and Women's Sensuality allows her to tour the world connecting with individuals on their self-healing journey.

CONTACT:
Organic Blood LLC
yonieggs.com
organicbloodline.com
855-Yoni Egg

KEARSE, ROBIN "KHEPERAH"
PERSONAL TRANSFORMATION

R. Kheperah Kearse, a powerful speaker and gifted storyteller, is a transformational leadership coach and marketing specialist. Fusing popular culture, multimedia, metaphysics, natural law and emotional intelligence, she created "The GEMNASIUM" (LLC), a learning model for growth and development. Kheperah's informative and inspirational style cause her to be sought after in the public and private sectors. She customizes seminars, workshops and keynote addresses specifically for each audience. Kearse works with numerous government agencies to promote dialogue and implement positive alternatives to youth violence and high-risk behavior.

Kearse's professional resume began in the early 90s when working at Def Jam Records, Sony Music and Arista Records/Bad Boy. At the height of her career she made a bold exit from the entertainment industry. During her personal sabbatical, while detoxing from self-doubt she created "The GEMNASIUM" which inspired her healing.

Essence magazine celebrated Kheperah's mentoring participation in the award-winning documentary, *The Hip Hop Project,* (producers Bruce Willis and Queen Latifah). Variety magazine calls her "ultra-articulate" for her compelling narrative in the film.

Presently, Kheperah Kearse travels nationally to share the Gemnasium curriculum for building healthy minds and fulfilling lives.

CONTACT:
R. Kheperah Kearse, Founder, Gemnasium LLC
646.902.4GEM (4436)
www.gemnasiumllc.com

KING SIMON
TAKE CARE OF YOURSELF

King Simon evolved from Reggae artist to top NYC Self-Knowledge, Health and Awareness—Producer, Promoter, Edu-tainer, Motivational Speaker, Author, and On-Air Multimedia Personality.

"Life-lights":

- **1995:** Interned at S.O.B; Assistant to Gayle Horio (Thank you);
- **1995:** Promoted debut of *Luciano*/ Palladium; Co-hosted (with Shadow) Exodus FM world beat music; one of the hottest, emcee-promoter hosts/NY-Tri-State; Co-hosted Monday Midnight Jams;
- **1996 to 2001:** Hosted "Caribbean Soul TV"; Joined WPAT;
- **Since 1998:** Hosted Annual Reggae Cari-Fest NYC;
- **2000:** Sent audition cassette to WWRL's then program director, Bob Law, the rest is history. Co-hosted (with Prince Kalunda);
- **2005:** Radio shows: "In the Mix with Simon Templer"; "Morning Talk Show" (Karen Hunter & Steve Malzberg); Waah Gwan Radio;
- **Presently:** Produces, promotes, hosts: Some featured presenters: Aton Edwards, Abundance Child, Lloyd Strayhorn, Amun Re Sen Atum Re/Brother P.O.L.I.G.H.T., Aseer The Duke of Tiers, High Priestess Het Heru, Noble Anpu, Taj Tarik Bey, Dr. Delbert Blair, Dr. Llaila O. Afrika, Dr. Phil Valentine, Queen Afua and others. (Dr. Sebi before his transition.);
- **Three decades:** Disaster Awareness & Preparedness Instructor with the International Preparedness Network founded by renowned Preparedness Guru, Aton Edwards.

CONTACT:
Instagram /Twitter/Face Book/
kingsimonproductions@gmail.com
kingsimonproductions.wordpress.com
http://www.readyforanything.org/
International Preparedness Network
Phone: 347.496.1022

LANE, MS, BS, BA, BETTY
VIBRATIONAL HEALING THROUGH THE VOICE

Betty Lane is a world-wide professional singer. She is a singing voice specialist, a vocal health educator, senior community wellness advocate, yoga therapist (RYT 500, C-IAYT), an Emerald Green Holistic Practitioner and serves on the Voice Faculty at Wayne State University in Detroit, Michigan.

A native Detroiter, Betty Lane is director and founder of *Vocal Pathways,* a voice training and vocal health resource for singers, actors and speakers, particularly those with abused, misused, troubled, injured and aging voices. Her primary focus is to utilize her many years of knowledge, skills and experience to help others rebuild, repair and restore wellness to the total body in which the vocal instrument is housed. Ms. Lane uses of a variety of physical, nutritional, energy practices and spiritual modalities to achieve her mission. She says, "If you take care of the body, the body will take care of you and the voice will follow."

CONTACT:
Betty Lane
248-414-7299
vocalpathways@yahoo.com
www.vocalpathways.com

LOVE, DR. GEORGE
QI GONG: BREATH OF LIFE

Dr. George Love, Jr.: BA (1966); MS Biology (Temple University, 1976); Ph.D. Sports Medicine (American College Sports Medicine, 1982); Oriental MD degree (Beijing Longevity & Rejuvenation Institute, VA, 1984). President of Love Chinese, Dr. Love, is a Florida-licensed primary care physician and Board-certified Acupuncture physician since 1986.

Dr. Love produces several South Florida local radio shows including: *Of Mind & Medicine, The Natural Doctors and Your Herbal Medicine Chest*. Co-founder of The Kitchen Physician School of Natural Healing in Boca Raton, Dr. Love teaches Meridian Qigong there and in Margate at the University of Martial Arts S.H.I.E.L.D. Wellness Centers. He says, "Avoid adrenal exhaustion and cultivate your essence with daily Qigong."

After thirty years of clinical experience Dr. Love has written ten books on health and nutrition and distilled the essence of illness and the nature of true health into a few select teachings. His private practices include:

- Physical Medicine: treating pain of muscles, bones, joints
- Internal Medicine: treating Yin/Yang organ function with foods and herbs
- Energy Medicine: increasing Qi and Blood circulation
- Psycho-Spiritual Medicine: treating emotional stagnation with Psycho-puncture

CONTACT:
Dr. George Qi Love
7035 Beracasa Way #104
Boca Raton, Florida
561-502-6200

LIDDELL, ELLIS
WEALTH IS OUR LEGACY, PASS IT ON!

Ellis Liddell is the President and CEO of ELE Wealth Management LLC, a client-based asset management company (Southfield, Michigan). With over 30 years of experience in the financial arena, Ellis is a wealth manager, insurance expert, retirement planning specialist and author of **Wealth Management: Merging Faith with Finance.**

Via print, radio and television Mr. Liddell's commentary has been featured in metropolises, including, Detroit, Atlanta and Dallas. He is a financial consultant for WXYZ Action News and a regular guest on News Talk 1200AM and WCHB *The Mildred Gaddis Show*. He has been featured in **Who's Who in Black Detroit** multiple times, selected as 'One of the Top Wealth Managers for 2010' and received the "Entrepreneur of the Year" Award from Alabama A&M University Alumni Association. In 2007, he became the first African American ranked #1 financial advisor, two years consecutively.

Mr. Liddell conducts seminars and workshops nationwide to businesses and churches, including Comerica Bank, Ford Motor Company, and TD Jakes' The Potter's House. Uniquely rooted in sound financial and Biblical principles, Mr. Liddell presents complex information in layman's terms, giving a wealth of knowledge, with homespun humor and common sense.

CONTACT:
Ofc: 248-356-6555
Cel: 248-388-6406
E: eliddell@elefamily.com
Web: elewealth.com

MA'AT, BARATUNDE & KAYAH
1. HEAL THE PEOPLE, HEAL THE PLANET
2. PRESERVING PARADISE

Baratunde Ma'at, is father of **The Forgotten Foods…Remembered** and manufacturer of Planetary Herbal Tonics. He has a 37-year history with Traditional Chinese Herbalism, Alchemy and Spiritual Sciences. From an early age, Baratunde spent time in nature where he learned about plants and discovered that they carry a distinct language; plants communicate with him directly. Similar to Dr. George Washington Carver, Baratunde has a natural relationship with the plant kingdom.

Intrigue with the Oriental Healing Arts led Baratunde to the study of Martial Arts and Kung Fu. He learned Hit Medicine and Qigong from herbalist masters. His travels to Africa and the Caribbean exposed him to the arts and sciences of Planetary Herbalism and Shamanism. The alchemy behind his proprietary herbal formulas and spiritual intent originates from Taoism and is very ancient. Appropriately, He often receives messages and instruction from the ancient ones for his formulations.

Baratunde's wife and soul mate, Kayah Ma'at, also has a three-decade history of natural health and transitional diet activism. A prolific culinary artist, she has owned and operated two vegan restaurants in Atlanta, GA. She blends raw culinary arts with The Forgotten Foods' sacred herbal sciences to create high-frequency superior-foods.

Kayah lectures on nutrition and personal health accountability and offers lifestyle coaching for those who desire to transform their lives wholistically. Kayah's natural intuitive gift spiritually complements her husband. With a background in health, business, law and marketing she has been an entrepreneur and self-employed for 35 years.

Together, Baratunde and Kayah make up THE FORGOTTEN FOODS…REMEMBERED.

CONTACT:
longlife@theforgottenfoods.com
www.theforgottenfoods.com
770-573-0488

MAAT, TASSILI
THE REMIX

Tassili Maat, Raw Vegan Master Chef is founder of **Tassili's Raw Reality.** The restaurant lounge in Atlanta, Georgia is known for its Afrocentric ambiance and raw vegan cuisine. Inspired by Tassili's international palate, her purpose is the improved health and well-being of patrons, one nutritious recipe at a time. Catering to flexitarians, vegetarians, vegans, transitional clients, and raw food experts she provides a unique variety of raw vegan entrees, salads, wraps, and more. Tassili passionately makes healthy, delicious dishes using the super food, kale. Her brand is recognized around the world as the best kale in Atlanta. Tassili's vision is to create an employee-owned, raw vegan restaurant franchise, to be truly homes away from home, globally. They will be identified by Tasilli's taste-exploding, signature raw delectables.

in June 2016, The Wonderful Wizards of Raw Food Extravaganza took place at Tassili's café. Some of the best raw food chefs in the country were featured. Tassili is also founder of I AM ASCENCION TEMPLE.

CONTACT:

Atlanta's Raw Vegan Cafe'
1059 Ralph David Abernathy Blvd.
Atlanta, Georgia 30310
I AM ASCENCION TEMPLE (located upstairs)
(404) 500-9405
tassili@tassilisraw.com
www.tassilisraw.com
Facebook; Twitter

MUID MHC, MSW, CASAC, FDLC, RJ, ONAJE
PLANET HEAL: SOCIAL HEALING

Creator of the SUSU Healing Circle System and The SEEDS BROTHERHOOD LEADERSHIP GARDEN NETWORK, Onaje Muid is WHM MSW (Weheme Mesu-national) Healer, leading the Maafa Healing Ceremony. (Whm Msw is a Maat national social recovery program designed to bring order, balance, harmony, justice, reciprocity and truth.) A student of Hazrat Inayat Khan, Onaje uses the healing breath as his foundation in his work. As a transformative, social work, human rights activist, his kazi (work) is the restoration of descendants of formerly enslaved Africans and indigenous peoples in the Western Hemisphere through reparations. His 30-year clinical experience—in substance abuse prevention, outpatient and residential facilities—laid the ground work for his advocacy of the third aspect of reparations: rehabilitation, along with compensation and restitution. Former advisor and current adjunct lecturer at Columbia University Graduate School of Social Work he continues to work on the theme of Decolonizing Social Work: The Reparations Imperative.

CONTACT:

Onaje Muid
321 Clearbrook Ave
Lansdowne, Pa 19050
muidmsw@gmail.com
646 662-0217
www.iamhealingfreeecourse.com

NATURAL (aka DOCTOR BROTHER NATURAL)
OPTIMAL HEALTHY LIVING

Doctor Natural - Holistic Health Instructor/Consultant, Raw Vegan Chef, Motivational Speaker.

Six-year-old George Gittens was an outspoken opponent of the killing of animals; by age 15 he was a strict vegan. In high school he changed his name to "Natural." While earning a BS in chemistry from SUNY/Westbury he methodically assessed the details of food preparation. He became known as "Brother Natural" for his diligence to consuming only nature's best. He is an experienced chemist and medical technologist with finely honed critical, analytical and intuitive skills. Brother Natural serves the community as group counselor, mentor for young males and fitness and a yoga/meditation instructor. An accomplished strategist and master of networking, Natural is a natural motivational speaker. His life's work rewarded him an Honorary Doctor of Divinity degree from Universal Life Church. Natural sharpened his skills as a Holistic Health instructor with Queen Afua. He considers his greatest achievement, "…after being self-taught in natural healing for over 30 years, I now effectively teach people how to heal themselves."

Founder/Director of **Temple of Illumination** (1998) Natural says: "…we teach the methods and benefits of positive mental attitude, organic raw vegan alkaline diet, and regular exercise necessary for an optimal healthy lifestyle."

CONTACT:
Consultation, lectures, workshops:
PH: (718) 783-3465
Website:
http://TEMPLEOFILLUMINATION.NING.COM

NADI
A WORLD DECLARATION OF DIVINE LOVE

*Flautist for new dimensions in beauty for your listening heart. Nadi Burton, with over three decades of service, and ministry, I am a spiritual activist through meditative music, and the "spiritized" written and spoken word. Listen to musical highlights and read my weekly writings on Divine Love.

CONTACT:
*NADI@Sound-Light Productions- Meditation & Innertainment Services
*nadi@nadi-om.com *
212.690.0535 nadi-om.com / *
*nadi's blog-music facebook.com/nadi.om

NASIK RAHM, ATURAH BAHTIYAH E.
WE CAN HEAL OUR PLANET

Aturah Bahtiyah has been on a journey in holistic living and a truth-centered life since 1998. She is a Crowned Sister (Aturah) and a government official in the African Hebrew Israelites of Jerusalem. Bahtiyah has been married for nine years and has beautiful children and grandchildren in the United States and in Israel. In 1998, she recognized the benefits of meditation and being a Live Foodist. She cleansed and has maintained the live food lifestyle and adheres to eating 100% live food and 95% organic food. Bahtiyah, obtaining the goals she set as a Live Foodist, has been vegan for over 18 years. She loves to travel nationally and internationally; if near the appropriate waters she takes the opportunity to scuba dive.

Aturah Bahtiyah is the founder of Tikeyah a conscientious company dedicated to offering holistically-based, educational programs and services promoting the longevity of life. The Tikeyah Regenerative Health & Wellness Center is an elegant and sophisticated atmosphere located in the Soul Vegetarian Complex in Atlanta, Georgia.

CONTACT:
404.916.5587
bahtiyah@tikeyah.com
www.tikeyah.com

O'UHURU, CM MS, SAKINA
HEALING THE PLANET EARTH: A CONSCIENTIOUS BIRTH

Sakina O'Uhuru, has been practicing the art of Midwifery for over 20 years. From 1999-2004 she was site Director of Midwifery Services of Morris Heights Women's Health & Birthing Pavilion. MHHC was the first clinic to offer out-of-hospital prenatal labor and delivery services in an underserved community in NYC. Ms. O'Uhuru is a Clinical Preceptor for SUNY Downstate Midwifery Program. Previously, she has been a preceptor for Midwifery Programs at Stony Brook, Columbia and NYU.

In 2002, O'Uhuru founded Gentle Spirit Home Birth Midwifery Services where she offers women comprehensive health care services. Her private practice is independently owned and operated with locations in both New York and New Jersey. She has attended well over 500 out-of-hospital births.

Publications:
"Can African American Women Conceptualize the Midwifery Model of Care As The Gold Standard of Prenatal Care For All Low Risk Women?" (Reality Bridges 2013 Volume 3.3)

Her first memoir: *Journey To Birth: The Story of a Midwife's Journey and A Reflection of The Heroic Women She Served Along the Way* (2013)

CONTACT:
Gentle Spirit Home Birth Midwifery Service
T: 212-368-2229
F: 866-308-6063
www.gentlespiritbirth.com
Sakina@gentlespiritbirth.com

ODUMS, LCSW-R, CCTP, M.S.ED. TANYA SHERISE
SHARING THE GIFT OF WELLNESS

Tanya is a Licensed Clinical Social Worker, from Brooklyn, with over 20 years' experience working with NYC's most vulnerable populations in a variety of private and city institutions. Founder of ***KhepeRa Counseling and Consulting Licensed Clinical Social Work Services,*** a mental health-consulting firm that provides therapeutic services to individuals and families and program development support to community-based organizations. Tanya uses her passion, skills and experience to design therapeutic programs and facilitate personal and professional development trainings. She is a Certified Clinical Trauma Professional and an EDIT Certified Eating Disorder Intuitive Therapist, specializing in the treatment of trauma and depression. She is studying Psychodrama and Cognitive Behavioral Therapy.

A former Professor of Psychology and Human Services at Touro College and the CUNY, she is currently an Adjunct Lecturer for NYU's Silver School of Social Work Advanced Trauma-Informed Clinical Practice Program. She has served as a School Building Leader for over a decade within NYC public high schools and is currently employed with the NYC Department of Education as the District Coordinator of Restorative Justice Programs. Tanya is a vital force, whose life purpose is to create opportunities for self-cultivation, healing and transformation to impact the world.

CONTACT:

Phone: 631-485-7473
www.TanyaSheriseOdums.com
Email: KheperaHeals@gmail.com
TanyaSheriseSS@gmail.com

MUHAMMAD, WAHIDAH
EARTH COOKERS

Wahidah Muhammad's name rings a bell wherever she goes. She is a mother, grandmother, pediatric nurse (specializing in infant and childcare); and an EARTH COOKER. Bronx born Wahidah is one of seven children whose mother, a caregiver and piano teacher and father a minister left a legacy of skills and service. The family lived in cities from New York to Florida, due to her father's outstanding ministry. Wahidah is well-known throughout the Muslim communities in Atlanta, Miami, New Jersey and especially in Brooklyn, New York. An entrepreneurial powerhouse who owned her first store at age 16, has also owned a juice bar, a record store, a clothing store, a jewelry store, and even a pillow factory!

A sister with a mission, Wahidah joined the Heal Thyself circle four decades ago. Offering her approach to food preparation with simplicity and love of God, she infused holistic cooking with healing mind, body and spirit. Her "Earth Cookers" philosophy first appeared in Queen Afua's ***Sacred Woman***. As an Ambassador of Purification, certified Heal Thyself fasting and nutrition coach and colon therapist, Wahidah says," I got into the field of nutrition to help myself and in the process realized helping others was more important."

CONTACT:

770 771 1912
wmuslimah7@gmail.com

PATTERSON, ND, WINSTON "KOKAYI"
WHOLISTIC ACADEMICS 101: "WHOLISTIC HEALTH"

A native Washingtonian, Dr. Winston "Kokayi" Patterson has two sons, a daughter, 4 grandsons and 3 granddaughters. He attended D.C. public schools and completed UDC Adult Education, Southeastern University and UDC Certified Addictions Counselors Program. Choosing a Wholisitic lifestyle at age 18, Patterson went on to become a vegetarian, martial artist and physical trainer. Observing health disparities Patterson decided to introduce the Wholisitic lifestyle into his community. While working in the addiction treatment field, he studied acupuncture and completed initial training under Dr. Mutulu Shakur at Lincoln Hospital, NYC. Kokayi cites, his grandmother, Pearl Ivy Lyon, (a Red Cross Nurse) and mother, Naomi Louise Lyon, (Clinic Coordinator at Walter Reed Army Medical Center) as his greatest influences. They promoted good family values, down home healing, healthy eating and service to mankind. Dr. "Kokayi" Is owner of: Wholisitc Health Academics 101 and Communal Effect Herbals/Aloe World, LLC.

Credentials:
Doctor of Naturopathy; Acupuncture Detox Specialist;
Reiki Master Level III; Wholistic Substance Abuse Specialist

Wholistic Activities:
HIV/AIDS Counselor; Youth Mental Health/First Aid Specialist/Trainer;
Family & Youth Empowerment; Motivational Speaker;
Students' Affairs & ADA Coordinator, KPU

CONTACT:
African Wholistic Health Association, Inc. (Founder)
713 13th Street NE, Suite 2
Washington, DC 20002
Phone: 202-412-4880
E-mail: Wpkokayi1@yahoo.com
Website: www.aloeandherbals.com

PEOPLES, CORINTHIA
ROCK YOUR LIFE

I am the first and only child of a clairvoyant mother who was misdiagnosed and labeled as autistic. Her clairvoyance is her blessing; the misdiagnosis was a curse. I am the last child of a father who thrived on material gains and 'making a way out of no way.' This mathematics was the onset of my flamboyant and isolated beginnings, which were nurtured and molded by a village of four women (my mother, benevolent grandmother and two aunts) and my grandfather. These beloved caretakers played deep southern and African rhythms. In my early years I was intensely sheltered, yet allowed time, space and freedom to express my natural talents as an artist and creator of beautiful things and movements. The environment was suitable for my subtle inner voice to be heard and leveraged. To my salvation my grandmother clearly saw ME, raw and untamed. She spent her final years cultivating my experiences, exposure, and outlets. Today, I recognize the power of dance and the education of youth as part of my earthly divine assignment. Consistently, I engage spirit in my gemstone work to reconnect to the power and beauty of the elements in Nature.

CONTACT:
www.corinthiapeoples.com
FB: corinthiapeoplesdesigns
E: corinthia@corinthiapeoples.com
IG: corinthiapeoples

PREMA (AKA LADY PREMA)
1. MOTHER EARTH SPEAKS
2. RITUALIZE, COME ALIVE

Vocalist, Poet, Songwriter, Lifestyle Transformation Coach and Author. She has served in the spiritual and cultural communities for over thirty-five years with meditations, healing workshops, retreats and entertainment. This pillar of power blossoms with her ability to bring fun and inspiration to spiritual development. Prema is the author of *Aligned with the Divine, Are You Buggin'?* and two poetry books, *My Soul Speaks, Jewels from Within* and a host of inspirational music and spoken word CDs.

CONTACT:
Email: ladyprema@gmail.com
Web: ladyprema.com

HEALERS DIRECTORY

QUEEN AFUA

Queen Afua is an internationally renowned and has been a devoted wellness advocate. Her certifications include holistic health practitioner, colonic therapist, yoga instructor and fasting specialist. With over 40 years of experience she has lectured globally, served as a consultant and educated and empowered thousands. Queen Afua has developed wellness programs that have been clinically tested and approved by prestigious doctors. She has been awarded nationally and internationally. Her ongoing mission is to assist individuals, families and communities who are on the path that includes balance and harmony for optimal wellness.

Queen Afua is the author of five best sellers:
- *Heal Thyself for Health and Longevity*
- *Sacred Woman: A Guide to Healing the Feminine Body, Mind and Spirit*
- *The City of Wellness: Restoring Your Health Through the Seven Kitchens of Consciousness*
- *Overcoming an Angry Vagina: Journey to Wellness*
- *Man Heal Thyself: Journey to Optimal Wellness;*
- *Circles Of Wellness: A Guide To Planting, Cultivating & Harvesting Wellness*

Recently, Queen Afua gathered the treasures here in
PLANET HEAL: What would you do to heal planet Earth?

QUEEN ESTHER HUNTER SARR LOVE AND BEAUTY OUR ULTIMATE HEALING!

Queen Esther Sarr (Olabisi, "The Beauty Doctor") a multifaceted artist, uses myriad modalities to facilitate healing. She writes poetry, create CDs and teaches, globally. Her Dance of Life™ movement workshops incorporate African rhythms and dance techniques to develop skills and encourage enjoyment. Under the pseudonym "Mother Nature", Queen Esther uses her poetry as 'medicine' to promote wellness. Healing of the Moon™ is her program to awaken the power of consistently aligning with the moon cycles for healing body, mind, spirit and prosperity towards a victorious life.

Some life-lights:
- Dancer 40 plus years; performed with Olatunji and La Rocque Bey.
- Extensive study of indigenous West African culture (resident 7 years).
- University study Legon/Ghana.
- Teacher: Nobel Prize awardee, Prof. Wole Soyinka (Univ. of Ife/Nigeria).
- Expanded her Cosmetology Certification into Holistic Beauty.
- Colon Therapist and Holistic Practitioner Certification (Queen Afua tutor - 1980s).
- Dean of Global Sacred Woman Village (Queen Afua founder).
- Resides: Las Vegas, NV; Serves as a Wellness Ambassador, encouraging women to enhance their authentic inner and outer beauty.
- Available for private consultations, group workshops and presentations.

CONTACT:
Invite Queen Esther to help ACTIVATE the GODDESS In YOU!
Email: queen_esther_s@yahoo.com
Cell: 702.542.5704/ Office:702 228 0441
web: www.queenesthersarr.com/
email: danceoflife360@gmail.com

QUEEN MOTHER MAASHT AMM AMEN
HET HERU HEALING DANCE

Queen Mother Maasht Amm Amen of the international Ausar Auset Society, has championed spiritual and economic empowerment of women, worldwide, for several decades. Her nation-building work has been recognized by the Ashanti Paramount Kings and Queens (Ghana) and the Yoruba (Nigeria).

An entrepreneur, Queen Mother helped establish Tchefa vegan restaurant, and *Senbeb*, a natural cosmetics line. Beginning in 1997, Queen Mother created Het Heru Healing Dance, followed by a book, DVD, Line Dance and Dance Circles. Her Healing Dance to assist women with awakening their innate healing power, has national and international outreach. Notable venues include: NYC: Bronx Community and Medgar Evers Colleges, the United Nations; Dallas, Texas: Shrine of the Black Madonna; Culver City, California: Agape International Spiritual Center; Mayaro, Trinidad: Radix Beach Resort; Brixton Hill, London: Lambeth Town Hall.

Having worked with acclaimed directors Bill Duke and Joseph Papp, Queen Mother's professional theatre background coupled with her wellness advocacy led her to write and co-produce a relationship-themed play, *The Rose Flyer: Peace, Pleasure or Pain*. She continues to heal the planet by teaching, relationship counseling, conducting Het Heru Healing Circles, and using her artistic talents to energize others.

RAHMAN, REVEREND HASIFA ABDUR
WOMEN NEED TO HEAL

Rev. Hasifa Abdur Rahman is a pioneer in uplifting and awakening Women to recognize the power of The Mother and the Womb of Life. She holds a master's degree in religious science from The Theological Seminary in Barrytown, New York.

Rev. Hasifa is The Keeper of The Shrine of Ast and she is a Chaplin in The Nation of Islam In New York City, NY.

CONTACT:

Rev. Hasifa Abdur Rahman through her daughter, Nassareen Rahman
Email: nassareen.rahman@gmail.com
Phone: 678-663-7773

RHA GODDESS, TRANSFORMATION COACH SACRED SELF...SACRED WORK

Healing Areas: Entrepreneurial Soul Coaching, Mindfulness, Spiritual Growth, Personal Transformation, Arts & Culture

Rha Goddess Founder & CEO of Move The Crowd has inspired hundreds of breakthrough changemakers and visionaries. From NY Times bestsellers to multi-million-dollar social enterprises, Rha's unique methodology empowers a new generation of conscious entrepreneurs to stay true, get paid, and do good. For over 30 years as a cultural innovator, social impact strategist and creative change agent, Rha has drawn on the power of creativity, culture and community to move hearts, minds and policy. Her have made an impact on millions of lives. Rha's work has been featured in Time, Ms., Variety, Essence, The Source, Redbook, Forbes, Fast Company and The Chicago Tribune, among others. A sought-after speaker, Rha leads the conversation around a "whole self" approach to entrepreneurship as key to a more just and sustainable economy and culture. Rha is galvanizing a movement of 1 million entrepreneurs who are dedicated to re-imagining "work" as a vehicle for creative expression, financial freedom and societal transformation.

CONTACT:
Email: hello@movethecrowd.me
URL: www.movethecrowd.me
@rhagoddess | facebook.com/rhagoddess
|Rha @TEDx
contributions Move The Crowd, LLC | P.O. Box 325 | Oradell, NJ 07649

RISINGSUN, H-ANKH CRYSTALS: PROTECTION, PROJECTION, MANIFESTATION

"If You Don't Have A Pistol, You Better Have A Crystal." H-Ankh Risingsun strives to create high powered magnetic water bottles, crystal orgone amulets for healing and personal empowerment. Inspired by his journey into plant based, Native American psychedelics and sexual cultivation through tantra, massage, reflexology, pranic healing, therapeutic touch, crystal therapy, and sound healing. Brother H-Ankh is a student of magnetism, orgone, and crystal science. He strives to follow the teachings of Ascended Masters, including the following: Saint Germain, Nikola Tesla, Cheikh Ahmadou Bamba, Simean Toko, Ptahotep, Akenaton, Enoch, Melchezidek, Buddah, Khrisna, Wilhelm Reich. Many of H-Ankh Risingsun's primary inspiration is help others "STRIVE TO THRIVE."

CONTACT:
Name: H-Ankh Risingsun
Organization: Healing Water Bottle
E-mails: teslabluequartz@hotmail.com
    hankrisingsunra@gmail.com
Phone: 347 – 788 -1865
Websites: www.healingwaterbottle.com
www.orgone4you.com

RICHARDSON MD, MSPH, WILLIAM "EMIKOLA"
CREATING HEALTH IN HUMAN COMMUNITIES

Dr. William Richardson aka Emikola Origbeara: Holistic Integrative Physician; Preventive Medicine, Public Health.

Founder (1986): Advanced Clinics for Preventive Medicine (ACPM.NET)/Atlanta, Ga..

ACPM is a comprehensive Holistic Medical Center staffed by Integrative Medical Doctors and Naturopaths

EDUCATION:

BS–Biochemistry/University of Pittsburgh (PA)–1975

Medical Doctor/Temple University School of Medicine (PA) -1979/ University of Alabama–1984

MS–Public Health–Science of Epidemiology/ The Mercy Hospital (PA)-1980

Rotating Internship–Northside Hospital/ University of Pittsburgh Health Science Center–1981-1982

Internal Medicine Residency–University of Alabama–1982-1984

Public Health and Preventive Medicine Residency/Hypertension Research Fellow – University of California – 1996

Medical Acupuncture for Physicians/Board Certified: Public Health and Preventive Medicine–1986

Certified: Chelation Therapy

MEDICAL MISSIONARY WORK:

Belize, Central America; St. Croix, U.S. Virgin Islands; Nigeria & Ghana, West Africa.

SPECIAL TRAINING AND EXPERTISE:

Intravenous (IV) EDTA Chelation Therapy ; IV DMPS Chelation Therapy;

IV High Dose Vitamin C for Cancer and Infectious Disease ; Nutritional Support and Herbal IV Therapies

Medically-Supervised Fasting and Weight Loss; Far Infrared Sauna Therapy to Detox Environmental Toxins

Herbology and Human Nutrition; Acupuncture and Meridian Medicine; Pyramid Medicine

SPECIAL INTERESTS:

Yoga, Meditation, Marshall Arts
Guitar-Lead, Rhythm & Bass

FAMILY:

Married 28 years, Father of six children

CONTACT:

www.ACPM.net
770-419-4471

ROLLE, CHRIS "KAZI"
HOW TO FIND LOVE AND KEEP IT ALIVE

Chris "Kazi" Rolle is an internationally recognized **matchmaker and relationship coach** who is helping people to find love and keep it alive. After 10 years of working in the music business, Kazi transitioned from artist development to personal development and began working with creative and corporate professionals across industry, helping them to achieve bigger goals and solve problems.

Kazi has *certifications in life coaching, crisis management, conflict resolution and business development.* He **speaks, writes, coaches** and **creates content** on how to successfully navigate personal and professional relationships. A **sought after speaker,** Kazi travels nationally and internationally lecturing year round. His intimate understanding of human relationships and inspiring life story has made him a sought-after expert for various media outlets. He has been featured on VH1, CNN, CBS, and The Oprah Winfrey Show. Kazi's work and life is the focus of the Bruce Willis and Queen Latifah award winning film, **The Hip Hop Project.**

CONTACT:
Chris "Kazi" Rolle
Matchmaker | Relationship Coach
NYC: 646.450.5294 | LA: 818.927.3291 | chris@chriskazirolle.com | chriskazirolle.com | Skype: chriskazirolle

CUSTOMER SERVICE
Camari Carter, Executive Assistant
646.450.KAZI [4625]
http://www.chriskazirolle.com

FOR SPEAKING ENGAGEMENTS/ MEDIA INQUIRES
Alaine Roberson, Manager
347.866.8279
robersonsartist@gmail.com

SALAAM, ABDEL R.
HARLEM IS A DANCE DIVINE

In 1981, Executive Artistic Director Abdel R. Salaam, his wife, Principal Soloist and Master Choreographer, Dyane Harvey-Salaam and Executive Managing Director Olabamidele (Dele) Husbands co-founded Forces of Nature Dance Theatre. Artistic Director of Dance Africa at the Brooklyn Academy of Music, Mr. Salaam directs and choreographs in multiple genres of dance and theater. He is Musical Director of Contemporary African percussion for his company, with additional skills in lighting, costume and set design.

Since childhood (1955), Abdel has been active in performance and visual arts. Throughout his nearly five-decades professional arts career, he has received critical acclaim in dance and dance theater. He has served on the faculties of Lehman College, The American Dance Festivals in the United States and Korea, The Alvin Ailey American Dance Center and the Chuck Davis Dance Academy. He is one of the directors of the Harlem Children's Zone/ Forces of Nature Youth Academy of Dance and Wellness @ St. Mark's Church in Harlem.

CONTACT:
Forces of Nature Dance Theatre
St. Marks Church
55 Edgecomb Avenue - 4th Floor
New York, NY 10037

Abdel Salaam
(646) 596 - 3708 (c)
abdelrsalaam@mac.com
forcesofnature.org
Facebook, Instagram

Dyane Harvey-Salaam
(917) 273 - 9424 (c)
ladydy161@aol.com

SANKOFA, PROPHETESS AFRAKA
HEALING YOUR MONEY MINDSET

I Am Prophetess Afraka Sankofa. I Am A Conduit Of Wholistic, Prophetic, Spiritual & Financial Healing. I Am a Knowledge Bearer. My purpose is being a spiritual guide and counsel to melanated womben and men in remembrance of their true identity and purpose, spiritually and physically. I want to assist them in restoring and renewing their minds and resetting their health, wealth and wisdom thermostat to its divine agree.

We have created a free community called the Q Experience. I extend an invitation to our radio show. Listeners can speak with us, ask questions and share in the knowledge that is being imparted. This platform is created for those who are seeking financial, spiritual and physical healing. In this space they can be reintroduced back to their true natural selves on Wealth, Health and Wisdom.

CONTACT:
Book appointment:
https://alendly.com/realestatesolutions3
Phone: 1-347-770-0189 / Mondays - Fridays 11AM Est – 3PM Est
Email: beaconinnerlightministries@gmail.com
Subscribe: https://mailchi.mp/48546db5a9b8/massive-passive-income
Website: https://omniversity-of-restoration.teachable.com/
Radio Show: http://www.blogtalkradio.com/thepropheticfinanciershow/

SANKOFA-EL, AUNDRIEUX (Prof. Khonsu)
D.A.D: DEDICATED AND DISTINGUISHED

AUNDRIEUX KHONSU SANKOFA-EL Is an inner-city youth activist. He has lived and studied the schools of Islam, Christianity & Judaism, also Buddhist and Hindu meditation. Usui Reiki, Tao sciences, Tantric yoga, Landmark education self-development, Holistic Health, and Khemetic spirituality as taught by master teachers Supreme Grand Master Neter Aaferti Atum Re and Dr. Ra Un Nefer Amen. He lectures on Modern Masculinity, Holistic Health, The Metaphysics of Hip Hop, and is Co-founder of The Manhood Academy for Boys in London, UK.
ThAnkhs
Aundrieux (Khonsu) Sankofa-El

CONTACT:
tel: +44 (0)7599504680
email: sacredman@mail.com
Instagram: aundrieux_sankofa
Facebook: • Sacred man • Aundrieux Sankofa
Author: SACRED MAN: From Boyhood to Manhood to Divine Masculine

SCOTT, MS, BA, GERIANNE FRANCIS
MY SOCKS DO NOT HAVE TO MATCH
(aka: Titi G, Midnight)

Blessings: Family Born and Gathered; Guyana Kings Family Reunion (Annually since 1970); Teachers

Mantra: Time-Space-Resources

Skills: Bridging. Editing. Archiving. Finishing.

Passions: Stories, Music, Dance, Travels, Scuba diving.

Home: tasks; singing a cappella in 4-part harmony; flash cards, Scrabble; jump rope, scattin' 'n' walking to LaGuardia Airport

Studies: Senior Prez/1969; CUNYBA/1974; Baruch (Honors) - MS/1982; First World Alliance; Abroad: Africa, Asia, Caribbean, North & South America, Europe…Dance: Caribbean, African, European Ballet, Modern

Awarded: National: Fellowships & Teacher of Excellence; Community Service (Mandala Center)

1983: Egypt: Dr. Ben +; 21-Day Detox: Queen Afua

Teaching: NYCBOE (33 years*): UFT, CUNY; Concordia College…

*Touching lives: Unprecedented Research Lab; "Use Everything Plans"

Literary: Editor: Queen Afua's publications; Editor/Co-author: *African/African American Curriculum Guide* (Coleman, Collymore, Scott, Washington, NYCBOE, 1988); Contributor (textbook): *African American History: A Journey of Liberation* (Dr. Molefi Kete Asante, The Peoples Publishing Group, Inc., 2000); Author: *The Dreams They Had:* a play of Sankofa and Discovery

Joy: Horizon watching: The sky kissing the sea…

Suggestion: Be Kind.

CONTACT:
Goods 'n' services:
1. **IT'S A WRAP:** hand-sewn scarves +
2. **EmmaJanePress:** editing +
3. **"Use Everything Plans"**
4. *The Dreams They Had*

C: 917 703 9303
E: scottgf51@aol.com

SCOTT, IMANI C.
CRYSTALLIZE YOUR LIFE

Imani C. Scott is Sacred Artist and holistic entrepreneur. A near six-octave vocalist, Imani is acknowledged as a Temple Chantress/Priestess by Baba Heru Ankh Ra Semajh and Mut Latrella Thornton; and ordained "The Wealth Empress" by the late Empress Akeweke. A Certified Holistic Consultant (Dr. Llaila Afrika), Imani is a graduate of "Sacred Woman" (Queen Afua), "Teer Technology of Soul" (Dr. Barbara Ann Teer) and "21st Century Women's Rites of Passag¬¬e" (Diana Pharr). She is a perpetual student of Lloyd Strayhorn, Lester Loving, Dr. Leonard Jeffries and formerly of the late D. Gary Young.

A member of the Harlem Arts Alliance, Imani is Corresponding Secretary of the New Amsterdam Musical Association. She features her talents and work in Healing Arts Studio housed in the landmark NAMA Building. Her nearly two-decade community involvement includes: Vibrational Therapy, Holistic Travel, Spiritual Development, Crystals & Gemstones, Sound Healing and Vocal Entertainment. The recently added Urban Aeroponic/Hydroponic Gardening is cutting edge. Imani's endeavors enhance Wellness, Empowerment and Pro$perity to build a Legacy of Significance and Success.

CONTACT:

Imani Scott/ The Wealth Empress
Exec Director & Project Coordinator
347-746-9749 Call/Text
ENRICH your HARLEM VILLAGE Experience, Amazing HOLISTIC Connections!
HOLISTIC HARLEM Project
HolisticHarlem@gmail.com
www.HolisticHARLEM.eventbrite.com
www.Facebook.com/HolisticHarlem
www.HolisticHarlem.com

SHABAZZ, WANIQUE KHEMI-TEHUTI
HEAL THE PLANET THROUGH NATURAL TIME & GLOBAL PEACE THROUGH CULTURE

Wanique Khemi-Tehuti Shabazz is a lecturer, Natural Time Scholar and an "Ambassador for Peace", awarded this title by The Inter-religious and International Federation for World Peace for his work with The Foundation for the Law of Time where he now serves as Officer of Internal Operations Emeritus. Brother Shabazz is a well-known community activist, radio talk show host and director of operations at Atlanta's progressive community radio station WRFG 89.3FM, streaming live at (www.wrfg.org). He also chairs the boards of ACCUSD (www.unty4power.org) & Sevananda Natural Food Co-op (www.sevananda.coop)

For more than 20 years he has produced and hosted the "Nightwatch" program MAPP-TIME JAZZ (Metaphysical Answers and Personal & Political Truths inside Musical Edutainment).

In association with the *Pan Atlantis Crystal Core Team (PACCT)*, The Law of Time Peace Calendar Change Movement and WRFG 89.3 FM radio, commissioned the Atlanta City Council and in 2005, July 25th has proclaimed 'Global Peace Through Culture Day' in commemoration of the annual "Day Out of Time".

CONTACT:

To learn more about Natural Time, living in harmony with nature, and the natural ways of the indigenous, visit:
The Foundation for the Law of Time (www.lawoftime.org)
https://www.melanatedimmortals.com/gps/
www.waniqueshabazz.com

SHARRIFF, REVEREND NAFISA
BE THE LIGHT!

Nafisa Sharriff is an ordained Interfaith Minister, Meditation Master and Dancer/Choreographer. Her spiritual journey included Ancient Egyptian temples, an Ashram in rural India and the One Spirit Interfaith Seminary in New York City, where she was ordained. Through ETHOH she conducts Healing classes and workshops for individuals and groups.

Sharriff is a Master Teacher and Choreographer of traditional West African dance and folklore. During her illustrious 40-year career, she has performed with Stevie Wonder, Whitney Houston, Spike Lee, TC Carson, C&C Music Factory and Kairaba West African Dance Company. She has television credits from the Richard Pryor Show, Dance Black America and Positively Black. Nafisa teaches free West African dance classes in Harlem, New York, where everyone is welcomed into her family of Love!

*ETHOH offers a wide range of services:
Meditation Classes, Spiritual Teachings, Seasonal Cleanses, West African Dance Classes;
Retreats: Stress Management, Spiritual Tools for Transformation; Woman's Rite of Passage; Reiki;
Reverend Sharriff is available for Speaking Engagements.

CONTACT:
Reverend Nafisa Sharriff
Founder & CEO Entering the Holy of Holies
PO Box 230144 New York, NY 10023
(212) 841 – 5449 (service)
(347) 526 – 2409 (cell)
www.ethoh.org; info@ethoh.org

SHEMSUT-GIANPREM KAUR, MUTSHAT
MAINTAINING PEACE OF MIND IN TIMES OF CHAOS

MutShat Shemsut-Gianprem Kaur is a healer. She is the owner of the wellness center, In Light Yoga and Health in the Bronx, New York. She has been practicing Kundalini Yoga and Meditation for over 15 years and has been a certified instructor since 2008. MutShat studied with Krishna Kaur in Los Angeles, Gurucharan Singh Khalsa in Espanola, New Mexico and in New York with Sat Jivan Singh and Sat Jivan Kaur. She is a Ra Sekhi Kemetic Reiki Master and Teacher having studied with Master Teacher Rekhit Kajara Assata Nebthet in Oakland, California. MutShat is currently a Ra Sekhi Snwt (priestess) in training. She received Medicine Buddha Empowerment through Lama Migmar Tseten in Lenox, Massachusets. In addition to teaching Kundalini Yoga and Meditation classes in the Bronx and Manhattan, MutShat attunes Ra Sekhi initiates, hosts workshops, speaks on wellness topics and leads monthly meditations at MMCC Beacon 142 in the Bronx. MutShat is the author of the soon-to-be-released ***Meditations for an Evolving People***.

CONTACT:
MutShat Shemsut Gianprem Kaur
Owner: In Light Yoga and Health
Ra Sekhi Kemetic Reiki Master;
Teacher Kundalini Yoga; Meditation Instructor
Bronx, NY 10466
www.inlightyogaandhealth.com
Inlightyoga108@gmail.com
646-571-9500

SHERIDAN MD, AAFP, BERNADETTE L.
IN THE FABRIC OF THE CLOTH

Dr. Bernadette Sheridan, founder/director of Grace Family Medical Practice in Brooklyn, New York, has been practicing family medicine for over 35 years. Her undergraduate degree is from Johns Hopkins University; her MD is from SUNY Buffalo. Diverse experiences including service on an Indian reservation and with prison populations helped shape her desire to provide comprehensive Family Practice care. Embracing the individual and the family, Family Medicine integrates the biological, clinical, and behavioral sciences, regardless of age, sex, organ system or disease entity.

Balancing career, family and self-fulfillment, Dr. Sheridan's services provide disease prevention, early detection, disease management and patient empowerment. A diplomat of the American Academy of Family Practice, concerned with reducing the gap in health disparities, Dr. Sheridan appropriately deserves her many awards and her consistent place on the list of New York's "Top Doctors." She is also a member of the Overseas Medical Assistance Team (Doctors and Health Care Professionals), who volunteer their time in underserved areas of the Caribbean and Africa. Truly global, Dr. Bernadette has become legendary as a passionate wellness advocate to thousands in the United States and globally.

CONTACT:
GRACE FAMILY MEDICAL CENTER
1222 E 96th St, Brooklyn, NY 11236
(718) 257-3355

LLOYD STRAYHORN, ASTRO-NUMEROLOGIST
THE POWER OF L-O-V-E... NUMERICALLY SPEAKING

Astro-Numerology is the 21st Century metaphysical art of merging two cosmic worlds; Astrology and Numerology.

As a child growing up in Harlem, New York, Lloyd Strayhorn had an interest in all things "weird" or "strange." Fascination with the study of astrology and related sciences held and attention. He enjoyed figuring out a person's astrological and/or numerical chart. After many intensive years of studying astrology and numerology,

Lloyd emerged as an Astro/Numerologist; perhaps the most renowned authority in this specialized field today.

Lloyd Strayhorn has written magazine columns and articles, as well as books, including the best-selling, **Numbers and You,** sold in bookstores, globally. An experienced radio and TV personality, he brings the audience insight and an informative approach to his very unique world. Lloyd's TV appearances include being on "Oprah Winfrey", "Geraldo", Regis Philbin and Kathy Lee", "The Montel Williams Show" and "Tony Brown's Journal." He has also made countless radio appearances across the country. His refreshing and warm delivery to the subject of Astro/Numerology is upbeat, positive and sincere. Amazingly on target, Lloyd leaves the audience mesmerized.

CONTACT:
lloydstrayhorn@msn.com
2266 5th Avenue #136
New York, NY 10037
Set up a personal conference:
800-581-4401

SSALI, STEPHEN WESTERN/AFRICAN HERBAL MEDICINE
OPTIMIZING SELF: WHOLENESS OF MIND BODY SPIRIT

Stephen Ssali is the CEO and Director of Mariandina and the son of the late Professor/Doctor Charles Ssali - Founder of the Mariandina Research Foundation. Stephen is the Sales & Marketing Director within Mariandina Research Foundation, responsible for Product promotion and distribution. Previously Stephen worked alongside his father Dr. Ssali to inform people about Professor Ssali's research and the range of nutritional health products. Currently he and his sister Christine Kas continue their father's Legacy. He is the founder of the Universal African Ancestral Alliance that is working to create a platform for empowerment through wellness, spiritual healing and collective cooperation. Stephen Ssali hosts a weekly health talk radio show on Conscious Radio 102 FM called the Holistic Wellness Show.

CONTACT:
Stephen Ssali
CEO and Director
Mariandina Research Foundation
Email: Stephen@mariandina.com
Mobile: 077659 61818
Website: www.mariandina.com

SUPA NOVA SLOM, WELLNESS ACTIVIST/ARTIST
EAT GREEN

Supa Nova Slom is a Celebrity Wellness Coach, Author, Creator of a supplement, Hip Hop's Medicine Man, Musical Artist and Dream Director. The son of a world-renowned holistic practitioner and author, Queen Afua, Supa Nova is a by-product of the hip-hop renaissance, and a survivor of the streets. Supa Nova, whose name means, 'Shining with the brilliance of a hundred million stars' is dedicated to the well-being of young people. He is galvanizing a new tomorrow for today's generation with multifaceted work which includes, his book: *The Remedy: The Five-Week Power Plan to Detox the Body, Combat Fat, and Rebuild Your Mind and Body;* his supplement line: Supa Mega Greens; his film: "Wholistic Wellness for the Hip Hop Generation", and several albums.

Nova is the pioneer of the 'Chlorophyllion' green lifestyle, creator of the Hip Hop Meditation Ciphers and founder of Unify the Hood and Heal the Hood. He has worked with A-list entertainers, accredited medical doctors and local street organization leaders. He has received recognition by the Association for the Study of African Civilization. Supa Nova Slom has spoken internationally and appeared on television programs on ABC, BET, and CBS.

CONTACT:
www.SupaMegaFoods.com

TAYLOR, JEANNE "MAJESTIC"
THE ESSENTIAL ENTREPRENEUR

Jeanne "Majestic" Taylor, born in Toronto, Canada takes her greatest pride in being a mother, homemaker, and family nurturer. An honored student of Queen Afua's wellness training, Majestic in partnership with Global Nation of Wellness celebrates 15 years of entrepreneurial experience. Co-founder of CAN Vending Solutions, she operates her successful vending machine company out of her hometown and serves customers across North America. Additionally, Majestic has founded F.L.O.W.W (For the Love of Wealth and Wellness), an umbrella company that is transformational on many levels of wellness and wealth building.

Jeanne "Majestic" Taylor has affirmed that her success is due not only to her hard work, sacrifices and dedication, but also to her *faith* in the Creator, her *gratitude* for the gift of life, and her *great desire* to shine her inner light so that others can benefit. "Majestic" believes in community and nation building. Every day she lives by:

1. Faith with work leads to success. Those who work their visions into reality create meaningful lives.
2. Using thoughts and ideas through entrepreneurship to achieve economic prosperity.

CONTACT:
E-mail: majesticbeautyco@gmail.com
Phone: 647-701-8479

TAYLOR, PASTOR KEVIN E.
MINDFULNESS: GRAB HOLD OF THE FLEXITARIAN LIFESTYLE

Senior Pastor of Unity Fellowship Church NewArk, Kevin E. Taylor is a noted author (***JADED; UNCLUTTER; ENVY: the darkest shade of green; GET OFF YOUR ASS AND DO SOMETHING***…and others). For three decades he has been a television writer and producer (BET) and runs TaylorMadeMultiMedia (TM3) his own company. Empowering and motivational, Taylor has spoken nationally and internationally before diverse groups. His creative writing, television and development workshops are enriching. Kevin wrote the discography for Natalie Cole's "Angel on My Shoulder"; and received Gold World Medal for International Programming (Dru Hill). He interviewed Aaliyah, Mariah Carey and Mary J. Blige and was double nominated for NAACP Image Awards.

Director of Administration for Turning Point Community Services, (women's and children's shelter), Pastor Taylor also heads the Essex County Consortium of Care to help eradicate homelessness. In 2017 he released his autobiography, ***NEVER TOO MUCH: this is my story of big words, big dreams and an audacious big life!*** Coming soon will be a novel and two empowerment tomes. Continuously guiding people to live their greatest lives, the theme at Pastor Taylor's church is: "LIFE…MORE ABUNDANTLY!"

CONTACT:
pastorkevinufcnewark@gmail.com
Instagram: KevinETaylor
Twitter: KevinETaylorTM3
Facebook: Facebook.com/NowWhatwithKevinETaylor

UZAN, MEMNON
HEALING THE SOUL

Mathematician Memnon Uzan is a skilled polymath, a polyglot, and a martial artist. He holds seven different ranks in a variety martial arts. In May of 2018 he was honored to take the preliminary exams into the MENSA I.Q Society in which he has scored in the 98th percentile. He has created eight theories of motion for intelligence, that will be published in the next two years. Recently he signed a four-book contract with Creation Theories for theories of physicality, Afrikan spirituality, I.Q. enhancement and on the perfection of the being. Memnon lives by the Dogon and Shona principles, "nesimba" (nee-sim-ba) and kileyo (kee-lay-o). Nesimba means perfecting the art of soul. Kileyo means living a pure life, immaterial, within and without.

Memnon Uzan says, "True greatness is a life fitness, it is an invincible energy of motion that never yields but is always in stillness."

CONTACT:
E-mail: memnonteze@gmail.com
Phone: 470 344 6572

UN NEFER HETEP RĀ (JAWANZA!)
CHANGE STARTS WITHIN

Un Nefer Hetep Rā (Jawanza!) is host of "Health Wealth & Divine" radio broadcast. "HealthWealth&Divine" is an inspirational and holistic dialogue that focuses on optimal living and wellness. Un Nefer Hetep Rā has had the honor of interviewing some of the most prominent Spiritual Leaders, Healers and Minds of this age including Queen Afua, Dr. Ra Un Nefer Amen I, Rev. Michael Bernard Beckwith, Iyanla Vanzant and Louis Gossett Jr. to name a few.

Tune in online at www.blogtalkradio.com/jawanza4life

CONTACT:
Email: j4lblogtalkradio@yahoo.com
Phone: 804 3009605
93 WORDS

VON DER POOL, LAUREN
THOUGHTS FOR PLANET HEAL

Celebrity Chef Lauren Von Der Pool's hunger for healthy living began in 2001 when she was only 16 years of age. When Von Der Pool realized that what was going on in her life and community was happening globally, she began to educate herself, her community, and the world about healthy living! The rest is history.

A graduate of Le Cordon Bleu Los Angeles and Paris Culinary School, Chef Lauren Von Der Pool has worked closely with renowned chefs and celebrity clients such as Wolfgang Puck. Her celebrity events include The Oscars, Grammy's, Screen Actors Guild Awards, American Music Awards, Golden Globes, The Olympics, Wimbledon, The Congressional Black Caucus, Bet Honors, The Espy's, MTV Video Music Awards and countless movie premieres.

CONTACT:
VON DER POOL GOURMET, LLC
www.vonderpoolgourmet.com
USA Tel: 770.856.9111
info@vonderpoolgourmet.com

WILSON, DACM, SMA, BISHARA
A HEALER IN EVERY HOUSEHOLD

Dr. BISHARA WILSON is a Pain Relief and Sports Medicine Specialist. He integrates Western diagnostics and Eastern Medicine therapeutics. He has refined his skills in over 18 years of clinical experience, treating over 3,000 patients and administering over 20,000 treatments. Bishara uses a non-pharmaceutical and non-surgical approach to eliminate pain. His professional credentials include: Bachelor of Arts - Wesleyan University, Bachelor of Professional Studies - Pacific College of Oriental Medicine, Master of Science, Doctoral candidate - Traditional Chinese Medicine, Pacific College of Oriental Medicine, Diplomate of Oriental Medicine (Dipl.O.M.) - NCCAOM, Licensed Acupuncturist (L. Ac.) and Certified in Sports Medicine Acupuncture®.

CONTACT:
888.375.5444
www.newyorksportsacupuncture.com
Info@nysportsacu.com
Facebook.com/newyorksportsacupuncture
Twitter.com/bisharawilson
Instagram.com/bisharawilson/
Bisharawilson.blogspot.com/

WISE, STEPHEN "KATRIEL"
MUSIC MEDICINE

Katriel uses sound to manifest transformation of planet earth. Through holographic light and harmonic resonance, he musically builds bridges from planet earth to the humanity living here. A metaphysical musical medicine man, Katriel's life-song is to awaken humanity to its infinite potential using the tremendous, healing power of music. As a recording artist, songwriter and producer he has worked with some of the music industry's biggest names such as, Stevie Wonder and Patti Labelle. A vocalist, Katriel is also an instrumentalist on flutes, saxophones, aboriginal Australian didgeridoo, native and African drums. blending his soulful roots with jazz, reggae, soul, world and meditative, he creates a musical alchemy of universal sound.

As a metaphysician, Katriel's spirit pours out of his soul with a healing effect that repairs and regenerates the spiritual DNA. The combination of his music and his wisdom raises the frequency causing the listeners to feel they are on sacred ground.

CONTACT:
Stephen Wise as Ras Katriel Wise
Bandleader for the Edge and Recording Artist
(484) 410 9473 US
876-857-5744 JA
www.stepwiseentertainment.com

WORRELL, MARILYN "IDAKA"
ART GUIDES MY LIFE'S PURPOSE

PERFORMANCE ARTIST, WRITER, TEACHER, ACTIVIST, Marilyn "Idaka"Worrell is trained in the disciplines of dance, theater, visual and literary arts. Additionally, Marilyn has studied alchemy and the African cultural and spiritual history by Natural healing nkisi nganga (masters). Some of her Master Teachers have been: Baba Fu-Kiau, Dr. John Henrick Clarke, Dr. Leonard Jefferies, Dr. Frances Cress Welsing, Dr. Joy DeGruy Leary, Dr. Marimba Ani, Diana Pharr, Queen Afua, Dr. Ivan Van Sertima, Dr. Cheikh Anta Diop.

Idaka says: "Early in life, I learned to always stand in my power and speak my truth. What I was taught, I learned. What I learned, I live. "What I live, I teach. I remain in the light. Keeping the spiritual, intellectual nkisi (medicine) content pure is a perpetual task. I dedicate my art, to the advocacy, support and education of our youth and families, and in turn, our community in the holistic celebration of our societal improved healthy development."

CONTACT:
OVO Productions
WESTBETH ARTISTS
Marilyn.worrell@gmail

"Give the world
a new humanity."

DR. JOHN HENRIK CLARKE